THE ALTERNATIVE SHAKESPEARE

A Modern Introduction

THE ALTERNATIVE SHAKESPEARE

A Modern Introduction

A M Challinor

… here is the strangest controversy
Come from the country to be judged by you.

King John

The Book Guild Ltd
Sussex, England

The Book Guild Ltd
25 High Street,
Lewes, Sussex

First published 1996
© A M Challinor, 1996

Set in Times
Typesetting by Adhands, Bracknell.

Printed in Great Britain by
Bookcraft (Bath) Ltd.

A catalogue record for this book is
available from the British Library

ISBN 1 85776 049 2

CONTENTS

*In Memory of Herbert Davies (1907–1960),
a lifelong reader and discoverer of information
through books*

PROLOGUE

This book is quite different from nearly every other in the vast stream of publications that appear annually on the subject of William Shakespeare. It is designed to arouse more widespread interest in a theme remaining thoroughly worthy of debate: are we really sure who actually wrote the plays and poems? To this end an extensive modern survey of the suggested alternatives is provided, along with the reaction to them. The book tries to cater for various levels or depths of interest; to inform, to encourage, to entertain, to promote reasoned discussion. While it leans towards unorthodox views, there is certainly no pretence that a cast iron case for someone other than the generally supposed author can be made.

There are four distinct aims:

First, to show the foundations of controversy, demonstrating that there remains today, at the very least, a genuine query to be considered – and if possible answered ('Acts 1 and 2'). Some people may suppose, wrongly, that all such debate must be bizarre, or 'old hat'. Others, sadly, have never really thought about it in the least; the 'quarrel' has tended to have an enthusiastic, but numerically very limited audience. Many of the arguments have been around for a long time. Yet it is far too easy, at present, for those interested in Shakespeare to remain unaware of their serious nature. Consequently, such people either miss out on the controversy altogether or note it only as something to be immediately discarded, via passive acquiescence in the might of the (so widely prevalent) 'official' view.

Second, to produce a short history of theories as expounded between 1900 and 1994, together with assessment of critical comment and rejoinders during that time ('Acts 3 and 4'). This is, at least potentially, the most demanding part of the book: there are naturally many names, as well as views, with which to contend. Some of these may be passed over fairly rapidly, especially on a first reading. In 'Act 4' sparks fly; for the serious doubts are not here all dismissed with scorn, as has been done by some previous commentators who used the natural strength of the well-established majority position as a stick with which to beat, often most ferociously, any dissenter.

Third, to put forward a highly unconventional theory, not in the least in a spirit of dogmatic assertion (as has too frequently been the case with doubters) but sketched very tentatively for consideration ('Act 5').

Finally, to offer throughout, not only an 'alternative Shakespeare', but also an alternative approach to Shakespeare's writings. Many people first come to these through the in-depth study of one or two plays; they often, for various reasons, stop there. This book touches upon every acknowledged Shakespearean work. Its study of the background to the whole enterprise, especially if simply used as a starting-point, may augment the customary approach to the great dramatist, widening knowledge and admiration of the plays and poems in their entirety.

For some this may all seem to promise a very academic volume on an academic topic, but since the debate is really worthy of much wider 'popular' interest, considerable effort is made here to present the essentials in an intelligible and accessible way. It is hoped that this book may be useful, as an exercise in investigative study, for university, college or even senior secondary school students, as well as for existing Shakespeare enthusiasts. It is aimed at anyone, in fact, who likes a provocative book, or has an enquiring mind; at those prepared to analyse, criticise, dig for genuine historical truth. The depth of the digging may well vary from reader to reader, but there is one chore which cannot be excused: it is imperative to think for oneself! In essence, the controversy provides a superb opportunity for just that kind of exploration which, regardless of the context, is of widespread general use in developing learning skills; for the sifting and weighing of evidence; for the forming of opinions, which can be modified if appropriate new information comes to hand.

It is unfortunate that many of the key works mentioned, being old (although not necessarily thereby dated) are out of print. Those seeking to hunt for further information, or check viewpoints at variance with my own, need access to books, even journal or newspaper files, via libraries. For anyone wishing to study the controversy extensively, a large reference library is essential. But, to change the earlier metaphor, it is not necessary to cover the whole ocean to enjoy a swim: the range must be dictated by accessible resources as well as inclination. Those wanting to stick to basics can cover much with enjoyment and profit just by using this book, or parts of it, along with appropriate consultation of Shakespeare's works. But it is hoped that some will seek out other sources, including some cited readings which adopt a stance radically different from mine.

Some other points must be made at the outset. One is that I distinguish between William Shakespeare (which we must, at the start of a debate like this, assume *may* have been a pen-name) as author of the plays and the actor who is almost universally supposed to be their author. I generally call the latter person 'William of Stratford' or 'The Stratford man'. This is not meant to belittle him, nor does it mean, in itself, that the actor and the great dramatist could not have been one and the same person. It is simply that, in a work of this kind, the alleged merits of the case for various others must be considered. The principal anti-Stratfordian schools of thought have established names – Baconians, Derbyites, Oxfordians, Marlovians and so on. Likewise, believers in the orthodox Shakespeare are here called Stratfordians (necessary if only to distinguish them from the anti-Stratfordians), while those who have made excessive claims for the Bard are sometimes referred to as Bardolators. The name 'Shake-speare' occasionally appears with a hyphen, like this, as its author-user sometimes employed it.

Other preliminary points largely concern the delicate balance between ease of reading and provision of technical detail. Footnotes are kept to a minimum, but all sources used can be checked in the bibliography. Because I see no intrinsic merit in perpetuating Elizabethan English purely for the sake of it, I have sought to explain archaic phrases, or convert a word or two into current language, whenever the meaning and beauty is not thereby adversely affected. If a little such conservative modernising offends some readers, I am sorry. On balance, this must be outweighed by its usefulness to others. It is insisted that this great historical theme, with tragic overtones, must be followed with enjoyment as well as zeal; some of the doubters have been too deadly serious. I thus try to present it in dramatic fashion with its five distinct sections as 'Acts', each having various chapters, shown as 'Scenes'. In the same manner, there is an attempt to inject some humour in parts, without detriment to the obvious overall serious intent.

These things may be pounced upon, as denoting a lack of sustained suitable gravitas, by opponents of my stance. Even some who might broadly support my view may dislike the lighthearted tone occasionally adopted, but there should be room for a little of such in a work which, despite some prolonged argument accompanied by references in a bibliography, is designed essentially to introduce, in an enjoyable way, a great debate for anyone prepared to at least question commonly received 'truths'.

Inevitably parts of the ground have been retrodden over the years, yet the newcomer to this controversy can still discover in it a fascinating story of suspected mistaken identity along with efforts to reassure us that this is not so. Equally inevitably, because of the long period of time involved, many of the combatants have now taken their exit from life's stage; yet, because the ideas live on, the present tense is often used in speaking of them. My contribution to the debate certainly offers opinions of its own, but tries to make clear, occasionally using their own words, the position held by various twentieth-century writers. Space and balance compel the reluctant omission of some names, but I acknowledge gladly my debt to the words of all who have, in their various ways, either walked what they saw as a compelling path, or endeavoured to show that it led nowhere. They are often – as I trust my own pages show – colourful characters, their zest adding momentum to the course of the controversy. I am most grateful to my family – Jean, John and Susan – for encouragement constantly given; to those various people, especially Derran Charlton, who provided helpful information; and for the editorial advice of my publisher. Particular thanks are due to my wife, and to Jill Bennett and Jean Garriock for reading the text in draft and offering some comment thereon.

The literature on the controversy is of mixed merit, yet some of it most certainly deserves to escape oblivion. Of course, an enquirer may form some other view, very different from mine, as the latter gradually unfolds here; or the belief held before exploration took place may be retained. The 'journey' would still have been worthwhile: investigation without prejudice must be superior to reliance upon assertion. There are, alas, those who quite simply resent all such enquiry. They would stigmatise it as an unhealthy interest in an area which they insist is (indeed must) remain on the periphery of Shakespearean studies – or even be obliterated if possible. It would be as well to ask, among other questions, why should this be so? The argument is one which should not be restricted to a few 'literary-minded' people, but opened up for more widespread debate. Far from being some kind of rebarbative aberration, it is a lively historical drama which should be examined with an open mind. In that spirit comes the request, as Shakespeare's prologue asks the audience of *King Henry The Fifth*, 'gently to hear, kindly to judge' this 'play'.

A M C
April 1995

ACKNOWLEDGEMENTS

Considerable effort has been made to trace appropriate sources for copyright clearance concerning some short quotations used to illustrate directly the standpoint of other writers. The author and publisher apologise if, unintentionally, anyone has been overlooked in direct acknowledgement. They are most grateful to the following individuals and organisations for permission to use extracts.

Cambridge University Press for an observation by J B Steane from his *Marlowe: a critical study*; Chatto & Windus for those from G Taylor, *Re-inventing Shakespeare*; *The Independent* newspaper, for a quotation from a 1991 report relating to our knowledge of Shakespeare; Methuen & Company concerning short passages from H N Gibson, *The Shakespeare Claimants*; the quotations from the 1991 edition of S Schoenbaum, *Shakespeare's Lives*, by permission of Oxford University Press; Reinhardt Books for those taken from R C Churchill, *Shakespeare and his betters*; both Sinclair-Stevenson and the Peters, Fraser & Dunlop Group for the use of a Shakespeare reference from *Jesus* by A N Wilson.

ACT 1
HISTORY, REST IN ME A CLUE!

Not truths unmixed,
But coarser levers only move the world,
Truths broken, flawed, or partial, party cries,
Passions and interests, custom, prejudice.

William Lecky, 1838–1903

SCENE 1

THE UNEQUAL STRANDS OF TESTIMONY

It is difficult to imagine a headline proclaiming that Shakespeare has been proved to be simply a pen-name. Yet the past, just as much as the future, has the capacity to astonish us. Beyond whatever minor secrets are held there, it can contain – in terms of what is really fact and what turns out to be mere supposition – the equivalent of unexploded mines. But surely not about the person behind what is the greatest literary achievement in the English cultural heritage?

Because this seems so unthinkable, the whole question of how much confidence can be placed in various accounts of former times is worthy of a little preliminary analysis. There is some reported history which is undeniably true, comprising statements about what all agree simply must have happened. There are also versions of what took place as revealed by the honest, but not necessarily always accurate, perceptions of those who were present at the time. If the event was deemed important, there will be many more, by later interpreters. These re-tellings, whether printed or merely verbal, may or may not closely reflect factual truth. Students or tutors inclining to say that we should accept always any long-established oral traditions have a potentially embarrassing problem: what to do when these, as does happen on occasion, contradict each other!

In relation to any actual historical theme, subsequent narrators, however diligent and faithful in their use of primary sources, need to abbreviate their account of events since the sheer volume of what is on record, fast growing all the time, demands compression – if only to enable contemporary minds to take it in and make sense of it. The necessity of such contraction carries an inbuilt tendency to simplify; perhaps, thereby, unwittingly introducing some distortion. There is a commendable wish to process information into a manageable bundle, with some 'value added', as a key to appreciation. This has potential weaknesses as well as strengths.

History is much more than facts, of course, but fact must be the bedrock of all good work within it, the foundation from which subsequent reflection, analysis or interpretation spring. Yet we inevitably inherit something of the standpoint of the commentator. Attractive tales have often been used, either to fill blanks in the records or to enliven and decorate what may seem the plain fare of historical details (this has been done for Shakespeare even more so than for many other themes). Such legends are often picked up by later writers who are either oblivious to their highly dubious status or feel that they enhance the appeal of the total 'story'. Some will go for a package overweight in legend if that supports a preconceived pet theory. Bias may well be unintentional, but in matters from bygone centuries, even the most scrupulous of reporters will be forced to say things like 'in sum, it would seem that ...', 'it seems to me probable that ...', 'it appears to most reasonable people that ...' and so forth. Many books on Shakespeare are riddled with such statements. They contain numerous unproved assertions. Sadly, what is merely the likely or most obvious interpretation becomes transformed, insidiously through constant repetition, into what people see as the 'definitely true' one.

Recognition of these qualifying remarks, concerning the essence of past deeds or achievement as handed on to us, does not seek to deny the excellent work done by scholar historians; they frequently enrich factual reporting by shrewd comment or skilful unfolding of its significance. The warning is simply an important reminder to suggest that, in some areas, the experts themselves frequently have no conclusive proof for some ideas on offer. Naturally, interpretation can sometimes be much more important than the facts. It might not have signified, for example, if King Robert the Bruce of Scotland was inspired by one spider rather than another, or in which cave (there are rival claims) this event took place – if it ever did! Or, for that matter, if Shakespeare of Stratford had died on 30 April 1616 rather than on 23 April of that year. But, in other cases, facts are absolutely essential to interpret the consequences properly. Even the exact location of a past battle may be important, as some debate in recent years between historians (over the site of Bosworth Field) has proved. Minor details may be unimportant if all one wants is the 'feel' of a historical period and its events. However, if the marginal blurring of some issues is tolerable, a radical mistake concerning significant matters would most certainly not be so.

Accuracy is crucial in certain factual attributions, such as the authorship of works revealing exceptional literary creativity. It is necessary to be as sure as possible that the fundamental premise corresponds with past reality, otherwise subsequent analysis is very wrongly skewed. Of course, flexibility is needed too. At times, our perspective of what was real concerning historical events can be changed by some new discovery; later, in relation to a book by R C Churchill, I find it necessary to point out that historical fact itself cannot alter, although our perception or understanding of it may change.

However, human nature is often very reluctant to abandon ingrained views of what truth is, especially if these have been implanted at an early age, if mass persuasion dictates otherwise, if a tourist centre might be seriously affected, or if 'loss of face' would arise from a change of mind. Thus some searches for factual accuracy which may strike at the roots of orthodoxy are unpopular; they could be met with ridicule, persecution or conspicuous neglect. Widespread beliefs become cultural institutions. Such institutions acquire strong defence mechanisms; they develop guardians who rapidly put a protective girdle around them. They tend to be remarkably good at surviving, with adaptations if the latter are absolutely necessary. Numerous people believe, if at all possible, what they want to believe: they support causes they want to support, sometimes regardless of logic, evidence, or even economics. However, we should be open-minded enough to examine, as objectively as possible, any key case concerning the reliability of accounts of past times.

The controversy over the authorship of the 37 or more plays and sundry poems attributed to William Shakespeare (1564–1616) of Stratford-upon-Avon provides just such a case. Most educated people have heard of it: few now read about it or debate it. Not so very many could name a rival claimant for the authorship other than Francis Bacon, although all the theories expounded in this book originated at least 70 years ago. Nowadays, there are occasional newspaper snippets, often mocking in tone, about those who claim the official attribution insecure. Yet the harvest of facts, ideas and opinions is far too great for any kind of meaningful treatment in a mere column or two. Could it really be a gigantic 'hoax' of some kind? Does (or could) 'official' history ever make a mistake on such a scale as this? Without any prior bias, some things can be said about legends and myths: they may well arise to explain gaps or incongruities concerning significant matters fervently believed to be true; they are not restricted in size; and, they may be hardest to recognise when they have already enveloped us.

This, of course, cannot mean in itself that the essentials within the usual account of Shakespeare are even possibly mythical. One commentator on the authorship controversy, F W Wadsworth, reasons that the validity of 'official' history in such matters must be accepted as received. If that normal view of Shakespearean authorship is false, he asks, how many more such deceptions might exist? Yet, in fairness, we do know for sure that imposture is not absent from the annals of English literature. There could also be said to be two other related questions to this one posed by Wadsworth. One concerns the issue of whether any other great writer has generated even a tenth of such a large literature proclaiming an authorship deception. The other relates, as we shall see, to how many great writers have a lifestyle apparently so much at variance with the ambience, values and aspirations of their work.

The debate covers much more ground than many would realise. Fundamentally it remains, warts and all, a fascinating one: helping to illuminate the works of Shakespeare and showing how astonishing he was; revealing the possible prejudice of commentators (including this one); saying something about the nature, variety and nuances of history. It is an intriguing tale that, whatever one's viewpoint, may well indicate the jealousy with which established views are protected when academic or literary reputations are at stake.

It was Delia Bacon, in the mid-nineteenth century, who made the passionate plea, demand even, in the context of the Shakespeare authorship question, that forms the title of this first 'Act'. It is interesting to note, whatever her various shortcomings, that a work by Martin Pares to mark the centenary of her death rightly emphasised her zeal to establish historical fact: he argues that she saw truth as a religion, but without intending thereby to belittle those who find some degree of make-believe necessary, to whom the truth is often less important than the story.

Well, we certainly know what the vast majority of people believe on the Shakespearean authorship issue. However, if they are right, they should be seen, demonstrably, to be right. Why give an unthinking 'knee-jerk' reaction to those who query? Yet clearly many among the 'vast majority' do view things uncritically, passively accepting whatever they are constantly told about history by specialists, provided that this is not obviously self-contradictory. They might say, if forced to articulate their belief: 'This is what the experts say happened. Therefore I accept it.' This does not make their belief necessarily right: it most certainly does not make it necessarily wrong. By the use of right and wrong here we are back to the basic issue of respect for whatever was the actual historical fact, or, in the enforced absence of sure knowledge, the strongest of the probabilities. If the latter, it should be recognised as only strongly probable, not absolutely certain. History has many examples of beliefs, once strongly held, which gradually

7

became discredited.

However, it really will not do to say that it does not matter in the least who wrote certain plays hundreds of years ago; that truth must be whatever current expediency dictates; or that orthodoxy should be left alone because poor Professor X would suffer if his views were shown to be inaccurate. Nor should it satisfy us to argue that if Mrs Y chooses to insist that Sir Walter Ralegh was really the great author, using the name 'Shakespeare', then that is a comfort to her and does no injury to others. In a curious way, to shrug off such matters supports the *status quo* by suggesting that whatever it makes people happy to believe can be considered 'true' in some sense, for them – although clearly false historically. Unconventional stances can then be passed off as 'a little mad, but harmless'. That is unreasonable. Truth is truth, as Shakespeare often reminds us: the search for it must be prized above either pleasant illusion or unquestioning acceptance of the prevalent view. We have to be brave enough to look for the most probable facts: to be intrusive, as required, rather than just blindly be loyal to what we have been told. There is need to recognise the difference between the various strands of historical testimony – certainty, probability, supposition, assertion, myth and legend; to seek honestly for what actually once was, not just for what one may want to believe, striving to follow the trail objectively, wherever it may lead.

What follows in this book justifies such scene-setting remarks. It is good to be proactive, seeking to establish an informed view in this way, whatever the outcome. Truth discovered for oneself by probing with due care has definite enhancement; such must always be superior to any dictated 'truth'.

SCENE 2

WHY INVESTIGATION IS WORTHWHILE

Everyone must know that there is a great deal of literature on Shakespeare, but relatively few would guess just how extensive this is. There have been, over the last 150 years, thousands of published items on the authorship controversy. Many of these writings, fortunately, cover very similar ground. Yet all this is almost a drop in the ocean compared with the many more thousands of (in authorship terms strictly orthodox) biographical and critical writings. Leaving aside categories like letters to newspapers or commentary therein, a large specialised bibliography would reveal the annual output of hundreds of books and specialised articles. Some are very specific; for example, 'a Marxist view of Shakespeare', or 'the place of strawberries in Shakespeare's plays'. Nearly all take the identity of the author for granted: could there really be the faintest possibility of any legitimate alternative?

Certainly, down the years, many people have wondered, despite the fact that the seed of doubt generally falls on stony, ungrateful soil. For some the wish to enquire, quickly buffeted by fear of taint or taunt, may have subsided into indifference. Yet several others, although often differing markedly in their view of the true Shakespeare, have answered the question concerning an alternative author with a bold affirmative. In the interests of truth, it is both unwise and unfair (although very frequently done) to repel hastily the views of every single disputer of the authorship as those of someone who is perverse, lacking in scholarship or literary awareness, or who has some peculiar personal axe to grind. Yet those who dare to query orthodoxy will find that it has a gravitational-type pull. Thus nearly everyone has a natural predisposition to believe strongly in it.

For most of these people this ingrained view, unfortunately, affects the ability to hear an alternative case objectively. Thus, even the suggestion that there might be one may encounter a blank look implying, 'What's this, why fuss over it?' It may even, on occasion, be met with a titter, a 'you must be a flat-earther' sort of stare, or with bellicose expletives! It has well been observed of the English, for instance, that they like to concentrate on sustained practical activity, taking long-received 'fundamentals' for granted. But for many, whatever their nation, rejection of an unconventional answer is because they possess a strong sense that any such dissent must inevitably scorn all previous experience, defying also specialists' official assertion.

This feeling combines with other factors to ring-fence the orthodox doctrine. One is an understandable desire to defend any belief, including attendant legends, received as a fine piece of tradition – surely it is too important for the majority to have erred? Besides, some will say, is there not a degree of irreverence in tampering with beliefs (even if possibly illusory) dear to many hearts? A potent factor, too, is fear of acute embarrassment. It is always easier to be with the crowd rather than against it. There is great comfort in conforming to what is seen as normality. Thus, silently to themselves, or even openly, some people will say, without indulging in any debate, that dissenting theories just must be futile, freakish, prurient, disastrous, even (if whispered in a Bardolator's ear) subversive or profane hogwash. Yet whether expressed or merely covert, such reactions are nearly always simply raucous noises or their equivalent, often from people who have probably never read even ten lines about the controversy.

So, in the name of reason, why should we discard all

doubters immediately as weird or misguided, even literary Calibans or Yahoos, without consideration of possible weaknesses in the orthodox case, or any critical review of the alternatives proposed? Perhaps indifference arises from a belief that 'it doesn't matter ... must now be a dead issue ... can be of no interest to me'. Or it stems, as already hinted, from that reverence for accepted expertise via the oft-repeated, clear authorship attribution implanted early in one's life. Conformity seems to be culturally desirable. People know the prevalent view is 'right' rather in the same way that many 'know' that chess must have originated in Persia, or that one can only ever 'learn' anything by sitting in a classroom, with teacher present.

It is also a characteristic of human pride that it wants to preserve views – to which there has been extensive, prolonged commitment – from any possibility of change. Academics tend to be dismissive, as they reiterate received 'wisdom' on an issue fundamental to their reputations; perhaps expressing, without due examination of the case, intellectual contempt. There are some who would have the possibility of an alternative Shakespeare forgotten. Yet we shall need to see how secure orthodoxy in these matters really is. One argument, advanced by those who are inherently scornful of the very idea of any genuine doubt as to who the author Shakespeare really was, can be found in the 'these people who put forward various other names can't all be right, so they must all be wrong' hypothesis. But it is self-evident that the plays and poems were written by someone. Why should it be thought misguided to seek assurance that it is the 'someone' generally postulated, rather than another, who was really their creator?

Nevertheless, any interested persons in the second half of the twentieth century, wishing to have reason for the faith that is within them, persisting in enquiry long enough to obtain background reading to the whole debate, could be directed (until very recently) only to surveys of the controversy which appeared to quash all reasonable doubts. The obvious lack of any final, totally compelling, material evidence can always be cited as an excuse for inertia. What is more, the power of established interests – in tourist revenue, as well as more

11

obviously within the academic world – in perpetuating the conventional view is far more than most people could possibly begin to guess.

The 'death' of the conventional Shakespeare would have incalculable knock-on effects. For 'Shakespeare' is today a vast, international, ever-growing, profitable industry. If an alternative Shakespeare were to be proved likely, let alone certain, massive stocks of books would become obsolete instantly. The credibility of innumerable learned articles, past and present (and the literary esteem behind them), is thus very much on the line. Automatically, therefore, the intellectual currency of the unorthodox is denied to be legal tender. Then there is the security of Stratford-upon-Avon (admittedly most charming), as a major historical attraction, with numerous 23 April traditions. These too are all at grave risk if orthodoxy even weakens. Never underestimate these things – but be prepared to believe that you may unwittingly have done so. If necessary, they will be defended 'by all the blood that ever fury breathed' (*King John*).

Those sceptical of the belief that the Stratford man was the real author of what is almost certainly the most magnificent range of work in all literary history will continue to probe, to reason, to protest. This notwithstanding the fact that their stance generally seems to receive only meticulous neglect or scathing attacks from the world of well-settled orthodoxy. They may argue that the orthodox scholars have closed minds and ranks. Perhaps they will add something akin to what cybernetics man Norbert Weiner once said in a different context: namely, that the constant repetition of clichés certainly increases the volume of noise, but may only prevent good debate, even genuine communication.

Stanley Wells, a leading Shakespearean scholar and one of the more reasonable communicators in our context, suggested in a 1994 broadcast that, should some revelation overturn authorship orthodoxy, professorial resignations would follow. Why should it be so: surely error, if made in good faith, does not demand such steps? But this does go to show how far existing writings and reputations would be damaged. Wells genuinely believes, of course, that it can never happen.

It is true that the lack of final, definitive, all-convincing proof helps to justify the established position. Yet it is really a two-edged sword. Without such kind of proof, the doubters are certainly never going to go away. They emphasise that their endeavour is not an attempt at lese-majesty; they do not wish to throw stones, metaphorically speaking, at a great cultural heritage. Nor would they see themselves as iconoclasts: they certainly do not want to belittle, in any sense, the wonder of the achievement, or a glorious English tradition; rather they want to be sure that the credit and fame go to the right person. Quality assurance is there for all to see in the plays; the issue for those who query or deny the received standard version is one of identity assurance.

If they are correct, the authorship dissidents argue, then 'Shake-speare' (and it was so hyphenated on the title-pages of some plays) was a pen-name signifying a literary lance-shaker. The true author, they urge, used this for some good reason.The person from Stratford-upon-Avon, an actor, perhaps too an aspiring dramatist, was an excellent front for the enterprise. A major reason for this state of affairs was his very similar name. Like many others it was spelt in many ways in Elizabethan England. It has about twenty variations: Shakspear, Shaxberd, Shagspur, and the like, even Breakspear is a related name. The form 'Shake-speare', occurs only rarely (never hyphenated) in records concerning the family of the Stratford man (as distinct from the literature attributed to him where that spelling, sometimes with the hyphen,is the norm). We shall have to weigh for ourselves the possibility that Shakespeare was a pseudonym, like 'Mark Twain' who, incidentally, is one of the people in literary history to deny that the actor could have written the works of Shakespeare.

At this point, some later argument can be anticipated by pointing out that, despite years of hard searching, we know little for sure that is significant about the man from Stratford: he out-tops our knowledge, as Matthew Arnold once put it, or seems to do so. The other dramatists of his age, the best being Christopher Marlowe and Ben Jonson, could not equal him.

But references to Shakespeare by his own contemporaries have a sufficiently ambiguous ring to make some of us wonder if possibly more than one person is meant. Praise mingles with some good-humoured disdain, even ridicule and accusation of copying. Sometimes, notably in the case of comment by Jonson, this 'mixed reception' comes from the same pen. By modern standards, of course, the Elizabethans took a relatively casual attitude to spelling, to literary ownership, even to authorship itself.

Trying to discover something of Shakespeare from the views and incidents expressed in the works themselves is very natural. Of course, these are not necessarily consistent revelations of his life and mind. Yet consider the book now being read: could not a few pointers about its creator be gathered from it, quite apart from the fact that there is a strong sympathy for the doubters? How much more, in that case, would one expect to learn of the knowledge and interests that Shakespeare possessed from 37 plays and several poems? Of course, plays are generally written to please audiences, not to show their author's character – yet over half of Shakespeare's were never published, some perhaps never performed, in the lifetime of the Stratford man. Always one might suspect too, in view of the many plays that do not fit the Elizabethan stage at all well, the writing was done with an eye to some self-expression, along with anticipation of the technological advances posterity would surely acquire. Charles Lamb once argued that, of all dramatists, the plays of Shakespeare were least calculated to fit a stage performance.

Moreover, the numbered sequence of Shakespeare's 154 sonnets is seen by most critics as intensely autobiographical. It carries an account of love, despair and banishment in the context of a friendship with a young nobleman. Whose life story is this? The sonnets are undoubtedly the most important single source of original evidence in the whole of the authorship debate. Many who know Shakespeare just from reading a play at school or from going to the theatre will know little of these sonnets other than a few very famous lines, like the opening of Sonnet 18. For consultation purposes, numbers

23, 29, 44, 50, 87, 89, 117, 120, represent a spread illustrating key aspects of dramatic events experienced by their author. First published, in highly unusual circumstances, in the year 1609, the 154 sonnets are full of mystery: it is like a literary striptease – the author reveals much, but never quite all ... although he sometimes seems to threaten the young noble, in addressing him, with his power to do so. There are various identities on which the curious may ponder, and often have: a 'Mr W H', to whom the sonnets are dedicated; the young lord; a 'dark lady'; a rival poet. The greatest identity search of all may well concern their author.

Many alternative 'Shakespeares' have been put forward. Therefore it might be thought, if any one candidature had probable validity, a marked realignment of the present majority view would have taken place. It must be reiterated that, to suppose so, would be to underestimate most seriously the might of the fortifications around the established citadels and reputations of literary scholarship. Holders of the conventional view have a valued, seemingly secure, world in these matters; could the god of this world have blinded their minds?

It is frequently suggested that investigation of who was responsible for literary work begun over four centuries ago cannot really matter, except perhaps to professional historians. The implication is to refrain from digging the dust. Since, despite what has already been said, it is possible to wonder whether that is the correct view to take, it may be useful to list some concise rejoinders to it.

First, it is morally wrong, an affront to learning or the author's memory, if we are even possibly attributing Shakespeare's 'hand of glory' (to use Stratfordian Ivor Brown's expression) to the wrong person. Remember, the doubters never query the achievement, only the identity of the achiever. The more the work of Shakespeare is admired, the more necessary it is to be sure we know our man. If some people insist on saying that whatever name is in the history book will do, right or wrong, that 'the play's the thing', then it is they who risk undermining the reputation of the author Shakespeare. Nearly all Stratfordians, including some who would never tolerate any of the contrary theories, would agree that, in terms of appreciating our heritage, knowing the identity of Shakespeare *is* most important.

Second, it would be most annoying to be hoodwinked in such a matter as this. Thus, to do some enquiring is, at the very least, a useful check on what might be a cosmetic acquiescence concerning the often-repeated, just possibly hidebound, 'fact' of who is the author. It proves that one is not prepared to risk being a prisoner of indoctrination. Furthermore, if the advocates of an alternative are all in error, it might be useful to decide how, or why, that error has arisen.

Third, to explore some rival claims is genuinely an unusual, but most valuable, *alternative way* – complementing usual routes – of learning more about the fascination of Shakespeare, indeed about Elizabethan drama in general: this is so whatever conclusion is reached: even some modern Stratfordians, such as Irvin Matus, acknowledge the value of this different perspective. If people only will examine the matter, even if they were then to declare the official story confirmed, the making of the investigation will still have been helpful. It cannot but encourage acquaintance with a wide range of Shakespeare's plays and poems, offering a 'global' view of the achievement, in contrast to the 'depth' study of a particular play. It could help to destroy some popular misconceptions concerning 'remoteness' from our age or the inaccessibility of the works, fostering wider appreciation of their cultural timelessness.

Fourth, many searches for the 'true Shakespeare', whether viewed as fact or fiction, offer (along with responses to them) a fascinating insight into the workings of the human mind. They also provide a lively, very readable story: think much of it fictional, perhaps, but be prepared for the passion, prejudice, party cries, mentioned in the quotation from Lecky, with which this 'Act' began – not to mention some jibes from both sides against their opponents!

Fifth, the controversy provides a stimulating arena for personal investigative study, or for debating groups; for reaction to the 'logic' of particular arguments; for considering conjectures and probabilities. The very distance of momentous events can seem to increase rather than diminish their fascination. There is a strong element of the 'whodunit' in this, with overtones of a possible hidden romantic tragedy. History may have hidden well some vital clues; or, of course, the very idea that there are such could be erroneous. The detection aspect is seemingly distasteful to some, who view such activity as an armchair game for amateurs, but it will appeal to others.

Perhaps this point may be extended by the brief riding of a personal hobby-horse. The very first editors of Shakespeare address a 'great *variety* of readers'; superb literature is not meant to be confined to a few 'highbrows'. But, to move to our own times, such literature is only obligatory reading for those at school. These individuals are often not ready for much of it; they may find imagination cramped by the learning approaches so often dictated by the spectre of an examination; several may not receive a play that might most readily kindle a flame.

Surely 'learning', in the wisest and best sense, should be potentially lifelong? Yet, for adults, that particular seed corn of schooling may yield no harvest whatsoever; in an age where so many things compete for leisure-time attention, the possibility of appreciating any classics via either theatre-going or relevant reading can be completely crowded out. The process of seeing the authorship as an instance of attempted detection may thus also become a means of general encouragement – helping rather more people, amateurs in terms of literary expertise, to find some responsive chords within the great range of scenes, moods and characters that constitutes Shakespeare. In judgemental matters, some amateurs may have perceptive comment to offer; if several of those in that category who enter the debate also enter the realms of error, the specialists should at least be delighted that an interest has been aroused. They should set out gently to encourage a maturer view, by logic and by scholarly method rather than by abuse.

Sixth, if Shakespeare were seen to be someone other than the Stratford actor, this would illuminate anew sections of some plays and the (surely autobiographical) story behind the sonnets. For this reason alone, the enquiry cannot be dismissed as 'other-worldly'. To attempt correct dating of Shakespeare's writings, says the *Encyclopaedia Britannica*, is not a futile pursuit, for the full appreciation of the work of the world's greatest poet rests upon it. We must agree, but how much more profoundly would such appreciation be affected by wrong identification of the author? In any case, those admiring Shakespeare the writer surely want to know something more about Shakespeare the person. And then, of course, it simply must be the right person.

Now, in spite of these arguments, several conventional scholars or critics seek to brush each and every flicker of authorship doubt aside, suggesting that this is really nothing but a wasteful diversion of potential talent. Received fundamentals are sacred for them, and thus not negotiable: Shakespeare the writer just must have been Shakespeare of Stratford. Anti-Stratfordian views, we are told in effect, are anti-scholarship. Yet, if historical truth is valued, contrary views represent a trail some must test. In this case, the prize (if it exists) is immense. So ignore discouragement: there is a compulsion to dig. The activity is certainly as valid as any other, and a pursuit far less harmful than some. For many people it can also be most enjoyable. Unfortunately, much of the large literature is composed of items each restricted to the views of a single camp; either orthodoxy or one particular 'sect' among the doubters. There is not much open discussion, verbal or written, reflecting earnest dialogue between the vast majority (Stratfordians) and the sceptics. It is not usual either for one group of those sceptics to know much about the detailed arguments of another.

Misgivings concerning the authenticity of the attribution of the plays and poems to William Shakespeare of Stratford-upon-Avon go back at least to the mid-eighteenth century, but it was a hundred years later before the stream of enquiries flowed freely. Some of the doubters did not suggest an alternative author, but most were Baconians or Groupists (this last term embracing those who believe that several persons, perhaps Bacon or the Stratford man being among them, were responsible for the output of Shakespeare).

A most memorable person who expressed her doubts was the

American, Delia Bacon, in *The Philosophy of Shakespeare's Plays Unfolded* (1857). Hers was an almost impossible book to read, perhaps because, despite the strength of her convictions, her views were still developing. Principally it is because of her style of writing when her physical and mental strength were failing, although she pressed on with a lonely quest. She once had a chance that some twentieth-century counterparts have longed for, but been denied: the opportunity to open the Stratford grave to search for documentary evidence. By then, her powers were totally on the wane. She died not long afterwards, unsound in mind, worn out in body. Her total commitment to her 'mission' had led her to disregard prudence in basic matters of food and health. Her very sad end shows that unbelievers should never, however great their zeal, become obsessive about such quests; or even too emphatic about the preferred 'solution', since it cannot – without some stupendous new discovery – be proved beyond all dispute.

Delia nevertheless blazed a trail. Some others, like her, have found a very gloomy side of it to wander down, but there is no need to do that. The trail may be false; if so, this has nothing to do with her breakdown any more than the illness of a major Stratfordian scholar would, in itself, invalidate the traditional authorship. Objective enquiry should not be prejudiced by her fate, nor for that matter be put off by any name or deed in the history of the controversy which may seem quaint or humorous. Each of us should be interested purely in the facts, to see, via relaxed and open-minded enquiry, the probable direction in which they point. Yes, perhaps 'probable direction' should now be stressed. The truth is what is wanted, but at the end of the day, probability that is based on some first-hand exploration (plus the retention of the capacity to be flexible if new ideas should emerge) may be as much as can be obtained to our own satisfaction, however worthwhile we may have considered the investigation.

In looking for facts and at the development of the debate, it is not the intention to linger in Delia Bacon's century, although the latter part of it was a most fruitful period in terms of the rise of unorthodoxy. The focus here is to be on arguments, together with the main alternatives, put forward since 1900. In passing, it may be noted that, over the entire history of the controversy, many of those submitting alternative names have themselves been specialists in fields as various as chemistry, natural history, law, music, social and economic history, the history of costume – to give but a few examples. Within the camp of the declared unbelievers are famous names: from the world of statesmanship and politics (Bismarck, Palmerston, Charles de Gaulle, Enoch Powell); from the world of psychology (Sigmund Freud); from the world of media entertainment (Charles Chaplin); from the acting profession (Sir John Gielgud – or so I am assured); from the world of social history (John Bright); there is even one from a protest movement (Malcolm X). Either they were all sorely deceived or there is, at the very least, a case to be investigated. Yet some commentators persist in presenting *all* the dissenters as people whose ignorance is equalled only by their credulity.

From the world of literature too, there are novelists who have doubted – Henry James, Mark Twain, John Buchan, Daphne du Maurier; poets, too – J G Whittier, Walt Whitman. In the wings, more guarded and ambiguous, although clearly unhappy with aspects of orthodoxy, are Charles Dickens (the life of Shakespeare was a mystery, he said, that left him trembling), S T Coleridge, and R W Emerson. But English literature teaching specialists tend to ignore the controversy. Many have just never thought of getting to grips with it; others might well sense a taboo, assuming, perhaps understandably so, that involvement could be rather like driving in the wrong direction when faced with an uncompromising one-way traffic system.

This great debate flowered most conspicuously at a time that clearly enjoyed such debates: the Victorian age in Britain, the real terminus of which was perhaps the First World War. Another controversy at its peak in those days concerns the impact of science on religious belief. It may be relevant to compare them very briefly. Both seek secure knowledge; both have a potentially perennial appeal. But religion and science may eventually have arrived at some sort of *modus vivendi*. Those proclaiming that scientific findings might require some

20

reconsideration of the nature of revealed religious truths made some impact – because recognised specialists from two distinct areas were involved. In the Shakespeare debate, it is impossible to use science or any other discipline as such to make inroads into the real or alleged expertise of the literary scholars. They are the sole acknowledged 'specialists'. Nor is there any hope of Stratfordian orthodoxy living happily with unconventional beliefs.

The mention of religion serves as a reminder that in the history of the authorship argument, a feature which may add spice to investigation, but is rarely pointed out, is the frequent use of biblical and other religious phrases and analogies. Any 'proof', like religious 'proofs', tends to be most acceptable to those who are already members of the faction concerned. But the similarities extend into the use of language. Let us look at just a few instances of this. Among the Stratfordians, G B Harrison speaks of the doubters (surely in most cases inaccurately) as 'agnostics'; Samuel Schoenbaum talks about rival sects; Louis Marder has said, in slightly different vein, that the deification of Shakespeare is a hard thing to combat. We might note, in relation to this last remark, that the great writer is often called '*the Bard*', and usually with a capital B.

Then, turning to move among those various doubters, Calvin Hoffman, in making his case for Marlowe as Shakespeare, says that the evidence is plain for those who have ears to hear. An earlier Marlowe supporter, Archie Webster, had claimed that his theory makes the crooked straight and the rough places plain. A dissident from a different camp, A J Evans, argued that the common belief that William of Stratford was the writer Shakespeare 'has the nature of a religion, supported far more by tradition and faith than by reason and logic'. One commentator on the whole dispute, F W Wadsworth, referring to its early history, noted a religious phrase used by Stratfordian turned Baconian, James C Cowell: 'a renegade to the faith I have proclaimed'. Really, I suppose, one is asked in this account of mine to start, to some degree at least, as a free thinker; so that, if the commonly received faith is accepted or retained, it is not done so blindly.

21

Religious parallels could be multiplied; they come mostly from the literature of the controversy, but there are exceptions. Thus, A N Wilson, in a book about the founder of Christianity, stated his contentious thesis immediately: 'The Jesus of History and the Christ of Faith are two separate beings with very different stories.' At the end of his penultimate chapter, he makes an unexpected sole reference to Shakespeare: 'The feelings of the historian about Jesus must be analogous to his feelings about Shakespeare, who managed to achieve fame, wealth and notoriety in Elizabethan London, and who left behind him a body of literary work without parallel, but whose "personality" remains almost invisible.' We shall return to this point. Since I find such comparisons interesting, I have tended to encourage the practice by deliberately adding, not necessarily within quotation marks, a few biblical phrases (sometimes adapted) or analogies at stages in this book where they seem to be singularly appropriate to the situation being described.

SCENE 3

AN INTERLUDE ON COMEDY

If there could be any possibility, however remote it may at present appear, that orthodox scholarship has been deceived into accepting the wrong person as Shakespeare, that surely provides us with a major tragedy. It also provides an interesting history of endeavour to rectify matters. Even if such a belief is patently false, both history and tragedy are still present in the development of the debate over several centuries. Along with comedy they represent the three categories in any classification of Shakespeare's plays. While the comical may seem out of place here, it can be rather more than an interlude; a valuable reminder that, while the debate is intensely serious, it is well to keep a sense of both humour and proportion. For some of the curiosities in the interchanges encourage laughter; others help to avoid any danger of what, for a few people, became a sad obsession.

What, then, of this comic dimension? An odd feature, perhaps linked to the controversy only in the sense that some supporters of the orthodox Shakespeare would have him supernaturally active, was once spotted by the author of a letter to a newspaper. This drew attention to features within Psalm 46, as it exists in the 1611 version of the Bible. The writer argued that Shakespeare (of Stratford) must have had a hand in the translation of the Psalms and would be 46 years old at the time.

It was pointed out that in this Bible, most curiously, the forty-sixth word of Psalm 46 is 'shake' and the forty-sixth word from the end is 'spear'.

A statement was once made, in jest, that 'Shakespeare' was written by an extraterrestrial being. Of course, this is mere frivolity; but, noting that some lawyers think the author must have had legal experience, soldiers that he had military experience and so forth, someone is bound to offer a sly suggestion not altogether dissimilar. It would be to the effect that the analysis, by computer, of the styles of various Elizabethan and Jacobean writers, to test similarities with that of Shakespeare, may only lead to one conclusion: that *The Complete Works* were obviously composed by some early form of machine intelligence!

The best-known of the dreadful 'howlers' are avoided here. But there is one very common observation that is made with a twinkle in the eye, which is nevertheless an opportunity to raise a serious point (since it is grim rather than comic in the ears of the doubters). This is the saying that the works were not written by Shakespeare, but by someone else of the same name. Any such comment is a deliberate side-stepping. One supposes it is sometimes intended to release the pent-up emotions of committed Stratfordians faced with determined unbelief, to divert their angry background of sibilance into the path of humour. But it does not help; there were certainly contemporaries with the very same name. The whole point, of course, is that those who insist there is an identity confusion believe that the true author was someone with a quite different real name. (A pen-name was required: this was based on that of the man from Stratford because the enterprise was essentially the shaking of a literary lance.)

A modern, wide-ranging, specialist encyclopedia edited by Charles Boyce sees the authorship controversy merely as a craze, saying that scholars of the Elizabethan period know there is no need to query the 'fact' that Shakespeare wrote Shakespeare. This is, given one of its two possible meanings, self-evident. That is certainly the name the author used, as everyone would agree! Given the other meaning of the quoted phrase (as intended by this encyclopedia), it is based – no matter how strong the conviction behind it – on assertion rather than definite knowledge. For if it were known and demonstrable, beyond every last lingering query, that the Stratford man wrote all the works, how then could there still be any kind of authorship debate?

It is even sometimes very wrongly half-suggested, by semantic juggling, that the doubters deny the very existence of William Shakespeare of Stratford-upon-Avon. This is a highly irresponsible implication: how could they do so? The orthodox have a duty to be more precise, at least when operating in the context of the debate. What they mean – and should say – is that they believe that, beyond all reasonable doubt, William Shakespeare (1564–1616) was the great author. Of course, anti-Stratfordians have responsibilities too. One of them is to recognise that there is no precedent for the use of a pseudonym by a great writer, where the assumed name coincided with that of a contemporary person who apparently claimed the works for himself. No Mr George Eliot, for example, came forward to assert falsely, against a nineteenth-century lady who used that name as a pseudonym, that he had really written *Middlemarch* and companion novels. For such a curious situation to have existed in the case of the author Shakespeare is not impossible, but certainly would seem most surprising.

This present scene, although seemingly a digression from the main argument of this book, perhaps has its own story to tell. So let us return to comedy of various kinds. There are over a dozen incidents (some told below) exhibiting different brands of humour, which might justly appear in any enumeration of various sources of merriment in the history of the controversy. One of these is a lovely tale concerning *Peter Pan* author, Sir James Barrie. When asked if he thought Francis Bacon wrote 'Shakespeare', he is reputed to have said dryly: 'I know not, sir, but if he did not it seems to me that he missed the opportunity of his lifetime.'

A Baconian once argued that the fair youth to whom the sonnets of Shakespeare are addressed was in line for succession to the throne, as a secret grandchild of the unmarried Queen

Elizabeth. He drew attention to the word 'succession' in Sonnet 2, pointing out that the initial letters of five consecutive lines of that sonnet spell out WHISP – signifying (he claimed) that we are dealing with a secret. I once mentioned this claim to a member of my family: she said, 'Surely it should not be "whisp", but whisper, where's the "er"?' I smilingly replied that, in so delicate a matter, the Queen's initials could not possibly be used!

Neither every humourous incident nor all the excess resides within the camp of the unorthodox, as we shall see. But another example which may amuse is that some of the more extreme Baconians have argued, quite incredibly, on grounds of literary style, that their man wrote not only his own attributed works and those of Shakespeare, but also those of several other contemporary authors. Then, somehow living on, he penned several of later centuries. One commentator on the controversy, R C Churchill, gleefully remarks: 'whether he now draws his old age pension ... is one of the points on which I have not been able to get any precise information'. It should be added here perhaps that The Bacon Society eventually changed its name to 'The Francis Bacon Society'. This was apparently because it kept receiving enquiries from the meat trade. Well, after all, there is a legend about the most famous son of Stratford-upon-Avon that, when young, he was apprenticed to a butcher!

Mark Twain, mentioned already as a leading doubter of the conventional Shakespeare, certainly presented the case in his own colourful, distinctive way. Thus, for example, he contrasted the anonymous verse on the Stratford man's grave, which (like some other readers of it) he regarded as doggerel (William's 'only poem' before he 'laid down and died'), with one of the finest passages in Shakespeare. Twain claimed that one needs to juxtapose good and bad closely, in this way, to recognise what dross the inscription on the grave really is. The point is driven home by typical Twain comic metaphor: 'You never notice how commonplace and unpoetic gravel is, until you bite into a layer of it in a pie!'

There is also an amusing anecdote concerning Twain. At a

Boston literary conference, he was apparently asked publicly a question similar to that put to J M Barrie, as to whether he thought Bacon could possibly have been the true writer of the plays. 'I shall wait until I go to heaven and then ask him,' was Twain's reply. The questioner had hoped for a more revealing answer. He thus commented: 'I do not think you will find Francis Bacon in heaven.' 'If that is the case,' Twain immediately retorted, 'then *you* will have to ask him!'

To take a quite different style of humour, a commendable attempt was made, during 1994, to display some possible relevance of Shakespeare for the population of a housing estate in Birmingham. One woman interviewed remarked, 'Wasn't he French?' As my final example of the comic, this could be associated with an episode in the large literature concerning the claims made that Edward de Vere (pronounced 'Ver'), seventeenth Earl of Oxford, was the real Shakespeare. One advocate of him said that *The Winter's Tale* was a meaningless title for the play concerned; thus there must be a hidden reason behind its choice, an attempt to reveal, or hint at, a name. An answer (of sorts) was found by translating both the title and the name of the supposed author into French: 'Le comte de Vere'; 'Le conte d'hiver'! The French connection, linking these otherwise disparate incidents, serves to remind me of the saying that some lovers in France, at the moment of sexual climax, are said to exclaim: 'J'éxpire!'

With this, we may safely leave a selection simply designed to entertain. My choice is very much a personal one; some of the items put forward in it are just good-humoured tomfoolery. Such episodes, not quite entirely confined to this chapter, vary in the nature as well as in the quality of their humour. Yet collectively they have, in a sense, some serious points to make. We cannot accept too many strange coincidences. Yet the citing of those letters, WHISP, may show that oddities do exist. Here is a similar one: the surname and initial of T Watson, a friend of Shakespeare's great contemporary, Christopher Marlowe, appears almost in full (but really only by chance) down the initial letters of consecutive lines within Sonnet 76.

Some of the other examples quoted as comedy indicate that

there are stylistic similarities between various Elizabethan writers. Many of the points noted were put forward seriously, and not everyone would agree with my contention that they represent ill-judged excesses of enthusiasm for one's cause. If such statements are extreme, this does not necessarily invalidate the case for Bacon or another; there may be much better evidence.

At any rate, we can be sure that it is important for students of a serious controversy to find points to chuckle over as well as issues of deep concern. At the end of the day those issues, about to confront us in more detail, must be taken seriously. History, it would seem, is determined at times to have a sense of humour, but truth remains its foundation. Of course, someone determined to adhere to the 'orthodox faith' can read parts of this book as fiction, or humour, and still reap enjoyment, even benefit, from the introduction to a great, potentially perennial, debate. It can be reiterated confidently, too, that the literature of this controversy remains a unique path (too infrequently trod, yet as good a method as any) for investigating and learning more about that great author, William Shakespeare.

ACT 2
THE WILL TO DISBELIEVE?

... the immense number of slight facts and coincidences, each of little importance in itself, but all collectively making the proof as good as certain. A fibre of hemp will bear only a small weight; but if we twist many fibres into each strand, and unite many strands into a rope, we can make a cable.

William Stanley Jevons, 1835–82.

SCENE 1

EXAMINING THE TRADITIONAL AUTHOR

With this quotation about using logical method for the reconstruction of the past, we can now return to the discussion which preceded our light interlude exactly where it was left. A N Wilson's analogy between Jesus and Shakespeare was mentioned. Transferring his general thesis to the realm of literature, can it not be asked whether the writer Shakespeare of actual history and the Shakespeare of the (common) faith are really the same person?

Of course, people may insist repeatedly: 'The specialists must have investigated this matter thoroughly. If there was anything at all in it, then they would know.' Let it be said again that part of the problem with coming to grips with truth in the controversy is that 'experts' are not likely to be sympathetic to anything that attacks even the margins of their track record, let alone theories essentially undermining the very essence of what their specialist judgement has backed in the past. Some may even be 'programmed' to accept only the conventional view, it being so difficult to run counter to the accredited academic norm in such basic matters. Unless or until there is proof positive, scholarly respectability will always tend to back away immediately, with some vigour, from those querying the authorship. But, since there are plenty of works by professorial or other orthodox specialists, the emphasis here is on those sceptical counter-arguments. I shall quite deliberately side with the doubters, from here on until the end of my book, as much as fairness allows.

One preliminary point not yet touched upon is a simple but key question. Why might anyone want to conceal identity behind a pen-name? In looking, in turn, at the main alternative 'Shakespeares' put forward, we shall see that one was an acknowledged great dramatist who was believed to be dead. If still living, he had very serious charges of atheism and homosexuality to face. Thus the case for hiding him, if indeed he was still there to be hidden, is easily made. The other chief candidates are all members of the upper classes. They had a quite different, but very real, reason for secrecy; one that may now seem quaint, but the extreme force it then had should be recognised. The reason was simply that to produce numerous dramas for the general hoard of theatregoers would be unthinkably inappropriate 'contamination' for men of their rank. One of them, as we shall see, had published some poetry, but even that was rather frowned upon. A contemporary writer of Shakespeare's, John Seldon, remarked: 'It is ridiculous for a lord to print verses. He may write them to please himself, but to publish them is foolish.' And *A Discourse on English Poetry* (1586) commented 'I know very many notable gentlemen in the court that have written commendably, and suppressed it again, or else suffered it to be published without their own names to it.'

The man from Stratford had a name which, quite unlike those of other contemporary dramatists, would make an excellent 'trading label' for any aspiring literary lance-shaker. Of course, this does nothing to prove it *was* a pen-name. But what is known (rather than guessed, or imagined) about the 'official' Shakespeare? The answer, unfortunately, in terms of value, is 'not a great deal'. Some modern commentators who deplore all the anti-Stratfordian sects say that lack of knowledge does not imply any mystery. It is just because there is a vacuum, they may contemptuously insist, that such 'rubbish' can float about.

There are four observations to be made on that. First, not all is rubbish. Second, not all of that which clearly is rubbish – the sillier or most distorted speculation – is by any means on the anti-Stratfordian side. Third, we may well come to feel that enough is known for sure to believe that the actor William Shakespeare surely lacked the right credentials (unless genius is to be equated with miracles) to write the Shakespearean works. Lastly, after tremendous effort by scholars to discover more, it emerges that all we do have for sure seems to distance him from those writings. It reveals a mind, temperament, attitude, range of activity, all at variance with them. He was also, it would appear, careless as to their destiny. Using the most 'modern' records unearthed about him, as well as older ones, what do we find? That there is total consistency in the ambience suggested by each single facet of his daily living – but that this is completely contrary to the ethos one must expect from someone who was, arguably, the greatest writer in all literary history.

There has been infinite speculation about Stratford's most famous person: some of it, with subtle mendacity, is passed on as though it were fact. Biographers of the 'official' Bard all too often reshuffle a thin pack of factual cards, getting by on legend, eloquence or guesswork. If two most reputable 'classic' biographies from the world of past literary orthodoxy are contrasted, we find that of Sir E K Chambers admitting to areas of ignorance, especially about the years 1585–92, while Sir Sidney Lee's earlier one strives skilfully to fill in such gaps through the use of traditional tales. But both deny, for instance, that the William Shackspere who is shown in the records as lending money to a John Clayton in 1592, and prepared to sue for its return in 1600, is their man. This despite the fact that he who was subsequently by far Stratford's most famous son did press for the repayment of debts such as these. Doubtless, if it helped the general cause of the orthodox, this reference would be claimed with alacrity. But how could their man have obtained money to spare for lending in 1592?

Probably that *was* a different Shakespeare. Yet about the one generally regarded as the literary giant, some things *are* known for sure. These include: that William Shaxpere (because his name was spelt in many ways, I deliberately use an alternative), from Stratford-upon-Avon, was born on or within a day or two of 23 April 1564, being baptised on the 26th; that he died on 23 April 1616. We also most certainly know, for example, that:

- he married a woman eight years his elder;
- he went to London and became an actor;
- he had three children by the time he was 21;
- he eventually returned to Stratford to retire;
- he left us a few shaky signatures (but these do not appear in literary works);
- his will left to his wife 'the second-best bed';
- she could not join him in his (unnamed) grave in Stratford church because he insisted that it should not be disturbed.

We know, above all, that certain plays and poems were published in the lifetime of this man carrying the name Shakespeare, sometimes hyphenated. These, along with others, were unmistakably attributed to this man in the First Folio of 1623. It is really due to the massive influence of these last two facts that most of us think it must be accepted, beyond all querying, that he is that great author. Yet there are certainly problems, one being that of compatibility. While there are various literary references of the time which we know refer to the writer Shakespeare, we can only assume (if we wish) that these simply *must*, beyond any doubt, also refer to the actor from Stratford. We also have references which indubitably do refer to the Stratford man. Alas for the orthodox cause, these do not relate to literature. They concern very mundane matters.

If commentary is mingled with the known facts, what do we know of the inclinations of the man? To aspire to be a gentleman property-owner; as one who pressed neighbours for small debts, according to some factual reports; to be a seller of corn and malt by others. Then there are the inevitable tales. He was a poacher of deer by an unreliable one; a heavy drinker according to one or two stories, but something of an abstainer according to yet another; a man who went to London to make his way in the world, at first doing a miscellany of things, such as holding horses for gentlemen outside the theatre, in his endeavours to pick up all the opportunities and information he could. At one time he was a butcher, at another a schoolmaster, according to the seventeenth-century gossip, John Aubrey. Perhaps he served as a soldier too?

Some modern commentators should certainly be prepared to 'hold their horses'. For much of what is told (the above being but a small sample) is sheer legend being added for the joy of decorative tale-weaving, often long after 1616. And when we are informed that a writer passing through Stratford in 1630 described it as 'a town most remarkable for the birth of famous William Shakespeare', we can only remark that by then the Stratford man's authorship, true or false, had been officially sealed; the basis for the vast ensuing acclaim begun. His adult lifetime plus the first five years or so after his death would be the crucial testing period for any planned, perhaps well-meaning, deceit. It would be far more significant if this 1630 remark had been said of Stratford's famous son in, say, 1613. But there was no such 'applause' then, nor any signs of widespread grief at the passing of a great man when he died in 1616. In our own time, Samuel Schoenbaum, a detester of all anti-Stratfordians, yet has a word of warning to give in his *Shakespeare's Lives:* 'If it would be an exaggeration to say that the materials concerning [the life] ... deny matter enough for a page, they hardly amount to a great deal; and they are fraught with perplexities for the biographer.'

Nor is there a fully reliable portrait. It is safest to consider any picture of Shakespeare as a mere representation. Most often seen of all is the 'Droeshout' engraving. There are problems with this in terms of the eyes; and also, as a tailoring magazine once pointed out, with the tunic. This most famous but curious 'portrait' is easily recognised. Some people consider that the line at the left-side of the subject's face indicates a mask. Others have thought that the reversed sleeve suggests he was two people rolled into one. Since Martin Droeshout, a Netherlander, was not born until 1601, he was surely too young for the dramatist to sit for him and was therefore copying from another picture. But then, if so, where is it? Could it be the 'Flower' portrait dated 1609, or is that a fake? Perhaps better than Droeshout's efforts, but unreliable as a genuine depiction of the Bard, is one described as the 'Chandos' portrait. Others may be encountered, too: they include the 'Grafton' portrait, found at Grafton Regis in Northamptonshire, dated 1588. The subject of it is certainly about 24 years old, but how would the Stratford man have enough influence, at that time, to have his portrait painted? More and more 'picture' questions jostle for priority of answer. The combined effect of it all is to leave us feeling very unsure of the man's actual appearance. Could that even be intentional?

In the Stratford church, alongside the unnamed grave, is a bust, or monument. It was produced by Droeshout's older countryman, Gheerart Janssen. Curiously, although it is known that in 1725 this monument looked much the same as it now does, there is a case, pounced upon by those sceptical of the orthodox Shakespeare, for arguing that the work currently on view there was not the original. William Dugdale, the Warwickshire antiquarian, had gone to the church to draw a picture of it in 1656 for his own purposes. The Dugdale sketch differs in several respects from the present monument; could that just be an example of carelessness? The problem is that Nicholas Rowe, producing a biography of the Bard in 1709, offered a picture which is different again, but much closer to Dugdale's efforts than to the bust on display today. Rowe and Dugdale show Shakespeare not as a writer, as he now appears, but rather as a merchant with a sack. Was Shakespeare originally remembered in Stratford as a man of business rather than an author? Was the bust altered, at some time early in the eighteenth century, to conform to the needs of a growing Shakespeare industry? Perhaps not. Like so many parts of the vast mosaic of doubt, the situation here remains tantalisingly inconclusive; but I believe that the bust, as originally depicted, is the best pictorial representation we have of the Stratford man's facial appearance.

Push the plays, poetry, glory, reluctantly to one side to concentrate on what is sure fact about the activity and experience of this Stratford man.

Examining, with neither preconceived ideas nor an axe to grind, what is known about his life rather than what is guessed at or imputed to him, one may well agree with the point made about the apparent gulf between the supposed author and the writings. He seems totally disqualified, in both quantitative and qualitative terms, to be the creator of that great range of literature. There is not only the absence of the necessary educational and experiential background; there is such clear lack of affinity. His interests seem essentially acquisitive; his true vocation to be social climbing. Of course, these things are not unreasonable. It is so necessary, as multitudes can testify, to have an interest in earning a living or making one's way. But the concern we see in the records (as opposed to the speculation) about this Stratford man for worldly affairs, along with the apparent indifference to those of literature or issues of the human spirit – that is what makes anti-Stratfordian hearts beat faster. For there is an enigma here which makes it difficult, as a major writer of later times, R W Emerson, admitted, 'to marry the man to his works'.

The stark dichotomy between the known deeds of his life and the known glory of the Shakespeare works has led to vastly different assessments, even by other poets. When John Milton, very soon after the age of Shakespeare, wrote: 'sweetest Shakespeare, nature's child', he was thinking chiefly of the literary output, which he believed to be from the pen of the Stratford man. When Alexander Pope said that Shakespeare 'For gain not glory winged his roving flight', he made a comment which has brought abuse on his head from Bardolators, but he was essentially looking at the known Stratfordian biography rather than the literature.

But perhaps this is premature. What is the evidence which doubters have found – and still find – so compelling?

The orthodox really should not point so emphatically to the 1598 testimony of Francis Meres, praising the work of Shakespeare, because this simply indicates that there was such an author. It mentions, for instance, some 'sugared sonnets', circulated privately among friends. But it does not identify him unequivocally with the Stratford actor. Indeed, as Enoch Powell once pointed out, the orthodox dating of plays, coupled with Meres's evidence, suggest that Shakespeare the writer was especially active between 1590 and 1594. Assuming him to be the person from Stratford, there is what Powell calls a double phenomenon: the combination of exceptional precocity of insight with productivity of wondrous speed and volume. By the time the Stratford man was nearing the age of thirty, Powell's logic continues, he had (if truly the author) written an epic poem plus most of the dramatic history cycle, together with several other plays. If we spread that output by pushing some plays further back in time to his younger days, we only increase the precocity; if we reduce the precocity factor, we increase the wonder of output – from a relatively uneducated man still in his twenties – still further.

One might add to Powell's comments the fact that there is no evidence that the Stratford man's associates had anything literary from him, unless we count a feeble epitaph for a certain John Combe. This too is of dubious authenticity. How helpful it would have been to the orthodox Stratfordian cause if some friends in the town had mentioned, or produced, copies of sugared sonnets penned by the man. In this, as in other things, there is painful silence where we might expect at least a glimmering of positive testimony.

In the same spirit, Enoch Powell has argued that *King Richard the Third* must relate to direct experience of political life. Of course, Powell must rank very firmly with the disbelievers. But orthodox Stratfordians, like Leslie Hotson, can still write that Shakespeare (of Stratford) had reached mature powers by the time he was twenty-five years old. The years 1585–92, remarks Hotson, were marked by amazing accomplishment. Well, yes, if orthodoxy is right, they really must have been! Our man was busy with daily work, while simultaneously absorbing culture, and writing extensively. Consider also his foreign travel, or the apparently wide education which would have to be acquired informally. Then there are indications of his range of interests, seemingly linked to the life of the high-born. There is his knowledge of law, the sea, warfare, the Bible, gardens, music, languages. These also seem to have all matured by the end of this period. He was actor, manager, investor too, says conventional critic Ivor Brown, while another such commentator, R C Churchill, tells us that actors had to be trained for proficiency in dancing, swordplay, musical knowledge, and acrobatics. (Since the author of the sonnets, written early in Shakespeare's career, was apparently mildly physically handicapped, dancing or acrobatics might seem out of his range.)

But the greatest enemies of all this are simply time and opportunity. Between them, the orthodox often seem to demolish their own case. True, our Shakespeare must have greatly lived in a small time, but there are limits. Does exceptional genius have a dimension which puts more than 24 hours into a person's day? We must return to this theme a little later, for it is all very puzzling. Little wonder that the doubters either smile or wince, depending upon mood, when historian A L Rowse (another hater of Shakespeare heretics) can comment that many people do not appreciate what a long, hard struggle Shakespeare (of Stratford) must have had! Certainly, those heretics will insist, it defies all realistic appreciation.

An equally eminent historian, Lord Dacre, then Hugh Trevor-Roper, Regius Professor of Modern History at Oxford University, once pointed out that the person from Stratford is still so elusive. We have only the outer shell. We must, therefore, look to the evidence we have of the mind he possessed. Professor Trevor-Roper comes across as apparently uncommitted rather than a declared disbeliever. Thus he must, one supposes, be classed as an agnostic. He sees the author Shakespeare from this 'mind examination' standpoint as, among other things, a devoted gardener. Also as one who knew cosmology, philosophy, foreign affairs. He depicted Italian scenes extremely well, says Trevor-Roper, arguing that the topographical precision in *The Merchant of Venice* is incredible if the author had not actually visited Italy.

As a yardstick for comparison, there were three near-contemporaries of the Stratford man who might be looked at in this context as men of quite humble origins who made their way by writing fine poetry or drama. Furthest removed in age is Ben Jonson, not a genius to rank with Shakespeare, but nevertheless a very able writer. But there is evidence to show that Jonson had an appropriate programme of education. Christopher Marlowe, humbly born the same year as the Shakespeare of orthodoxy, proved his genius in early works. He had the immense advantage of a scholarship to attend Cambridge University. He was also associated with high circles, partly through his espionage activity. Yet he could surely never have produced these earliest Shakespearean plays with the mature (although now very dated) wit of *Love's Labour's Lost*, or the character of Falstaff. Michael Drayton, born in Warwickshire the year before Stratford's Shakespeare, had educational opportunity through his links with a wealthy household. Incidentally, Drayton's doctor, John Hall, spoke of him as a fine poet. Dr Hall was married to Susanna, William of Stratford's daughter, but never mentioned literature in the context of his father-in-law. Was this just family modesty? Later, in 1643, a surgeon visitor found the only books or manuscripts in Susanna's home to be those of her late husband.

It might, of course, be legitimately objected, as a caveat concerning the direction in which the above indubitably points, that, when William of Stratford laid claim to the plays and poems (as presumably he must have done at times in conversation) some people may have been surprised, but nobody said: 'Hey, just a moment ... these are mine!' But of course, if it were a planned deception with the real author wanting to keep his identity secret, no one would make such exclamations. Nor would we need to dub the official Shakespeare a thief, either, if we assume another the true author, but holding good reason for wanting the 'willing' (no pun intended), and so appropriately named actor to be his 'official representative'. But, if the glorious heat of Shakespeare's genius was really all his, there was surely a metamorphosis required far greater than that shown by Prince Hal in *King Henry the Fourth* in achieving maturity to be the next monarch. Then, even more incredibly, the Shakespeare of convention, as we shall see, changed back.

So it is that, when we scrutinise this man of Stratford, the great sun that was the author is seemingly masked in perpetuity by what investigation shows to be the 'base contagious clouds' of sound, but uninspiring, everyday living. The William Shakespeare of conventional belief must have been gradually perceived, in London, as an author, since the works were appearing there and he claimed them. But, in his lifetime, it seems he was never so regarded in his home town.

Let us look beyond his death in 1616. That went completely unremarked. If he was a big fish in the small pond of Stratford, he did not seem to be known there for any reason other than as a local man of property. But in 1623, there was published the First Folio edition of Shakespeare's plays. This most unambiguously points to our Shakespeare of Stratford-upon-Avon as the great author. It carries some plays unheard of before, plus some others which, although played in the theatre, had not previously been published. It omits *Pericles*, later to be generally accepted as Shakespeare's on the grounds of internal evidence as well as his name on the title page. The sonnets are also omitted. There is high praise in verse about the author from contemporary dramatist Ben Jonson, tributes to William Shakespeare of Stratford from fellow actors John Heminges and Henry Condell. There are also shorter verses of commendation from others. One of the latter, Leonard Digges, who had personally known Shakespeare of Stratford, doubtless must have believed him to be the author. The Janssen bust was placed in the church at Stratford-upon-Avon. The Droeshout portrait of Shakespeare appeared in the Folio.

Although there is nothing in any of this that absolutely prohibits an imposture having been arranged, it seems, at least on the surface, to be most unlikely. Indeed, at first (even second or third) sight this, certainly the best Stratfordian evidence, comes across as remarkably final. It thus appears highly improbable that there could be major deception here, but then a good deception would make things appear so.

Beneath a calm surface may be strong undercurrents. Be prepared to consider, at least, that Digges may have given a tribute simply accepting the word of others that William

Shakespeare of Stratford was the great author; that Heminges and Condell rather curiously copy their remarks from the classical author Pliny. (These two actors also received the legacy of a ring in the Stratford man's will in 1616, although this bequest is interpolated between lines in what seems a different hand.) Wonder why their own eventual wills were superior in tone and content to that of the man from Stratford. Think that Jonson just might have been put up to writing what he did, by some influential person or persons. The Stratford bust can scarcely be said to do justice to any human mind, let alone Shakespeare's. And why wait until 1623 to honour the man who died in 1616? All such suppositions, again on the surface, seem highly dubious. We could never tolerate them or any other such 'mays' or 'mights' promoting doubt were there not other reasonable grounds for probing. For the moment we continue to range over the evidence in a general, discursive way. There will shortly be some focus upon ten specific points of argument to suggest that there are such grounds.

Ben Jonson, however, had things to say about Shakespeare which contrast strangely with the handsome tribute he pays in the First Folio. He was later to suggest, for instance, that Shakespeare 'wanted art'. In the lifetime of the Stratford man, there are two items by Jonson worthy of study. One is the sketch of this William Shakespeare as the character Sogliardo in *Every Man out of His Humour*. The individual comes across as something of a bumpkin, eager to get on in the world and 'ramping to gentility'. We know just who is meant since Sogliardo's motto, 'Not without mustard', is clearly a parody on the Stratford man's 'Not without right'. Then, in one of his *Epigrams*, published in 1616, Jonson speaks out boldly. There can be no doubt here as to the person intended:

> Poor Poet-ape that would be thought our chief,
> Whose works are e'en the frippery of wit,
> From brokerage is become so bold a thief,
> As we, the robbed, leave rage and pity it.
> At first he made low shifts, would pick and glean,
> Buy the revision of old plays, now grown

ACT 2. THE WILL TO DISBELIEVE?

To little wealth, and credit in the scene,
He takes up all, makes each man's wit his own,
And told of this, he slights it ...

All caricature carries some exaggeration. I do not mean to suggest by quoting these lines (nor did Jonson), that the actor from Stratford was a dolt. What is suggested is that he claimed to be a play-broker, then a writer of plays, that other dramatists were somewhat sceptical; but, lo, the plays appeared. Yet they noticed that some were 'revisions' of plays circulating, presumably without an author's name, at an earlier date. There can be no doubt too that Shakespeare (the writer) did, on occasion, take up other people's works for enhancement in his own distinctive way. Perhaps Shakespeare of Stratford did not strain the credibility of dramatists of that age when he claimed to be a writer, but he certainly seems to have done so in presenting himself as a great and original one. They could see that this Mr W S somehow had the freedom to draw on earlier work (clearly not by himself) with impunity – or (they assumed) by buying the right to revise it. By 1623, when Jonson made the wholehearted tribute which can still be read in the introductory pages of most modern editions of the *Complete Works*, he offered a different view. Perhaps he had curious reasons of his own for this. If not, he was either insincere in that tribute (surely not), or had received information (with instructions) which radically changed his perception of the nature of what constituted Shakespeare.

There is one other piece of important evidence for the conventional view of Shakespeare. This is often hailed with delight by Stratfordians. Although over-quoted, it is worth mention in relation to points about it which seem to be so easily missed. The passage in question is a published statement by the dying Elizabethan dramatist, Robert Greene, in 1592. He is scathing about several people, but warns three other playwrights (one of them clearly Christopher Marlowe) against an upstart crow, an actor 'beautified with our feathers'. This actor aspires to be a playwright himself: he is described as a factotum (a jack of all trades). And, most crucially, with his

43

'tiger's heart wrapped in a player's hide', he thinks himself 'the only Shake-scene' in the country. It is highly probable that William of Stratford was meant, although not quite the cast-iron certainty that so many Stratfordians insist upon. They are so very much less ready to pick up name similarities by suggesting that the characters 'Black Will' and 'Shake-bag' ('two rougher ruffians never lived in Kent'), appearing in an anonymous contemporary play, *Arden of Feversham*, must be based on their man also, although Arden was his mother's original name. Curiously, there is also a character called 'Greene' in that play, a drama surely penned in part by Christopher Marlowe.

Some followers of the unorthodox paths within the history of the authorship controversy have queried the 'Shake-scene' identification as being a pun on the Stratford man's name. I am content here to accept that this is what Greene meant. The 'tiger's heart' reference comes from *King Henry the Sixth Part III*, but it may well be lines which Shakespeare took over in revising and developing that old play. Significantly, after Greene's death, there came an apology to one person. This expression of regret was from the publisher of the outburst, Henry Chettle. It is not at all clear that the one to whom the apology is addressed was the 'Shake-scene', since Greene had also criticised playwrights. If Chettle is read with care, the disclaimer could equally well be intended for one of them. A consensus of modern scholars supports the idea that it was meant for the upstart actor/playwright, but then, that is the interpretation that concurs with the stated views of that consensus! At any rate, two of the people concerned had been offended by Greene's attack. One of these (generally reckoned to be Marlowe) has learning which Chettle admires, but he does not care for this man – is happy to be never acquainted with him. There is no apology from Chettle to that person: it is offered to one of the others only, either the actor who aspired to be a playwright, or to one of the dramatists.

Perhaps, indeed, Chettle did, as Stratfordians insist, mean it for the 'Shake-scene'. Let us assume that he did; also assuming, at least for the time being, that this was the Stratford actor. What does this apology say? In essence, it is most fulsome: it has been described by various members of Stratfordian orthodoxy as a glowing tribute, even the most handsome apology of the age. Henry Chettle says, as part of the passage concerned:

> I am as sorry as if the original fault had been my fault, because myself have seen his demeanour no less civil than he excellent in the quality he professes. Besides, divers of worship (many people with high social standing) have reported his uprightness of dealing, which argues his honesty, and his facetious grace in writing, that approves his art.

What we are being asked to believe by the orthodox, in their endeavour to find an early reference of some literary worth for their man, is that a young actor of humble birth, presumed to be at the outset of his career as a dramatist, could bring forth an apology on this scale. Furthermore, he had many worthy people taking trouble to speak up for him. Why should they be so interested in defending his reputation? It is surely far more reasonable to assume, with a long retrospective view, that there were aspects of this situation undreamed by Chettle when he published Greene's attack. He would subsequently be advised, by a representative of the many worthies, that apology was in order. If the apparent 'Shake-scene' was but a 'front' for a much more powerful and significant person as author, the apology becomes much more easily understood. A young commoner, new to the world of the theatre, could surely never, whatever his natural genius, have commanded such praise and support from people of high rank at the very beginning of his career. The apology then, it may be argued, was surely ordered in 1592, by a significant personage, to protect an emerging enterprise with more behind it than Henry Chettle could possibly imagine.

So the Greene/Chettle episode, while retaining intense interest, becomes, if put into true perspective, somewhat counter-productive as argument for the man commonly acclaimed as Shakespeare really being that great author. In sum:

the Stratford man was probably meant by Greene, who would take apparent contemporary happenings at their face value; the subsequent publisher's apology was likely intended for Shakespeare. Its wholeheartedness, based upon the (presumably verbal) testimonials given to Greene's publisher, speaks of a situation most definitely *not* what it appeared to be, but quite extraordinary. Chettle, in such circumstances, would by no means be given a full explanation. He would simply be told, on the authority of worthies and in no uncertain manner, that an apology was required.

Much nearer the end of the writer Shakespeare's career something else happened which uses language that seemingly echoes that of Chettle's apology. It was in 1609, close in time to the first publication of Shakespeare's sonnets, that there appeared a quarto edition of the play *Troilus and Cressida*. This has a most curious preface. The writer of that preface (not Shakespeare) tells playgoers that they are lucky to be able to obtain this play now. We are assured that if the 'grand possessors' of the Shakespeare manuscripts had their way, then the theatre audience would not yet have received it. The doubters are entitled to ask (and do), 'Who were these grand possessors?' It surely cannot be a name for the acting fraternity, or the company for which Shakespeare (of Stratford) worked. If it were Shakespeare himself, why is the plural form used?

Thus it is that we need to note another startling double phenomenon or curiosity. That 'William Shakespeare' (the writer), whoever he was, had (it would seem) the support of many worthies at what was apparently the start of his career; then, later, his manuscripts were under the control of 'grand possessors'. Enough may have been said to indicate that there is genuine cause for doubt about the 'Will' Shakespeare of common everyday belief. Of course, people may cling to it from loyalty; because of early indoctrination; or because doubters are consistently brushed aside, being denied credibility, as academic ranks quickly close. There may be every wish to be fair, recognising that judgement in cultural issues cannot be a precise science, but professorial reputations are understandably paramount, and may override such intentions: 'Nature must obey necessity' (*Julius Caesar*).

Perhaps, over the centuries, to luxuriate in a positive flurry of further quotations both direct and indirect, things have not too infrequently been so – at least in the instance of some academics in English literature. I am first reminded of a rather waspish remark by Francis Bacon about his personal experience of the reception of new ideas by a group of his own dons: that the last thing anyone in that particular circle would be likely to entertain was an unfamiliar thought. In areas requiring sustained critical or aesthetic judgement, we may see that the establishment must be held to be correct. For the most inflexible of these specialists, accumulated 'wisdom', published endeavour, can never be allowed to have been wrong-headed. It represents reputation's lifeblood, their intellectual immortality. Heaven and earth may pass away, but their words must not do so. Specifically, in this field of ours, all today's English literature dons have their 'honest Will' of tradition; rightly or wrongly, it is their will to uphold him; they certainly do not intend to be vexed by 'eccentrics' who offer much circumstantial evidence, but lack overriding final proof. Yet, since there is no such incontrovertible proof available to either side, we can only seek to advance knowledge by honest debate, using the best tools available to us. One might say, thinking of a comment from the philosopher Artur Schopenhauer, that 'when [any] "Will" crowds out knowledge (or efforts to progress towards it), we call the result obstinacy'!

One last reference may be appropriate. Another philosopher and psychologist, William James, did not (unlike his younger brother Henry) write words suggesting denial of the traditional assignment of the works of Shakespeare. But he did write a book entitled *The Will to Believe*. Perhaps, right here, there is a Will to disbelieve? It may take courage as well as conviction to do just that, but let us look systematically, even at the cost of a little repetition, at major anti-Stratfordian arguments.

SCENE 2

TEN ARGUMENTS AGAINST HIM

Little has been said above concerning the general evidence in favour of William Shakespeare from Stratford for three reasons: the wish to be succinct in an introductory work; because the evidence itself, although seemingly all-powerful, is not extensive, being based on a few key matters; and because he has hosts of commentators who repeat and press home what there is. Since this book does not aim to supplant the efforts of others in attacking the Shakespeare of orthodoxy, the anti-Stratfordian arguments may also be dealt with reasonably briefly. Below they are condensed into ten key points. These are essentially a personal choice. They are meant to be illustrative areas for starting investigation for oneself rather than a comprehensive statement. Thus each is presented only in very concise form, to give its flavour.

1 It is clear that the Shakspear, Shaxpere, Shakespeare, Shaxberd (or whatever of the several other variant spellings you wish) of Stratford and his immediate family lacked both learning and opportunities to learn

We know that William may well have gone to the local grammar school. It is not certain that he did. Despite the confident assertion of so many books on this point, there is no

48

clear evidence. Let us assume that this was so: there was certainly no more than that to his formal education. Interestingly, noting some alleged Catholic leanings of the father, John Shakspear, one Stratfordian commentator, J Dover Wilson, denies that William went to the local school at all; he must, Wilson claims, have acquired education privately as a singing boy in the house of a Catholic nobleman.

As for the immediate family, John Shakspear, although at one time an alderman, signed his name by means of a mark. One of William's daughters, Judith, later wife of Thomas Quiney, could not write; the other, Susanna, could sign her name, but could not read well enough to recognise the handwriting of her husband, Dr Hall. Some Stratfordians even think William was removed from the grammar school early, to help support the family, when his father's financial position deteriorated. That would add to the burden of overcoming a built-in educational handicap. Now, it is sometimes suggested that any such objections are but a form of snobbery, based on the idea that only a wealthy, very well-educated person could ever possibly even aspire to write such plays. It is not so. There are many anti-Stratfordians who would gladly hail the route to success of one from the working classes or lower middle class, giving extra applause in recognition of obstacles overcome, provided the route is (even faintly) visible or credible.

2 To redress the balance by extensive intellectual effort, the Stratford man would have needed books

Yes, there were books in sixteenth-century Stratford. Yet for our key man, there is no evidence of their possession, of interest in them, or of access to a library. This does not prevent orthodox literature of our century, recognising that the great writer possessed much more knowledge than Ben Jonson had admitted in the 1623 First Folio, offering comments such as Kenneth Muir's to the effect that even if we read all books still available that were published before 1616, we could still be sure that we had not encountered all of those known to Shakespeare.

Many anti-Stratfordians would agree. The author must have read voraciously. The whole point is that the evidence for this comes from the Shakespearean works: the background needed for them together with the love of reading expressed, for instance, in *The Tempest*. It is only by assuming that William of Stratford was their author that we can make such statements of him. His own sure factual biography, as relevant testimony, is so conspicuously counterproductive. (It may be noted, in passing, that one of the many wild legends, an anonymous document of 1728, suggested that he had neither the time nor the need to do reading, but 'kept' a historian to do his background research for him! Here we see very well how history *can* be distorted. How would a man of his background acquire or afford one?)

3 The works of Shakespeare exhibit particular knowledge of a wide range of subjects and scenes

The subjects concerned include law, music, war, sports, the sea, plants, the Bible. Books and articles have been written on these links, often specialising in just one of them. This is especially true of the legal knowledge:* in that respect, after making due allowances for the interests of the age, there is such a residuum of technicalities in Shakespeare's legal references, delivered with such precision.

Here, while saying so much less than the various specialist works do, it can at least be recognised that there are limits to what one person, however talented, can deliver. Shakespeare the author seems to many of the doubters happiest in the milieu of the court: he knows hunting phraseology. He appears to be much travelled.

Robert Giroux is a modern American critic who, like the vast majority, accepts the Stratford tradition. He has

---

* It is illuminating to see, as just one example via my bibliography, an indication of the interest this once provoked in the journal of The American Bar Association.

nevertheless felt obliged to point out that early dramas, such as *The Comedy of Errors* and *Titus Andronicus*, were soon followed by Italianate plays which show familiarity with the lifestyle of wealthy aristocrats. Those who do not believe that Stratford's William Shakespeare was the great author argue that he would have had to undergo a stupendous educational and cultural transition in an incredibly short time. And, somehow, he would have had to have bridged the chasm while engaged in earning his living. That writing, so wise, so glorious, must have been superimposed on acting, learning parts, acquiring education, fraternising with the nobility, listening to gossip from all ranks as one important source of ideas. Moreover, we should remember that several plays, including one of mature courtly wit, had been completed before this man was thirty.

Then we might ask, for instance, how many languages did he know, and how well did he know them? Consider the following remarks on seven Shakespeare plays, reflecting comments from orthodox writers on some of their sources:

> *Timon of Athens.* Source: a work on the same subject by Lucian. Shakespeare may have known it in Latin, French or Italian, but no English version existed for him.

> *Othello.* Source: a novella by the Italian, Cinthio. There was no English translation; our dramatist may have read it in Italian, French or Spanish. The situation is similar with regard to *Measure for Measure*.

> *Comedy of Errors.* Source: Plautus. Only available in Latin when Shakespeare wrote.

> *Cymbeline.* One source was Boccaccio's *Decameron*. There was no English translation, so we must presume Shakespeare read it in French or Italian.

> *Two Gentlemen of Verona.* A Spanish romance, not to be published in English translation until 1598, was one source.

(Did he, for this and other sources, see the manuscript of a translation before publication? Surely not.) Likewise, Italian sources were used for *Much Ado about Nothing*.

Perhaps there are other legitimate presumptions concerning access to sources for the origins of these plays? Here are two, but I would not advise any honest Stratfordian to clutch tightly at either. Could he have obtained his data orally, having been told about the sources by someone who had read them; or was an English translation for some of them available at the time, only to be subsequently lost? One scrupulously orthodox writer, Kenneth Muir, tells us that Shakespeare, in fact, had fluent knowledge of Latin, some knowledge of French, Italian and perhaps a smattering of Spanish. Well!

Most Stratfordians, alas, have their eyes fixed only on one man. Unable to acquire a gaze transplant, they cope with these remarkable pointers by a curious circularity. They *insist* that their man wrote the plays, the plays need knowledge of foreign tongues, therefore their man must have had such knowledge – though how, neither they nor we know. Apart from the not unreasonable supposition of at least some years at the grammar school, he must have been, in Matthew Arnold's phrase, 'self-schooled'. In such circumstances, what is described above would certainly need genius, but other ingredients too. Is there not a fundamental contradiction in all this? It would demand much time, both in the sense of the number of years required to gain the knowledge and daily pressures of time due to his normal work as theatre factotum. Would not such opportunity be denied to a busy actor earning his living?

If we assume him to be the great dramatist, we must also assume that beyond his interests, or capabilities (springing, presumably, from what has been termed the genius of a supremely articulated commonsense), lies the question of what he experienced. Despite sustained searching of archives, we have no record of him ever leaving Britain. It begs the question to say that his description of foreign scenes is not always exact; that is artistic licence. Some detail certainly seems first-hand. Can genius provide such experience of places one has never visited? Consider, as one instance here, the Italian view suggested in Sonnet 33:

Full many a glorious morning have I *seen* [my emphasis]
Flatter the mountain top with sovereign eye.

Or as another, the so authentic Venetian name of the character 'Gobbo'. The sea imagery, too, may speak compellingly of things its writer had witnessed. But examples could easily be multiplied.

Scrupulously honest as well as strictly orthodox, Ivor Brown wonders how his man was finding time, by the early seventeenth century, to study and perform parts; to turn out two or three plays a year; to compose sonnets and poems; to have an eye on property in Stratford; to follow leading managerial and commercial interests with the Lord Chamberlain's men. Brown thinks it was not impossible that, in his early days, William of Stratford was in turn glover, butcher, schoolmaster, and serving in a lawyer's office. He travelled round England as an actor. He doubtless somehow found room, in his crowded days, to be omnivorous of the human scene in swapping yarns, taking in the ideas or experiences of others to be polished for future use. It is also conceded by Ivor Brown that the Shakespeare he visualises, to write as he did, had himself spent time at sea; while he could have improved upon his botany (we are told) by going no further than Piccadilly. His life must have been filled with the bustle of continuous activity, argues Brown, yet accepting that the great writer left (as the introduction to the 1623 Folio testifies) 'not a blot in his papers'. This really will not do. Brown's willingness to admit the facts concerning the knowledge and experience of the great author only underscores the insuperable problems for his 'Shakespeare'.

4 The sonnets speak of some deeply moving personal experiences which do not accord with what we know of the Stratford man

These are the best primary evidence of the fault line in

orthodoxy. Their message, surely biographical, is of a friendship with a youth of noble birth. This had been put under great strain by affection having reached levels of intolerable intimacy. There was an extremely painful rift, a departure by the poet, a shared lover. This despite the fact that the original love between the two young men had surely been homosexual or, at the very least, potentially so. Subsequent to his quitting the company of the friend, the poet gives us a mixture of enduring ardour and bitter recrimination from one who had

> ... passed a hell of time;
> ... suffered in your crime.
> *Sonnet 120*

Perhaps most importantly, there is a need to conceal the poet's 'branded' name and some of his knowledge of the past, lest the noble youth be disgraced. Now, the Stratfordians would have us believe that the young Shakespeare could publish some early plays so modestly that he omitted his name from the title page. They would also have us believe, because the evidence is there for Shakespeare the writer, that the aspiring young actor from Stratford was simultaneously bold enough to implore the noble youth to marry and beget children 'for love of me' (Sonnet 10). He was also sufficiently self-confident to dedicate, at the very outset of his career, two major poems to the Earl of Southampton (who may well have been that mysterious noble youth). These dedications are in language so warm that it suggests great friendship, even physical intimacy. Is this another part of the biography of our Stratford man? When did he become an outcast (Sonnet 29) or disgraced (Sonnets 33, 34)? Despite the intense spotlight thrown on him by archivists over the last hundred years, there are no records found to support the idea that it is he whose 'life has in these lines some interest'. Then again, to presume that it is nevertheless so, we must cram still more activity into his early adult years.

5 The alleged authorship achievements of the Stratford man are ignored in contemporary records until the publication of the First Folio, seven years after his death

By this is meant that the work of Shakespeare is certainly mentioned, the name Shakespeare appears on title-pages, but he is not unequivocally identified with the man from Stratford until 1623. As an example, a contemporary scholar named William Camden praises Shakespeare the author in his work *Remains* ... (1605), but omits William of Stratford from his list of worthies of that town, published a few years later. Nor, in his *Annals* for 1616, does he mention the Stratford man's death as one of the significant events of that year. Anti-Stratfordians, rightly or wrongly, pounce on things like this. Are we, they might ask, trying to gather figs from thistles? Any imprint Shakespeare's fellows in Warwickshire may have made upon his imagination escapes us, says arguably the best Stratfordian biographer of all, Sir Edmund Chambers. He might equally well have said the same of the impression his Shakespeare left on the imagination of the latter's Warwickshire contemporaries.

6 As an alleged author, he is seen as rather a figure of fun in some literature prior to 1623

Comment has already been made upon passages by Ben Jonson, quite different from his eulogy in the First Folio, ones in which Shakespeare (of Stratford) is a figure of good-humoured fun, as a 'poet-ape', and as 'Sogliardo'. We know he had the (not at all unreasonable) wish to better himself and be a major property-owner at Stratford. He is surely one of the ambitious actors referred to rather scathingly in a late sixteenth-century poem (author unknown) entitled *The Return from Parnassus*:

> With mouthing words that better wits have framed
> They purchase land and now esquires are named.

7 Prolonged and assiduous efforts to add to our biographical knowledge of the Stratford actor reveal nothing of a man of letters

Sometimes it is remarked how much more is now known about him than was the case in 1900. But what is this 'more' worth? Perhaps the best British example in comparatively recent times comes from the Public Record Office in a beautifully presented digest of all the relevant public records about Stratford's Shakespeare. Apart from contributor Jane Cox's startling conclusion therein that not all of the six 'known' Shakespeare signatures are by the same person, it is essentially prosaic: the concern is with property deals, street refuse, the sale of corn, fines, pressing for the repayment of debts, tax bills. This despite the fact that it examines all known references to him in these records, including some recently discovered documents. It is frankly what might be expected if detailed biographical records of Elizabethan times were extant on a powerful computer – and if we had chosen to search them in order to come up with a random example of a man of humble origins who became reasonably prosperous through having a good head for business.

But someone may still object: 'We know as much about him as we do about most of his contemporaries.' Even if we do, it is only after an exponential degree of effort. Sadly, it must be repeated, the extra details have no literary merit. The gulf between the Shakespearean splendour and this threadbare life is immense. There are not even letters to friends or others associated with the stage. We know embarrassingly little that is of value, and what we do know is often embarrassing.

One is reminded of Hugh Trevor-Roper's comment that much less searching would enable much more worthwhile biographies to be written about any of Shakespeare's dramatic contemporaries. It may be noted that twentieth-century archivist C W Wallace, checking out millions of documents in unremitting labour, has been reported (by George Greenwood) as being driven to the extreme of concluding that Stratford's poet perhaps had a contemporary neighbour of the same name, to whom the disappointing references must, presumably, relate. Or, to go back to earlier times yet essentially in the same vein, we can consider the remark of the Stratford teacher–clergyman Joseph Greene. He commented, in 1747, that William Shakespeare's austere last will and testament was 'absolutely void of the least particle of that spirit which animated our great poet'. It only reveals him as a relatively wealthy small-town gentleman.

8 Orthodox history would have us believe that Shakespeare of Stratford rose from modest beginnings, reached incredible heights of wisdom and culture in middle life, but reverted to the earlier pattern in his closing years

These three periods of Shakespeare of Stratford's life are well recognised, but they do not cohere. To paraphrase a remark once made, it is like a grub rapidly becoming a beautiful butterfly – even of a variety denied by its origins or opportunities – then turning back into the grub! One of the most innovative of the doubters (who we shall encounter as the first to state the theory that the seventeenth Earl of Oxford was the real Shakespeare) sums up the problem very well:

> It is impossible to believe that the same man could have accomplished two such stupendous and mutually nullifying feats…. The perfect unity of the two extremes [of his life] justifies the conclusion that the middle period is an illusion.

To this idea that the middle period of life, holding all of his great achievement, is but a dream with regard to William Shakespeare of Stratford, one can add that there were controversial literary acts which must have affected Shakespeare the writer, during the lifetime of that Stratford man. An example of such was a combination of some of Shakespeare's poems with those of others in a work attributed to him in 1599, *The Passionate Pilgrim*. Another was the appearance of his name (presumably for 'enhancement value') on inferior plays; on stylistic grounds, everyone agrees that these were not his. In 1609, there was the publication of the apparently pirated edition of *Troilus and Cressida*. Then there were his sonnets, also first published (without the author's permission?) in 1609, with such embarrassing revelations. Writing about them in 1899, novelist Samuel Butler surmised that the great man's gorge must have risen at the sight of the skull of his dead folly being dug up. Well, certainly one could not be impervious. Somebody must have been shocked to the core. Yet historical records can only suggest that to all these events the Stratford man exhibited sublime insouciance. The question to be asked, since the reason was surely not lethargy, is whether it could have been superhuman detachment ... or were they simply just not his concern?

9 He appears to emerge instantly as a great writer

Assuming Shakespeare the writer to be the man from Stratford, there are no apparent exploratory beginnings: no juvenilia, unless we were perhaps to count *Titus Andronicus* as such, marking the first sketches of his genius. Take *Love's Labour's Lost*, already mentioned here indirectly as an early work, yet one speaking volumes concerning the author's great assurance. It is essentially a play of its time; in fact, it may now seem a complete oddity to some of us. Yet consider its courtly emphasis, mature wit, the brilliant euphuisms. These do more than stamp its date: they speak of the sophistication of its creator. In it, once again, it seems we are receiving the fruit of some European experiences; could it really just be based on travellers' tales? For a member of the nobility, having journeyed appropriately, to have written it early in his literary career would be a very considerable feat. That a young grammar-school boy (even a genius) just making his way, never having left England, ignorant in the ways of the court, should nevertheless produce it – this defies comprehension.

Slightly earlier still, in 1593, the name Shake-speare had appeared as an author for the very first time, in association with a long, relatively mature, classical poem: *Venus and Adonis*. In dedicating it to Henry Wriothesley, Earl of Southampton, the writer described it as 'the first heir of my invention'. This is most curious, because some plays, later to be (quite correctly) attributed to Shakespeare, clearly precede this poem. The expression quoted does not seem to be fully satisfied either by saying that this was the first item actually published or by arguing that poetry has a higher status than drama. How then do we reconcile the expression 'first heir of my invention' with the clearly earlier existence of plays? There is a point to be made here which doubters by and large have missed. Since the poem represents the first use of the name 'Shake-speare' as author, could it have been that name, as a pen-name, which was the 'invention', with the classic poem the very first instance of its use? It would be subsequently added to those earlier plays.

10 Shakespeare the writer expected literary immortality for the works, but clearly feared he would not receive the credit himself; a pen-name would explain this paradox

There are various references which support this statement. As just a brief example:

> Not marble, nor the gilded monuments
> Of princes shall outlive this powerful rhyme.
> *(Sonnet 55)*

but

> ... I, once gone, to all the world must die;
> The earth can yield me but a common grave.
> *(Sonnet 81)*

> My name be buried where my body is
> And live no more ...
> *(Sonnet 72)*

A majority of the commentators, orthodox or otherwise, believe that the youth to whom these sonnets were addressed, who would lie 'entombed in men's eyes' because of them, was the Earl of Southampton. Archie Webster, an early advocate of

59

Marlowe as Shakespeare, certainly agreed. He pointed out that Shakespeare said to the youth concerned:

> I may not evermore acknowledge thee ...
> Nor thou with public kindness honour me.
>
> (*Sonnet 36*)

– a further indication of the 'disgrace' already mentioned. Yet the poet *did* acknowledge Southampton, dedicating his two long classical poems to that earl. Webster suggested that the situation could only make sense if the poet was not making the acknowledgement under his all-revealing true name. The name 'Shakespeare' (which obviously *would* be immortalised along with Southampton) must thus be a 'mask' enabling him to do so safely.

It may be reiterated that all that we know of the actor from Stratford suggests his complete indifference to the fate and lasting appeal of Shakespeare's works. He took no personal steps to ensure their publication. True, in his day, it was somewhat unusual for a dramatist to publish collected works. But he, if the author, risked over half of his being for ever lost. Yet this, we are asked to believe, is the same man who speaks with such transparent sincerity of his conviction that his work is timeless. It was this attitude in Stratford's Shakespeare, together with what we know of his biography, that led Alexander Pope to conclude that he was, at heart, a worldling. But, of course, it may simply have been that the perpetuation of the work of Shakespeare, the writer, was someone else's business!

Commentary

These ten points are but a framework, with necessarily selective comment, by way of illustration: a foundation with some scaffolding of argument (for individuals to build upon or seek to demolish) rather than finished stone. In constructing such, I have used the language of the 'heretics': my sympathy with them doubtless shines through. This is because I am convinced that there is a case to be answered. Yet those Stratfordians who are resentful of all probing or questioning might run quickly through the list, insisting that each item is of no consequence. Slightly misquoting the Bard they would argue that 'among a number *all* are reckoned none'. A metaphor might be that of a jar of assorted produce, which has been mentally emptied, the content being dismissed as all worthless – but this being done in many cases without ever looking at it properly, and in some instances even without actually turning the lid of the jar.

Let us suppose that these and other arguments, fully developed, do give rise to queries, have obvious potency, or are even thought conclusive. Such belief would not mean that Stratford's most famous figure was a knave, a fool or a mere cipher, as some doubters have portrayed him. On the contrary, he may well have been a crucial figure in a well-planned enterprise, its vital official representative. The fortunate coincidence of his name and his availability as a 'mask' would be an essential feature for its feasibility and secrecy. He must have been capable enough to learn lines as an actor. Wearing the 'mask' as the nominal Shakespeare would be, on occasion, a test of that acting ability. He would need to refer occasionally to the plays as ones he had written; perhaps sometimes to give the appearance of a shrewd person of deeper thoughts than he was prepared to express in conversation.

But for him to have actually done enough to encompass that incomparable span of words and wisdom? No: for his 'disbelievers', the odds are impossibly long. In April 1981, the British Broadcasting Corporation's children's television programme, *Blue Peter*, celebrating Shakespeare's official birthday, included a remark to the effect that William would have laughed to think that one day he would be hailed as the greatest writer the world has ever known. We may be pardoned for the audacity of wondering if (even if just ever so possibly if) the comment has an infinitely deeper, much more ironic, significance than could possibly have been intended.

The doubt about the validity of the majority viewpoint on Shakespearean authorship springs not from any one of the ten points, nor other specific queries which could be provided to extend such a listing. It lies in the mutually supportive nature of a whole range of diverse and disturbing facts. We may say that some of the queries are exaggerated; that in other cases the Stratford man could have got access to the necessary information (although this sometimes itself requires exaggeration to make it plausible); that others are just coincidence. The problem is that, as the 'coincidences' mount, the odds against them being just coincidence mounts rapidly. A passage in an altogether different context, from a bygone specialist in the detective story genre, happens to express this perfectly. His investigator is allowed but one dogmatism. It concerns:

> the matter of accumulative probabilities ... two trivialities, pointing in the same direction, become at once, by their mere agreement, no trivialities at all, but enormously important considerations. ... [Other apparent trivialities] reinforcing ... bring the matter to the rank of a practical certainty.

Some will be quick to dismiss examples from fiction, despite the fact that they may illustrate truths. Those distrustful of it may look to modern management techniques for a parallel. There exists, at present, no absolutely final proof as to who was the author Shakespeare: if such proof were accessible, there could never be an authorship problem. Very well, but the worlds of industry and education abound with processes or achievements which are not susceptible to precise quantification. Thus management tries to find suitable 'performance indicators'. These are proxies or surrogates for measurement; they are signposts rather than indisputable facts. As such they must be used in clusters: one or two alone could be misleading. A strong consensus, however, is regarded as most powerful evidence. We might therefore transfer the concept by assuming that Shakespeare's works had come down to us anonymously, then asking a question: Would the accumulation of grouped indicators, on balance, point to the Stratford man as responsible for that unique literary performance?

ACT 2. THE WILL TO DISBELIEVE?

Those more prepared to tolerate fiction might find a useful analogy by noting another BBC television programme's message on the growth of attractive legends. This, in 1987, marking the centenary of Sherlock Holmes, drew attention to the myths (the curved pipe, the deerstalker hat) that grew up only after the stories were written. One opinion expressed was that, for maximum impact, when faced with fact and legend, one should publish the legend! We need to realise that the accounts, or legends, of an upwardly mobile Stratford boy, soaring to the heights, rest on relatively few known foundations. This remains true even for those who are convinced that the foundations are probably sound. The latter then have to explain how his genius not only brought him education and culture beyond his reach, but also apparent first-hand knowledge of events beyond his experience. Then, at the end, there is that apparent voluntary return to mundane obscurity.

For some of us, a simple metaphor might be to imagine a small sum of capital being invested, remarkably wisely, in the late sixteenth century; then to find that it is now, because of appreciation and accumulated interest (including, dare one say, much 'vested interest') worth millions. But, if fact is really wanted, might not our eyes turn, at least briefly, away from what may be glittering fables, to examine the honesty by which the original capital was acquired? Around whatever is true about Stratford's Shakespeare, there has been woven a vast, complex web of speculation and gossip. Some of it is contradictory; much of it chosen to appeal to the popular imagination. The lay person's usual view of a tolerably secure biography, linked to the writings, becomes first dishevelled, then nearly shattered if, gradually, those layers of myth and guesswork are exposed.

So it was that Charles Dickens trembled every day lest something turned up; that Henry James went further, rejecting in this context his elder brother's 'will to believe', wondering in a 1903 letter, if 'the divine William' might be 'the biggest and most successful fraud ever practised on a patient world'. Walt Whitman thought the frequent aristocratic tone or setting of these dramas pointed to their likely author being one of the earls, some 'born descendant and knower' of the characters from the medieval aristocracy so plenteous in the plays. In providing a lively introduction to a book by Hilda Amphlett on the authorship controversy, the then judge, Christmas Humphreys, summed up admirably:

> Insert the edge of the chisel of doubt in the plaster of this legend and it is frightening to watch the wishful thought assumptions tumble to the ground ... even if fifty per cent [of queries posed] are rejected as far-fetched or in any way unproved there remains an abundance ... . The proof mounts rapidly, with geometric progression, as the number grows.

Of course, there are very many people who do not agree with all this. Since they include the Shakespearean specialist experts, their views must be most carefully considered. However, it should always be recalled that those experts have a reputation and track record to defend. It is for honest enquirers, trying to view argument and counter-argument objectively, to decide whether we can safely dismiss virtually all the arguments presented by doubters. It will not do to say, in effect, 'There's no real mystery, it's just that we don't happen to know much about him.' The above surely shows the incongruities between what we do know of William of Stratford and the Shakespeare glory. The disbelievers in the conventional 'Will' certainly sometimes overstate their case. Moreover, the rival sects also sometimes argue quite fiercely against each other! Neither of those undoubted facts invalidates the general thrust or strength of the anti-Stratfordian cause. It is time to look at aspects of this cause in the twentieth century. We shall start with an examination of the major candidates proposed, references being made to the advocates who, in this author's view, best present their case from the standpoint of the modern reader.

ACT 3
THE CONTROVERSY:
TWENTIETH-CENTURY THEORIES

> … I have bought
> Golden opinions from all sorts of people.
> *Macbeth*

SCENE 1

PRELUDE TO THE SECTS: GENERAL TURBULENCE 1900–1918 (GREENWOOD, TWAIN, ROBERTSON)

This 'Act' focuses briefly on a vast area – trying to catch the flavour of major aspects of the debate throughout the present century. Only the chief contenders, among the many that have been put forward as the true Shakespeare, are presented. Moreover, to keep the argument concise, just a few advocates are chosen to represent each of them. There were also, however, people with no particular candidate to propose who had strong suspicions about Shakespeare, most notably Sir George Greenwood (died 1928). His stature in the history of this controversy is such that it is necessary, as well as worthwhile, to begin with consideration of the character of the quite prolonged cut and thrust arguments in which he and various opponents (we concentrate on one) became involved.

The turn of the century could, in a sense, be viewed as the golden age of the Shakespeare authorship debate, at least from the viewpoint of a doubter. True, many of the rival candidates had not then been proposed. But the period of late nineteenth-century questioning perhaps reached its real culmination in the years 1900–18. Greenwood's contribution to this was immense; it was also destined to be enduring. In various books over a decade he first stated, then defended against critics, his basic beliefs and position. This was essentially that the works of Shakespeare were written, not by the Stratford man, but rather by an unknown aristocrat.

His ability in presentation was generally recognised, though there were those who saw the views expressed as essentially pestilent – perhaps the more so because they knew not how to deny them. One device used was to claim that they were a slur against the work of Shakespeare. However, Greenwood could justifiably indicate his deep admiration for that glorious literature, for he could apparently quote passages of the Bard by the page. He drew attention to the gulf between what we know of the life of the 'official' Shakespeare and what we know of the mind and achievement of the great author. He wrote about the writer Shakespeare's knowledge of the law, of his use of classical sources and allusions, of his familiarity with hunting, arguing that his natural stance and tone was that of the upper classes.

Discussing the issue of whether one of lowly birth could write great literature by sheer genius and unstinting effort, he contrasted the claims for the Stratford man with what was achieved by writers like Bunyan and Burns. One aim was to show that the output of even the greatest genius would be shaped by circumstances concerning opportunity or environment. An apparently very ordinary man, at those times, feasibly might undergo informal self-education, perhaps of a spartan kind; then go on to produce good, even great, literature. But the mode of achievement would reflect both the path trodden and compatibility with growth from his origins. It would also take time: one must take in culture before one can pour it out. So, for example, consider *The Rape of Lucrece*, written no later than 1594. Lucrece embarks (lines 1366 onwards) on a long digression about Greek aesthetics, being inspired by a particular painting. The poet had clearly been impressed by seeing this (surely not in England!). The passage is another clear reflection of his own appreciation of the arts, gradually accumulated via both reading and travel. No genius could create that knowledge spontaneously. Greenwood quotes, with approval, Coleridge's comment that Shakespeare the writer had 'studied patiently ... meditated deeply'. This is evident in the very earliest works.

At the time Greenwood was writing, the only other individual claimed emphatically by many of the unorthodox as Shakespeare was Francis Bacon. Sir George retained an open mind on this matter, but was careful to dissociate himself from any Baconian excesses. He was perhaps canny in being reluctant to name an alternative author; it may be argued that any such commitment, being unavoidably based on extensive speculation, can only serve to loosen the bricks within the general wall of doubt. His several books represent a large mine of fact and opinion. The sceptics of various persuasions have quarried (and will continue yet to quarry) there in pressing the negative side of their seemingly enormous allegations – the case against the Stratford man. Of what is probably his major book, *The Shakespeare Problem Restated* (1908), one reviewer commented, 'it breeds irreverence for the literary mandarins'.

One of the people impressed by it, the noted American novelist, Mark Twain (1835–1910), was always prepared to be irreverent. Those determined to undermine all who are unorthodox in these matters, embarrassed at finding a man of literature there, might argue that Twain was an eccentric, that he loved attacking established beliefs, or that his relevant book *Is Shakespeare Dead?* (1909) was written in his embittered last years. Yet, whether we agree with him or not, he provides lively reading that is full of characteristic blunt wit. He might be thought of as a Baconian or a Groupist, but is perhaps most safely seen as an uncommitted unbeliever like Greenwood. He writes: 'I only believed Bacon wrote Shakespeare, whereas I knew Shakespeare [of Stratford] didn't.' Always interested in religion, he is quick to pick up relevant analogy and speaks of the comfort given by an anti-Stratfordian faith.

The tone of his commentary evokes throughout pleasant memories of his Huck Finn. To the comment quoted earlier, about finding gravel in pies, he adds others in the same vein. He claims we know as much about the life of the Stratford man as we do of the biography of Satan; that the Stratford tradition is for him like a reconstructed brontosaurus (a few sure bones as facts plus an enormous amount of plaster of Paris representing speculation). 'Habit-sodden' Stratfordians make too much of their evidence: 'do chipmunk trails through the dust of Stratford village tell the reasoning race that Hercules has been along there?' He also pretends that he does not really seek to convince us, and that this is because he knows the nature of humanity too well, with its loyalty and devotion to the creeds that have been implanted at an early age. Thus he is

> aware that even when the brightest mind in our world is trained up from childhood in a superstition of any kind, it will never be possible for that mind, in its maturity, to examine sincerely, dispassionately and conscientiously any evidence which shall seem to cast a doubt upon the validity of that superstition.

Perhaps something has been conveyed, even so briefly, of Mark Twain's vivid contribution to the debate. Of course, he is not everyone's favourite: there are those who want him to be disqualified on account of his 'idiosyncrasies', as a major biographer of the orthodox Shakespeare, Sir Sidney Lee, put it. It is not the purpose here to put forward pro-Stratfordian replies which, in any case, dominate Shakespearean literature, if only by inference. But there was one other leading figure in the controversy of that time, sometimes claimed by the orthodox, who must not be omitted. John Mackinnon Robertson, who died in 1933, had left school at the age of thirteen, and so gained much of his education only through prodigious reading. Then, but after due passage of time, he became a prolific writer – on literature, on free thinking, and on social science themes. In all these areas, his works bear the clear stamp of his own personality. The major book for our purpose is *The Baconian Heresy* (1913). In this, he set out at length to refute Greenwood's 1908 book and the whole of the Baconian argument, also firing a few shafts at another candidate whose name was just beginning to appear (the Earl of Rutland). Robertson saw the case for Bacon as being based on just the sort of faulty reasoning that Bacon himself would have been swift to condemn. He insists that it was a reaction to excessive 'bardolatory'.

Anti-Stratfordians are victims of misinformation: both learned and unlearned people, Robertson claims, have been led down this path by garbled and erroneous teaching. He very naturally (and rightly) attacks the views of those Baconians who would attribute the work of many sixteenth and seventeenth century writers to Bacon. It is argued that coincidences with Shakespearean language are not limited to the works of Bacon, but arise with many other Elizabethan writers; if one studies the whole of Elizabethan literature the truth will fall clearly into perspective. Robertson claims that Shakespeare's many legal references did not require exceptional knowledge. He points out that John Webster, a dramatist writing immediately after the Shakespeare era, made many legal allusions too, but had no special law background. As for classical references, many were passed on verbally, in distilled form, to ordinary people through the words of divines and moralists. Twain had accepted Baconian dogma unquestioningly, without knowing all the facts: his 'unhappy mystification was evolved by others and taken by him on trust'. The real target is Greenwood. Robertson takes up issues concerning the education of any humbly born person who achieved greatness in literature, say Bunyan, Burns or Keats.

Parts of Robertson's book can undoubtedly offer solace to Stratfordians. Many of the issues remain open ones. We should proceed as far as possible, on the grounds of reason and probability, then decide. However, there are powerful arguments against calling J M Robertson as champion witness for the defence. It is not just that, while Stratfordians claim that the unorthodox keep on churning out ideas from Greenwood which Robertson had smashed to pieces, neither Greenwood nor other doubters could find that their position needed revision. More potent are the problems arising from Robertson's own very distinctive stance. In numerous books, emphasising the search for the genuine by literary detection, he dismantled the orthodox Shakespearean canon. He claimed that there is evidence of extensive collaboration in some plays; that Shakespeare's hand was absent completely from a few of the plays attributed to him; that many plays bear the mark of considerable revision. Most significant are his remarks, in his *Marlowe: A Conspectus* (1931), on the 'tiger's heart' passage from *King Henry the Sixth* that is linked to the identification of the 'Shake-scene', that upstart of whom Greene warned his fellow dramatists. For Robertson's emphatic view on the play in question is that there has been collaboration. But he finds, from studying styles, that Christopher Marlowe's work dominates it, Shakespeare's share having been of the smallest.

In his 1913 book, Robertson says: 'if only the specialists had done their proper work of discriminating between the genuine and the alien in Shakespeare's plays, much of the Baconian polemic would have been impossible'. Yet many of those same Stratfordian specialists would have to discard Robertson along with the doubters, viewing him as damaging the unity of their Shakespeare. Indeed, if I were a stalwart member of the orthodox church, as it were, in this intriguing literary debate, I might see J M Robertson as akin to a theologian who picked the gospel into minute fragments, thoroughly undermined the unity of its traditional message, told the faithful they worshipped a graven image, yet still proclaimed himself a believer!

Greenwood and Robertson, both Members of Parliament, had very different backgrounds. But the largely self-educated man from the Isle of Arran remained a friend of the old Etonian. Sir George took up the debate in later books. (It would have been fascinating if Twain had been alive to do this also.) Bunyan and Burns were aired yet again as Greenwood argued back. As for Jacobean dramatist John Webster, he wrote relatively little, as Greenwood was quick to point out. Webster was also known to be an admirer and imitator of Shakespeare's writing. To follow the notion of using legal references and foreign scenes in one's drama is rather different from being a bold pioneer in introducing them, decisively and generally with apparent direct knowledge, as Shakespeare did. To the suggestion that the plays contain unusual Warwickshire words,

Greenwood retorted that while some were little known or technical, use of these was not restricted to Warwickshire.

For anyone interested in researching the controversy as it stood early in the century, the work of these three is indispensible. They set the stage for much that was to follow, though their standard was not always maintained. Robertson, writing just before the First World War, offers a unique extra reason for studying the Shakespearean authorship issue. In a sense, his comment helps to dismiss the idea that investigating is but a dissipation of mental endeavour. *The Baconian Heresy* ends its attempted refutation of the theories with it and we may likewise end this 'scene': 'It may be as humanly useful to settle aesthetic questions of this sort as to develop the law of projectiles to the end of more easily and surely destroying life in war.' The orthodox should be able to join with heretics in saying 'amen' to that.

SCENE 2

BACONIANS (THEOBALD; PRESENT-DAY ADVOCATES)

Francis Bacon was, of course, both a contemporary of William Shakespeare of Stratford-upon-Avon and a distinguished author (although certainly not a dramatist) in his own name. A prominent statesman, he was raised to the peerage relatively late in life, as Lord Verulam. The argument that he was really also the writer Shakespeare goes back at least to the late eighteenth century, and had numerous adherents of note in the second half of the nineteenth. They include Mrs C M Pott, who in 1885 founded The Bacon Society, as it was originally called. The concern of this book is neither with the nineteenth century theories, nor only with Bacon's advocates; were it so, these enthusiasts would certainly demand much space.

But the early years of the twentieth century show the continuation of much of that hectic Baconian activity. The writers involved are interested in matters such as possible cipher messages, Shakespeare's legal knowledge, parallels of expression between him and Bacon; the fact that their philosophy is so entirely compatible. Some books of that period, including one by Sir Edwin Durning-Lawrence, are bullish, flamboyant works that proclaim their revelations most emphatically. There are also more restrained supporters;

indeed, right up to 1950, various writers vie for selection as representatives of the Baconian cause. It has been decided to focus on just one from this period: in terms of scope and date, he provides a good conspectus of Baconian views up to the end of the first 30 years or so of this century.

The chosen writer is B G Theobald, who died in 1940. Illustration of his arguments here is solely through one book, *Enter Francis Bacon* (1932). This is partly because this work does not seek to make a case via codes and cryptograms, although Theobald was certainly a believer in them and extols them elsewhere. (Some who have read Baconian arguments before may feel that the case minus cryptograms is like *Hamlet* without the Prince, but due reference is made to them later – along with reasons for distrusting them.) Theobald came from a family which contributed to the Baconian cause over several generations, most notably his uncle at the turn of the century. Like most of the doubters, Theobald spends some time in seeking to explain factors undermining the conventional authorship attribution. In his case, this had been done in an earlier work; the one mentioned above could thus be said to represent the positive side of his thinking.

From the 1932 book, five arguments for Bacon as Shakespeare have been selected, mostly for extremely concise description. They may serve to illustrate that, in general, the points raised by Baconians are of uneven weight. First, there is the question, already raised, of the interest shown in law within Shakespeare's plays: many doubters have suggested that such provides evidence of legal training. Stratfordians protest that there is too little reference to legalistic details for this to be the case; the frequent law allusions are said to arise because Elizabethans, including Shakespeare of Stratford, were interested in them. The doubters then protest again. It simply must be someone known to have more specialised legal expertise – who better than Bacon?

A second matter raised concerns the fact that in a letter to Sir John Davies, seeking a favour, Bacon begged him 'to be good to concealed poets'. This shows that such poets existed: it may or may not mean that Francis Bacon considered himself to be

75

in that category. Most certainly it cannot, by itself, signify that he wrote under the name of 'Shakespeare'. Other arguments used by Theobald relate to documents. One of the most constant themes, in the Baconian camp as in others, is claims of parallelisms between the writings of their man and those of Shakespeare. There is a need to be careful in such matters. They are not necessarily inconsequential, but we must remember that there was much parallelism and unacknowledged 'borrowing' across the literature of the Elizabethan and Jacobean periods.

But Baconians will point particularly to the existence of *The Promus*, a collection of Baconian papers constituting a sourcebook of proverbs, metaphors and other allusions. This work was definitely Bacon's. It may or may not predate the Shakespeare plays. Its references are said not to be used in the published works bearing Bacon's name – even only rarely in other literature of the time, except that of Shakespeare, where they are reproduced frequently. It is undoubtedly an interesting piece of evidence, the use of which precedes the references to it by Theobald, Mrs Pott having published it in 1883. Stratfordians will normally agree that this is a notebook of Bacon's, designed to be used as a storehouse of ideas, but may say that he did use some of these sayings in his acknowledged published works, adding perhaps that some of them are used by other writers of the age. It is thus maintained that Shakespeare could have had access to them from sources other than *The Promus* itself. Nevertheless, some observers may contend that this collection, apparently freely used by Shakespeare, suggests some writing link, even if only a tenuous one, between our greatest dramatist and Francis Bacon.

In similar vein is another Baconian 'package' discussed by Theobald. This, discovered in 1867 in Northumberland House, London, became known as the 'Northumberland Manuscript'. It comprises material acknowledged, I think by all, as having once been Bacon's property. It consists of a number of sheets, the outer one of which appears to have been used as a scribbling page, although perhaps it was originally a list of documents belonging to Bacon. The writing is in two or more hands. The sheet is crammed with comments and doodlings, rather like a heavily used blotting pad. *Richard the Second* and *Richard the Third* are two titles upon it, with no author's name. The names Francis Bacon and William Shakespeare also appear on the sheet, along with various words and phrases of no obvious significance. It is a really intriguing historical document: one of many possibilities is that the scribbler (whoever this was) mentally associated Bacon and Shakespeare, as writers of the age. However, as clear evidence for them being the same person, it is clearly inconclusive.

These items put forward by Theobald (there are others offered, too) have been dealt with very briefly, because I want to concentrate upon one element in his case in rather more detail, perceiving it to be of greater stature. In fact, it seems to refute the suggestion that no one at all in the lifetime of the Stratford man challenged his right to be considered the true, sole author of those immense Shakespearean writings. Theobald was not the first to 'discover' this, but for a fuller account than is possible here one should turn either to him, or to an earlier survey of the controversy than mine, H N Gibson, *The Shakespeare Claimants* (1962). The latter, apart from some pro-Stratfordian commentary, repeats Theobald's version. Like me, Dr Gibson, whose survey is considered in more detail later, believes this to be the best of the Baconian evidence. However, those who want to explore it beyond what is said here will find that it involves some somewhat complex Elizabethan wordplay.

The argument, basically, is as follows. In Joseph Hall's satires of 1597, we find gentle fun being made of a contemporary who is perceived to be the secret part-author of a particular poem. Hall refers to this person only in a concealed way, as Labeo (this being the name of an ancient Roman lawyer):

> For shame write better Labeo, or write none
> Or better write, or Labeo write alone …

The authors being commented upon are not identified here, but one of them (Labeo) is obviously being encouraged to do one of three things – write better, drop his collaborator, or give up altogether. Hall goes on to observe that it seems that there are people who cannot produce poetry and yet (strangely) they do so; this is only apparently true – that is, it is accepted as so by those who do not know of the collaborative assistance that is involved. Later in the satire, Hall (who seemed to disapprove of the poem he is describing, perhaps because of its theme or treatment) comments further of it: 'While but Big Ohs each stanza can begin', and also:

> In Epithets to join two words as one
> Forsooth for Adjectives cannot stand alone.

The 'Big Ohs' are seen by Theobald as referring to Shakespeare's *Lucrece*: both this and his *Venus and Adonis* frequently use hyphenated words as epithets.

Hall had support. In 1598, John Marston, an Elizabethan playwright, also produced some satires, called *Pygmalion's Image*. Labeo is mentioned again, in rather telling circumstances:

> So Labeo did complain his love was stone
> Obdurate, flinty, so relentless none.

This reference is seen as being to lines 199 and 200 of *Venus and Adonis*. Later, Marston, again referring to the mysterious Labeo, protests: 'What, not medioca firma from your spite!' These Latin words constitute Bacon's family motto. Theobald thus concludes that Hall and Marston had both identified Bacon as the secret part-author of *Venus and Adonis* and *The Rape of Lucrece*.

Gibson, discussing the Baconian case in his 1962 overview of the authorship controversy, agrees that Hall's target was a lawyer; also that the 'Big Oh' reference certainly alludes to *The Rape of Lucrece*. That 1962 survey accepts that Marston clearly had Bacon in mind, but suggests he may simply have been making a guess at who Hall meant. Dr Gibson, who certainly would never be accused of making too much of anti-

Stratfordian evidence, says that only two facts can be deduced, with absolute certainty, from the late sixteenth century satires of Hall and Marston. They are, first, that Hall believed he had guessed the real part-author of some work published under a pseudonym, and second, that Marston thought Hall meant Bacon as the author and *Venus and Adonis* as the poem. 'Anything further', Gibson adds, 'takes us into the realm of surmise.'

Stratfordians would never enter such a realm in their own theorising – or would they? But, leaving this aside, these passages, whatever our precise interpretation of them, are illuminating. Of course, Hall and Marston write in a teasing style that may irritate modern readers. Both may have been mistaken about a hidden author being involved. However, it seems certain that they had in mind these two Shakespearean epic poems, dedicated to the Earl of Southampton. We can be equally sure of some other things, namely that they thought the part-author concerned was a man of law, collaborating with William Shakespeare of Stratford. And that Marston, at least, thought this man was Bacon. It would certainly seem reasonable to wonder why two Elizabethan writers should assume that such poetry had been partly produced by a man of high office, with strong legal connections. Presumably Hall, at least, must have had some reason for originating such speculation? Presumably Marston, a man of the theatre no less, must have had a reason for supporting that view and for thinking Bacon was involved? Surely anything less than these modest assumptions takes us into the realm, not of surmise, but rather of intense pro-Stratfordian bias, even bigotry!

There we must leave Theobald for more modern advocates of Bacon. In Britain, Thomas Bokenham and Francis Carr are both closely associated with the journal *Baconiana*. Carr, a writer on art and music, has been a vigorous and combative supporter of the anti-Stratfordian cause in general, and the case for Bacon in particular, over a number of years. His considerable energies in this area have been partly given to running the Shakespeare Authorship Information Centre. From this, he produces regular compilations of recent news extracts about Shakespeare, but designed particularly to show inherent weaknesses in the orthodox authorship theory. He has also written various articles proclaiming the Earl of Pembroke and Mary Fitton to be the young lord and Dark Lady of the sonnets, or on other specifics within the Baconian framework. Elsewhere, in various press interviews, examples of which appear in my bibliography, he has voiced his scepticism of orthodoxy in general, along with his support for Bacon's candidature. Anyone choosing to examine his stance directly might well read of him fulminating about the Stratford industry violating the Trade Descriptions Act!

T D Bokenham is less obviously dramatic. His 1982 monograph sketches, perhaps all too briefly, some aspects of the debate. It concentrates upon his own strong preference for cipher evidence, said to be hidden in the plays of Shakespeare, or other records, which may give Bacon's name as true author.

Having spent some time on Theobald, though without covering all his arguments or doing full justice to the ones highlighted, I have chosen to be much briefer on 'the moderns'. In fact, it should perhaps be emphasised that it is more difficult to do justice, in concise fashion, to the Baconians than to any other 'school' or 'sect' in the controversy – except perhaps the Oxfordians. On the other hand, there may be disadvantages as well as benefits in being the earliest 'heresy'. So many are the other contenders who have been proposed in our century that, unreasonably, for some enquirers, the Baconian argument may now seem superseded.

Yet this undoubtedly remains the only case of which many of those who have never read about the controversy before may be vaguely aware. Even so, Francis is not even the only member of his own family for whom claims have been made, for among the 'minor' (in terms of volume of support) claimants is his elder brother, Anthony. But, with one most important exclusion, it can be said that my comment on the views of Theobald, augmented by reference to modern Baconians, give a fair, if necessarily succinct, statement of the case for Francis Bacon.

The exclusion mentioned concerns the inherent value or

otherwise of cryptograms. While Baconians do not have a monopoly on these, the idea of 'keyed-in' messages represents a very substantial part of all Baconian 'evidence' put forward, perhaps especially nowadays. This is despite the fact that W F and E S Friedman, in a 1957 book, had shown the inherent untrustworthiness of the early ones claimed. I have already stated my own deep distrust of most anagrammatic evidence or hidden word messages of any kind. That is a personal view which Bokenham, for one, certainly does not share. People picking up a copy of *Baconiana*, the periodical published by the Francis Bacon Society, will find claims of many messages of this kind in Shakespeare. Indeed, those wanting to be unkind might claim that it is possible to mistake some issues for a word puzzle magazine.

We are told that the ciphers now being found in Shakespeare are vastly more sophisticated than those advanced for Bacon much earlier in the century, by Durning-Lawrence and others. Another modern Baconian, Omaha attorney Penn Leary, contends that there are plenty of genuine ciphers to show who was Shakespeare: the Friedmans demolished only exploratory ones based on insufficient understanding of Bacon's methods. Some of the 'improvements' now on offer claim to provide an unanswerable challenge; yet those who disbelieve them have remained unconvinced! Are these cipher techniques immune from throwing out various conflicting messages and numerous authors, if carried through with sufficient knowledge or empathy? The techniques are complex enough, for sure.

Of course, if ciphers or other codes claimed are all invalid, this does not necessarily mean that the Baconian case is so; nor would their error prove, in itself, that Shakespeare the writer was the same person as the man from Stratford. If false, it simply represents excess by people looking for fresh and compelling evidence. Clearly, I do not lack sympathy for the authorship doubters, and would also commend the liberal stance taken by *Baconiana* to the expression of strongly held, often diverging, views. Thus Baconians may see my attitude to coded signals as a curious blind spot, a failure to come to terms with the methods for identifying them. The 'messages' cannot be faulted for ingenuity of concealment, since this is often dazzling. Yet they may be rejected on four distinct counts. The first reason for so doing is that there are too many of them being found by so many people. (If that seems true of alternative Shakespeares in general, remember that *one* of the alternatives, including the Stratford one, of course, must be genuine. We cannot be sure with all these alleged cryptograms that any are necessarily genuine.) A second reason is the work of the Friedmans: despite Leary's attempted reassurances, I think this convincing enough to crush at least nearly all such 'hidden message' theories. A third cause for rejection is simply that all these alleged Baconian messages keep on repeating the same fact. Would not such constant repetition be superfluous?

The last reason may be the most convincing of all. How could anybody, even the greatest genius of all time (needing to keep a contemporary secret, but wanting to give hints to posterity), write superb literature *and also* hide away numerous examples of a message within it? It would come down to a choice between one or the other, for the constant need to tuck away coded signals would inevitably affect, most seriously, the beauty, flow and resonance of the literature containing them. Yet virtually all 'new evidence' for Bacon as Shakespeare is now of just this kind.

It is certainly not part of the intent to display here, in any kind of detail, examples of such alleged hidden messages; several examples can be found by the enthusiastic or the curious in, for instance, the work by Bokenham cited in my bibliography. To get merely a little of the 'flavour' in a very simple way, as it were, we may refer here to the first of his many diagrams. This, a typical example, arranges the letters of a tribute (that appears on the official Shakespearean bust in Stratford church) in a 14 x 16 square. There can be found, in some sort of pattern within this square, groups containing respectively (but out of sequence) the letters FRANCIS, BACON and AUTHOR (U and V are the same letter in the Elizabethan alphabet). As has been shown with other cryptograms, from various people down the years, one can often find other messages too. I seem to see the name of

Sir T More in this one!

Now, since some Elizabethans certainly loved acrostics
and concealment, such ciphers and anagrams may well have
been used by writers of the age to some extent. Moreover,
it is widely accepted that Bacon had an interest in
cryptology. But ever since the time, early in Baconian history,
that the most curious of all Shakespeare's many words –
'Honorificabilitudinitatibus' from *Love's Labour's Lost* – was
said to contain Bacon's name, and it was then found that it
could give other messages, the credibility of ciphers has been
under pressure. If anyone feels that my treatment of arguments
like Bokenham's is not sufficiently sensitive or detailed to do
justice to the hidden messages claim, one must consider that
the more intricate any such message, the more difficult to
weave it into the literature with a confidence that it would be
later not only found but generally believed.

Some ciphers, if valid, would have Bacon as the author of
much of the literature of his time, even later works. This is
claiming far too much for any one person, even 'Shakespeare'. I
do not subscribe to it for one moment. Also, I can accept
neither the view that Bacon might have been the secret son of
the (unmarried) Queen Elizabeth, nor the secret society
overtones that reside in some of the Baconian literature. But
there are those who resist any calls for restraint. Some
advocates in this 'heresy' have long evacuated even the
outskirts of common sense.

Of course, if we accept that most (perhaps all) ciphers and
codes are false, it may be wondered why Baconians and some
others continue to 'discover' them. There are basically two
reasons. First, sheer enthusiasm. Once the idea that cipher
messages may be there has been ignited, it burns like a fierce
forest fire in some breasts, along with a hope that something
both original and valuable is being contributed by any new
offering of this kind. Second, those frustrated by their inability
to prove to all, beyond any remaining doubt, that Shakespeare
the great writer was not the actor from Stratford may well feel
that somewhere there is (or ought to be) a hidden message that
would satisfy even the most obdurate champion of the

traditional authorship ascription.

More significantly than pondering the credibility of numerous codes of mixed ingenuity, could Bacon possibly have used his own name for some works, and 'Shakespeare' as a pseudonym for the writing of others? He has always had – indeed, continues to have – some noteworthy supporters. Daphne du Maurier was one. Or perhaps, if we may judge by her letter to Dorothy Ogburn in July 1952, she was a 'Groupist', with Bacon viewed as the group leader. It is rather nice to think of him, whether Shakespeare or not, as 'that precious gem of a concealed poet' as one writer once described him. Officially he is not a poet at all, although Baconians must insist otherwise.

Relatively speaking, the argument that Bacon was Shakespeare certainly thrived not only a century ago but for many later years; at one time its adherents even possessed a separate 'females only' offshoot. Currently it could be running out of steam somewhat, although Baconian ideas are always varied and interesting. Sadly, there is also evidence that, of all the main 'sects', this one carries the largest number of extreme views. Some of its followers would have Bacon, apparently immortal or nearly so, travelling down time to write other works. A few have even bestowed upon him illustrious illegitimate descendants such as Benjamin Franklin. It is difficult either to understand or to excuse such blatant excess, which earns ridicule. Alas, it then brings that ridicule too readily upon the whole literature of doubt.

But there may be good arguments for Bacon too. Was he really the same person as the greatest of the contemporary writers, 'Shakespeare'? Personally, I must disappoint Baconians, who I have always found earnest, friendly people, by answering in the negative. While the language of the two is sometimes similar, particularly in the use of pithy sayings, the known works of Bacon exhibit to me a different sense of priorities, interests, even personality from those suggested by the Shakespearean ones. I am also convinced, as most people are, that Shakespeare was dead by 1623 when the momentous First Folio edition of his plays appeared. My own stance in this matter does not, of course, make it impossible that Bacon was the true author. It certainly does not mean that he could not, in at least some minor way, have had influence, thus fulfilling his intent to do good to mankind through 'a despised weed', as he put it. The 'weed' (meaning dress or cloak) could have been the medium of plays. If (of course, it is very much an 'if') there was some secret collusion, then through an advisory role at least – despite his clearly professed aversion to some of the contemporary drama – he could have made some contribution without actually being identical with William Shakespeare.

SCENE 3

DERBYITES (LEFRANC, TITHERLEY)

Immediately after the First World War, two important new theories were emphatically proclaimed. One proposed the idea that 'William Shakespeare' was a pen-name for a nobleman with the same initials, viz William Stanley, sixth Earl of Derby. This thought actually had origins in the 1890s, for it was then that an antiquarian found two similar references in searching the *Calendar of State Papers* for 1599. These concern investigation into possible espionage. They suggest that Derby, far from being involved in a Catholic plot to overthrow Queen Elizabeth, was actually 'busy in penning comedies for the common players'. Derby's plays, if there were any, have not officially survived. However, the find was destined to establish him, in some eyes, as a secret dramatist of great stature; a member of the Elizabethan nobility, who might even be the true Shake-speare. (There are, incidentally, Elizabethan plays bearing simply the initials 'W S' on their title-page: these, decidedly inferior to the work of Shakespeare, are not comedies. Nor can it be certain who their author is.)

The case for Derby was taken up with vigour by a French Professor of Literature, Abel Lefranc, in his *Sous le masque de William Shakespeare*. The religious heresy parallel rears its head high with Lefranc: a certain party actually tried to buy up copies of this 1919 book in order to burn them! I can only refer selectively and very briefly to the argument in its two volumes, but the reasoning includes the following.

- That the author of *Love's Labour's Lost* must have been at the Court of Navarre and witnessed important incidents which are used in the play. The character Biron is seen as representing Baron de Biron, a person Derby had met. Lefranc found this play intensely French in style and language. He insists that the author knew France and the French court.

- That sixteenth century poet Edmund Spenser's reference to 'our gentle Willy' concerned a poet. It occurs in a work dedicated to the wife of the fifth Earl of Derby. Spenser elsewhere refers to a poet as 'Aetion', meaning 'eagle'. Several Stratfordians agree that the reference is to Shakespeare: it is noteworthy that Spenser was a friend of the Stanleys and that the crest of the House of Derby includes an eagle.

- The inner play in *A Midsummer Night's Dream* is seen as a reference to the activities of amateur artisans in midsummer plays produced at Chester, which was a favourite town of William Stanley's.

- Lefranc believed that the character of Malvolio in *Twelfth Night* was based on that of the steward to the Stanley family.

- A justice of the peace, named Stephen Proctor, brought an action against Lord Derby's agents for killing deer. This is seen by Lefranc as the source for Justice Shallow's accusations of Falstaff in *The Merry Wives of Windsor*. Lest this seems very nebulous, it must be pointed out that the name 'Proctor' was actually introduced into the 1602 quarto of the play, being removed later. (It is also suggested that the Garter references in the play arise because Derby became a Knight of the Garter in 1601.)

Lefranc, born in 1863, wrote in this vein until the middle of our century, and may justly be regarded as the true founder of the Derbyite cause. Some orthodox soul, obviously worried by Lefranc's literary credentials, said the views were formed in his dotage – yet he had held them for over thirty years! He had his followers in France, notably Georges Lambin with *Voyages de Shakespeare en France et en Italie* (1962). But, by 1950, there were certainly advocates to be found in England too. One was a university lecturer in chemistry, Dr A W Titherley (what colleagues in the Department of English thought we scarcely dare guess). In 1951, then more briefly a decade later, Titherley embraced the Derby cause in print. He advocated scientific method in the search for literary evidence, favouring induction in his stated quest for 'objective truth'.

Titherley lays some emphasis on genetics, mapping out the genealogy of the House of Derby to show that its pedigree was sufficient to bring forth a genius. He also offers interesting appendices on Shakespeare's handwriting. Basically, he sees Derby as one of a number of possible candidates from the nobility. However, he is advocated as the right one for various reasons. He had the appropriate Christian name (the sonnets seem to insist: 'my name is Will'); the right (we are told) sincere, unassuming personality; the familiarity with the Welsh people shown by Shakespeare; similar Lancastrian sympathies.

The point is made that a noble author is suggested by the hundreds of falconry images embedded in the Shakespeare writings. By this is meant the use of terms and phrases, such as tassel gentle, jesses, haggard, bate, eyas, staniel (as examples, see *Othello* Act 3, Scene 3, lines 260–5, or *Romeo and Juliet* Act 2, Scene 2, lines 158–9). This, of course, does not necessarily imply Derby as the noble author concerned. Titherley refers to Lefranc as a great French savant, about whose theory he was sceptical at first. The commentary is very dispassionate in some parts; less so in others where, despite the insistence on scientific method, Titherley strays into subjectivity. An obvious instance is where he surely succumbs to pleasant memories from his own youth, saying that Derby as Shakespeare knew the Isle of Man and drew on experiences from it for the fairy scenes in *A Midsummer Night's Dream*. Such references had 'eluded' Lefranc.

For an update in English on the Derbyite position of Lefranc, one could refer then to Titherley, or (preferably, in my opinion) to A J Evans, about whom more later. From time to time, even in the last decade, as my bibliography shows, press items have appeared connecting the writer Shakespeare with the Derbys. But could the sixth earl, who has at least one modern supporter of his cause in Canada as well as a few in Britain, possibly have been the real Shakespeare?

The case for William Stanley is a cryptogram-free zone, so we have to weigh arguments put forward from events, references, inferences, as they are expounded by Lefranc and his followers. A personal element can easily enter into such judgement, but some seem more significant than others. Certainly the young actor from Stratford worked for the Lord Chamberlain's company, which previously came under the patronage of William Stanley's brother. We can note, too, how well the House of Stanley is regarded in Shakespeare's works. One could argue from these factors that the sixth Earl of Derby, yearning to write, pounced on the idea of using as cover an individual associated with the theatres, this man having the same initials as those of Derby's family name and thus making his an ideal pen-name.

On the other hand, I feel that, if one argues that the true author was not Shakespeare of Stratford but someone at present unknown, it is pointless to claim in any seeking-out process that the hidden author must have had the real name 'Will'. In postulating the circumstances of authorship in the form which Derbyites and other doubters do, it must be merely the 'adopted' name. By no means do people using a pseudonym always employ their actual first name. If, for example, we did not know Mark Twain's real name, and if he had made puns in his writings on the word 'mark' (as he certainly would have done had he so wished), we would be completely wrong in thinking, simply from that word play, that Mark was the name given to him at birth.

Nor, of course, should any personal leanings or wishes sway us. This is said with a smile, because for the present writer, as a Lancastrian, any temptation towards bias in favour of William

Stanley must be denied. More seriously, I have to add that I find Derby's dates (1561–1642) most unsatisfactory for any case to be made for him, except possibly as an early source of advice or ideas for input. The date of his birth presents no problem. The difficulty is that he remained alive, yet completely inactive in his literary capacity (that is, if he was really a dramatist and poet of consequence), for so long after the Shakespeare enterprise came to a definite end with the publication of the First Folio in 1623. It may be repeated that, in this matter, I side with only some doubters but with all Stratfordians. For it seems indisputable that the whole tone of that major publishing event, together with the words of tribute accompanying it, signified that the great author, whether Stratford-upon-Avon's Shakespeare or not, had died before that date.

SCENE 4

THE OXFORD MOVEMENT
(LOONEY, AMPHLETT, OGBURN)

With due regard to other theories, it may be justly remarked that the claim that Edward de Vere, seventeenth Earl of Oxford, was actually the writer Shake-speare, is the most striking one to originate in the century under review. In fact, it now surely runs ahead of the Baconian claims as the most strenuously publicised alternative. This has been achieved, one might well suggest, despite the surname of its founder. Thomas Looney, a Gateshead schoolmaster, prepared his case during the First World War years; his *Shakespeare Identified* was published in 1920. Looney (apparently the correct pronunciation is Lorney or Loney) disregarded the offer to publish under a pen-name, pointing out that there was no need to be ashamed of his, with its long Manx ancestry. He emphasised, most particularly, that those who were put off a serious argument by a mere 'label', or derided it, would not under any circumstances be looking for the truth in these matters.

This is certain enough: one does not have to look too far to find other names, or even initials, on either 'side' in the controversy which might excite laughter. But people must be judged by the case made, not the accident of a name. Looney, a very serious and determined person, had been a convert to the positivist thinking of Auguste Comte, which he sought to apply to this problem. Writing with clarity, he covers the Stratfordian view; the nature of the difficulties encountered with it; the method proposed for their solution; features of the author; the fulfilment of these in Edward de Vere, seventeenth Earl of Oxford; de Vere's life and poetry. There is, incidentally, one poem by Oxford (as the earl is generally called) in the well-known anthology Palgrave's *Golden Treasury*. This is in the same metre as Shakespeare's *Venus and Adonis*.

The case, as we shall see, has at least one major weakness, but some enquirers have found much to be commended in it. By the time Looney died (early 1944), a strong following had been established. On the negative side of the problem, he has some telling remarks to make about the supposed writing career of the Stratford actor. We are told that, in his beginnings, this man 'emerges from (at least relative) squalor and ignorance, without leaving a trace of the process or means by which he accomplished the extraordinary feat'. The closing of his life, assuming him to be the great author, seems equally baffling: 'as destitute of an aftermath of literary glory as the first period was devoid of promise'. Looney adds, later in his book, that to suppose that 'he was so indifferent to the fate of his own manuscripts as to leave them to drift among unknown actors', without preparing for their preservation, is to suppose him incapable of realising their enduring worth.

Looney's first step to a solution was to look at what the writings of Shakespeare revealed about their author. That seems logical, and doubters from other camps have followed his example. Before touching upon some Oxfordian arguments, we may look at examples from such a list of attributes.

- Shakespeare must have been a person of some learning, with knowledge of the classics and some on special subjects such as astronomy.

- He can create comic characters from the ranks of the masses, replicating their talk convincingly, but seems most at home in a courtly setting.

- He must have tried out his 'pupil pen' in lyric poetry before the publication of the epic poem *Venus and Adonis*.

- Interests (and corresponding knowledge) include music, law, war, the sea, hunting and heraldry. The actual degree of specialist knowledge may be disputed, but it is desperate reasoning that suggests he would have needed none on any of these themes (and also no relevant personal experiences) to write as he did.

- He had travelled on the continent, seeming to know several areas particularly well. This may be especially true of northern Italy.

- In financial affairs, the great writer comes across to us as casual, even lax (whereas we know from the scant reliable biographical record of the Stratford man that he was a 'snapper up of trifles' in such money matters). The message of the works is that one's good name is much more important: the sonnets suggest that their writer's name had been sullied or defamed in some way.

- The sonnets also suggest that he may well have been rendered lame at some time (Sonnets 37, 89).

- He has Lancastrian sympathies.

- His attitude towards women is somewhat equivocal.

We need extend the list no further. It is sufficient to say that Looney, from his own original exercise of this kind, identified his man in Edward de Vere. Such a list is useful, least as a broad guideline. The strength again is in the whole. To justify Shakespeare of Stratford, say all those who are sceptical about him, we have to demolish not one or two coincidences, but a whole series. We have to ask how he had knowledge of events he had not experienced; countries he had never visited; how he had access to at least some biographical detail from the lives of his social superiors. Some points shown above, in a sequence by no means exhaustive, indicate the transformation he would need, whatever his genius – and that relatively quickly. They illustrate why the more able doubters at least deserve serious attention.

Arguments for Oxford's choice of the pen-name are that his family crest was of a lion shaking a broken lance. (Compare Ben Jonson's eventual tribute, in the First Folio, to the lines of Shakespeare – 'in each of which he seems to shake a lance'). The idea existed in the contemporary drama: George Peele wrote in one play, the line, 'Shake your spears in honour of his name.'

Much more significantly, say Oxfordians, there are the words written to the young Earl by Gabriel Harvey, designed to discourage de Vere from his early poetic efforts: 'throw away the insignificant pen, throw away bloodless books and writings that serve no useful purpose … your eyes flash fire …your countenance shakes a spear'. It would be a fine pen-name for him. And, most wondrously, there was an actor to hand with a very similar name to act as official author if questions were asked. Harvey may have been influenced in his words by Oxford's family name suggesting the Latin *veru*, meaning a javelin or spear.

We have evidence from contemporary sources that Oxford wrote one or more plays under his own name, perhaps restricted to a small private audience. None has officially survived, even though he heads a list compiled by one writer in 1598 of 'the best for comedy'. Shakespeare is listed too: that may mean much or little. The writer concerned, Francis Meres, would have no ready means of telling if two dramatists on his list were actually only one with different names used. He does not mention the titles of Oxford's plays; his list may well have been based on (incomplete) comment supplied from various sources.

Oxford's family affairs certainly seem, at least to his advocates, to be echoed by passages in the plays. Even several Stratfordians would accept, for instance, that the character of Polonius in *Hamlet* is based on William Cecil, Lord Burghley, who was Oxford's father-in-law. Oxfordians would cite many more examples of incidents in the plays which reflect the life of their man or characters which seem to be drawn from his relations. Of course, some comparisons may be forced, but the list has enough credibility to ask questions of orthodoxy. It is also well known that Oxford, at least when young, was fond of making puns on his name, Edward de Vere (pronounced 'Ver'). So, for instance, in his youthful contribution to an Elizabethan poetry anthology called *A Hundred Sundry Flowers* (1573), he noted his initial (E Ver) and his nickname 'Ned' (Ned Ver) in signing some contributions by 'Ever or Never'.

Another poet of the age, Thomas Watson, picked up the idea in expressing a hope for one of his own poems that it would find a place on the learned bookshelves of Oxford, 'ever the friend of the Muses'. (There are other contemporary observations which play on the theme, two examples of which are: a VERy ancient family; the best VERse he EVER wrote). So it is that Shakespeare's Sonnet 76, where 'every word does almost tell my [real?] name' is often cited by Oxfordians. There is too the link between the stem 'Ver' and the word truth (as in words like verify or verity). This is borne out by advice to Oxford's wife that she should be 'an ever lover of the truth'. Besides, the family motto was 'Nothing truer than truth'. Incidentally, concerning the more speculative possible puns on his name, the play *King Henry the Eighth* was originally entitled 'All is True', but was later changed to conform with the other titles in the history play series.

Admittedly, finding a reference to Oxford in each Shakespearean variation of 'true' is straining credulity well beyond reasonable limits (though this does not stop some modern Oxfordians from apparently doing it). But at least we know that de Vere (and others in referring to him) did sometimes indulge in such word play. Perhaps more significant, for our purpose, than examples so far quoted is the 1609 quarto edition of *Troilus and Cressida*, the first year of its publication. This has already been mentioned as having been wrested from the hands of 'grand possessors', according to its preface. De Vere was by then no longer alive. But could his memory linger in its most curious dedication: 'a never writer to an ever reader'?

If not, how is this to be explained?

We have barely begun to consider the arguments made for Oxford by Looney or subsequent writers. The case made an impact on a number of people, notably Sigmund Freud and John Galsworthy. By the mid-century years, it had a large literature of variable standard. By choice, I would select, from 1955, a fiery, sometimes witty, book by a painter and naturalist, Hilda Amphlett, showing how far the Oxford theory had progressed. It is of very readable length and perhaps, in Britain, not too difficult to see still. Oxfordian 'evidence', of variable status, abounds there. We read, for instance, of the strong elements of autobiography in *All's Well that Ends Well* and in *Hamlet*. Amphlett, who died in 1981, is said to have started enquiring about Shakespeare after seeing the bust in Stratford church.

'The Oxford Movement' (I am not the first to so describe it) has many followers in the United States, whence comes the third advocate selected for special mention here. Representing, as he does here, a Georgian family most industrious in Oxford's cause, he really could not be omitted. Charlton Ogburn's *The Mysterious William Shakespeare: The Myth and the Reality* (1984) is a most detailed (nearly 900 pages), handsomely produced work; until or unless new facts or striking new suspicions emerge, it must surely be the definitive statement of the case for de Vere as the true Shakespeare. Some readers may prefer (or be able more readily) to consult a subsequent British abridgement of it by a descendant of the Earls of Oxford, Charles de Vere (Lord Burford). Ogburn, born in 1911, has published successfully on other themes, but holds a long interest in the authorship controversy. His parents, Dorothy and Charlton Ogburn, had themselves published, in 1952, an extensive book, *This Star of England*, advocating Oxford.

The work of the second Charlton Ogburn cannot be faulted for coverage or endeavour. For those who gain access to it, there can be no alternative if what is wanted is a comprehensive 'Oxfordian read'. It is a measured, sustained effort to accumulate the evidence until the case can become overwhelming. In addition to its warm reception in the (New

York based) Shakespeare Oxford Society, it has won several other converts. We have a presentation of the life of the true author as matching the vicissitudes in the life of de Vere which, if seen as fact, is startling; or, even if one insists that it must be largely fiction or guesswork, is still a moving story. One does not have to agree with the author on all points to be impressed by his obvious sincerity and the flow of the argument. There are valuable glimpses too of the history of the Oxfordian cause and how it had gathered momentum as research gradually provided more information on the life of de Vere. Right, wrong, or somewhere in between, this 1984 volume has to be reckoned the most scholarly work in the whole large literature of unorthodoxy. Several reviewers, not bearing the albatross of being necessarily locked into orthodoxy, were equally ecstatic. A critic in the *Boston Globe* claimed that a literary Watergate was being revealed.

Could Oxford have been the real William Shakespeare? Some arguments are stronger than others: desperation has not led supporters into too many claims of hidden word codings, but some of the (so very numerous) comparisons claimed between the plays and the biography of his circle seem forced. Other arguments are faint rather than strong suggestions. One example of such is that the 1573 anthology *A Hundred Sundry Flowers* contained a poem about a sparrow called Philip. This is echoed in Shakespeare's play *King John* ('Philip? – sparrow!'), where the name is rejected as unworthy, because its former owner is now 'Sir Richard'. The allusion is clear enough, but its use does not necessarily mean that the writer of the play had been a contributor to the 1573 volume. It might simply mean that Shakespeare knew it; felt too that his audience would also know and appreciate the reference, which also arose before 1573, in the poetry of John Skelton.

Other good examples of association which is frustratingly inconclusive concern Malvolio's reference to the 'sweet Roman hand' (handwriting) in *Twelfth Night*, (de Vere used this modern handwriting style; the Stratford man, to judge by his extant signatures, certainly did not), or in the observation that Oxford brought back from foreign travel a pair of scented gloves for the

Queen, in which she took great pleasure. This gift may seem to be recalled in one or two of the plays, notably *Much Ado about Nothing*: 'These gloves the Count sent me; they are an excellent perfume.' Cynics may say that, as emphatic evidence, this reflects the title of the play. Certainly, the Queen's delight with her gift could be widely known. Yet, despite some clear excesses from his followers, the actual or possible links with Oxford's life and deeds in Shakespeare's plays do seem extensive. We shall come back to consideration of pro-Oxfordian arguments.

As with the Baconians, a large Oxfordian literature leads to some overreaching in the desire to find new ground. It certainly is not necessarily a help to the cause to be told that he was Queen Elizabeth's secret lover, and that the fair youth of the sonnets is really a 'Ver' youth. (Oxford was some 17 years younger than the monarch, but there are bigger obstacles to this strand of argument than that.) However, as with other theories, it does not matter if some advocates run to even the wildest excess, provided there is some prospect of the essentials being correct.

But it was mentioned earlier that there is one very big stumbling block concerning claims for the seventeenth Earl of Oxford. For he died in 1604, while several Shakespearean plays, if their usual dating is to be accepted, were undoubtedly later than this. Looney's response to this problem was to deny that some plays (*The Tempest*, for instance) were really Shakespeare's. Amphlett sees that play as being started by Shakespeare, but completed by an inferior hand. Several later Oxfordians, including Ogburn, would have us accept a different solution. They urge that the conventional dating of the plays must be revised. This may seem a better answer, but it has difficulties of its own in endeavouring to remove the impediment. We cannot revise the dates of Shakespeare's plays in isolation, for all demonstrable improvements in the drama were noted by others, with an eye to imitation. Thus, if we say any plays were written earlier than conventional thinking allows, there are implications for the revised dating of other writers' works.

If some Oxfordians seem unrealistic in this, my three chosen writers from their ranks may be seen also to have been so in an important respect – the sense of expecting their case to be accepted readily in scholarly circles. All doubters need to be hopeful, but Oxfordians do seem to me to be particularly optimistic. Looney himself had written, in a letter of December 1932 to Carolyn Wells, that he felt confident that the truth was clear to minds prepared to see it. If this seems highly presumptuous, we should note in fairness the 'positive thinking' outlook held: having done all possible to solve a problem as he saw it, it was time to turn away to something else. But, in a rallying call, near the end of her 1955 book, Amphlett too exclaims: 'the proofs of its truth are accumulating so fast that the day is at hand when even ... the most diehard Stratfordians will out of their burrows like conies after rain'. And Ogburn tells us that he set out to press home the case as never before by putting orthodoxy on the witness stand, to contrast their claims with the facts, so as to illuminate what he saw as the irresistible truth. Even if the cause is just, the optimism of all three is unjustified.

The Shakespeare Oxford Society has thrived in the United States of America; a de Vere Society newsletter is also published regularly in Canada. Within the United Kingdom, the de Vere Society, founded in 1986, had mixed early fortunes: there was, among other events, a simulated Elizabethan banquet and ball which seemed to overstretch the group financially. The British group now works more closely with their longer-established American 'cousins' as the Oxfordian camp strides on. The march is primarily in literature, lecture (where Lord Burford has been especially active) or debate; unlike *Baconiana*, which has struggled for new copy in recent years, Oxfordians are almost queueing to write. There is another portrait to consider also: the enigmatic 'Ashbourne', which has been claimed as Oxford and as Shakespeare – although it may be someone else altogether.

Many archive collections are now being examined for 'hard' evidence, notably through the work done by D K Charlton within the Wentworth Woodhouse records in Yorkshire and elsewhere. At the very least this endeavour should enable considerable enhancement of the historical details given in an article on the seventeenth Earl of Oxford within the *Dictionary of National Biography*, and in those background works on his life of which my bibliography cites examples. The finds to date also throw light on others, including the sixth Earl of Derby.

There has been 'popular advertisement', too: for instance, via 'The Earl of Oxford is Shakespeare' T-shirts; via actual or sought television 'exposure'; by asking people to sign a petition pressing for more objective investigation into the authorship. It remains at least notionally feasible for the Oxfordian claims, like those of any other school of doubters, to gain substantial extra support. To have any chance of doing this, in my view, unless some entirely new find in their favour comes to light, they need to be refined somewhat. More importantly, they would also need to be 'heard' (the Oxfordians are admittedly working very hard on this) by a vastly larger, much more open-minded, audience.

SCENE 5

THE RUTLAND HYPOTHESIS
(POROHOVSHIKOV AND SYKES)

One of the problems for any of those who propose a member of the Elizabethan nobility as the true author of Shakespeare is that there are a good many pointers that seem to them to suggest that the great dramatist drew on the biography of these nobles, their experiences, the habits of their acquaintances – but these pointers do not always direct us to the same person. The fifth Earl of Rutland has had relatively few supporters, but has attracted some good intellects. He was advanced as a candidate early in the century, before the Earl of Oxford was proposed or the Earl of Derby seriously considered, by writers from Germany and Belgium. A most striking enthusiast then, from the latter country, was Professor Celestin Demblon. His specialism was French literature, but it has been claimed that he had read 5000 items on the Shakespeare authorship controversy. However, the fifth Earl, Roger Manners, is introduced here through two other advocates.

One of these, Pierre Porohovshikov, distinguished in law and history, left his native Russia at the time of the Revolution to work in the United States. His *Shakespeare Unmasked*, published there in 1940, appeared in Britain later. Professor Porohovshikov points out that Rutland was a great friend of the Earl of Southampton (to whom some Shakespeare poems were dedicated and who may well be the 'fair youth' in the sonnets). In terms of the dramatist's mood, it is seen as significant that the Shakespearean tragedies were written over the period of time when Rutland was imprisoned in the Tower of London; another great friend, the Earl of Essex, was executed during that time.

Porohovshikov draws attention to an anonymous drama produced at Cambridge University when Rutland was there. This is seen as a clear forerunner of *Twelfth Night*. We are then shown details of a handwritten speech from the latter play, the hand being claimed as Rutland's. If he was the author of this Cambridge drama, called *Laelia*, he could not have been copying Shakespeare, because of the date of production. ('Can echoes resound before the horn is blown'?) So Shakespeare must have copied from *Laelia*. On such arguments, the case for Rutland becomes a moral, if not mathematical, certainty.

Claud Sykes's sanguine book for Roger Manners (Rutland), *Alias William Shakespeare* (1947), is introduced by the historian, Sir Arthur Bryant. Sir Arthur does not accept the conclusion, but found the work 'absorbing, erudite, ingenious'. But the strategy of Sykes, imagining Sherlock Holmes seeking the true Shakespeare, has excited unjust ridicule elsewhere. (Surely it can be regarded as an exercise in literary detection no less than searching through historical records would be?) Sykes finds flaws in the case for some other high-ranking Elizabethans. Neither Bacon nor Derby had reason for the black mood shown by Shakespeare from 1603 to 1608; Oxford was 43 when *Venus and Adonis* was published. Bacon did not know Italy as Shakespeare seems to have done, nor was he so interested in forestry and field sports. A key play once again is *Hamlet*. The bad feeling between brothers, shown in this play, was mirrored in the Manners family. Rutland alone had the direct experience of Denmark. Sykes contends that he knew people there named Rosencrantz and Guildenstern. It was Rutland, Sykes insists, who was always in the right place at the right time: the man who shook the spear must have been the man who visited Denmark.

ACT 3. THE CONTROVERSY: TWENTIETH-CENTURY THEORIES

There are interesting points to consider if the claims made for Rutland as Shakespeare were to be investigated in more detail. While some of these may seem quite strong, the difficulties seem even stronger. A basic problem lies in the relatively short life span of Roger Manners (1576–1612). We know for sure that, although some plays were not published until they appeared in the 1623 Folio, Shakespeare did stop writing around 1612. Yet he had started, with a mature classical poem, in 1593 and the *Henry the Sixth* plays attributed to him were available, probably in an unpolished form, earlier than this. Could young Roger (later Earl of Rutland) when aged only 16 or 17 have composed *Venus and Adonis*? Then, so soon after, many dramas of varied, often highly sophisticated, wit?

My answer has to be very firmly in the negative. Sykes tries to persuade us otherwise, speaking of a child prodigy at a time when men matured earlier: he makes a nineteenth-century comparison via the early writing of Byron. All doubters have a chasm to leap in taking on a new faith. For the Rutland school, the date of his birth makes this the widest of those described here (although not as wide as that for many others only touched upon in my book). It may be significant that Porohovshikov could be said to be something of a Groupist. He gives all the real glory to Rutland, but thinks that the classical poems and the early play *Love's Labour's Lost* came from the pen of Francis Bacon.

There are other aristocrats of that time whose names have been put forward, but we have now seen just a little of the main ones. Could any of them be revealed as a dramatist of consequence? Could Rutland have been even a major dramatist *manqué*, let alone the real Shakespeare? Provided doubts about orthodoxy can be accepted by now, each may have something in his favour. How important are these pointers that suggest that Shakespeare had special interests and experiences; that he was most comfortable writing about the high-born; that there are oblique references in his plays to actual events in the lives of noble Elizabethans; that some plays reveal first-hand experience gained through continental travel? Some of my readers may feel that no one candidate fits the bill. If this is so, could it possibly be someone else altogether, even that shadowy personality from Stratford? Or, if the aristocrats do not provide a satisfactory answer singly, could they possibly do so in combination?

Before looking at advocacy for that theory, we must examine a quite different one. This is the supposition that Shakespeare was really a mask for a professional author rather than a gentleman amateur – the man regarded, despite the early date of his official death, as the second most accomplished dramatist of the Elizabethan age.

SCENE 6

MARLOWE'S SUPPORTERS
HOFFMAN, HONEY, WRAIGHT

Christopher Marlowe (1564–1593), son of a Canterbury shoemaker, is unique among those who are contenders, in the eyes of their advocates, for the title of 'Shakespeare'. He was known to be a fine dramatist in his own right, but was also officially dead during Shakespeare's productive years. 'Kit' Marlowe was the greatest of a group of young writers from the universities at that time: the transformer of blank verse and the drama; the writer, while still young, of fine plays that form a natural preface to those of Shakespeare. *Tamburlaine the Great, Doctor Faustus, King Edward the Second*, and *The Jew of Malta* are the four major ones. Other works included a long epic poem, *Hero and Leander*, neither finished nor published by the date he is believed to have died violently. Naturally, this exercised a powerful influence upon the epic poems of Shakespeare which soon followed. It is widely acknowledged that, but for his early death, Marlowe would have equalled (or come very near to equalling) our supreme Bard as a writer of great tragedies.

His own life certainly reads like one. Partly through his readily demonstrable ability, he rapidly became involved with leading personalities of the time; he was caught up in aspects of the espionage service, having himself served as a government spy; he was a man seemingly contemptuous of lesser minds. His willingness to challenge and flout convention can be seen in his beliefs and habits, although had he not been so recklessly outspoken charges of atheism and homosexuality may not have been brought against him. They were, and matters of this kind could certainly lead to execution. However, at a time in May 1593, when he was attending the court daily in the context of such charges, the literary glory of Christopher Marlowe was seemingly cut short; history tells us that he was stabbed to death by a man named Frizer, in a brawl with a group at a Deptford inn, concerning a quarrel over who should pay 'the reckoning'.

This life of his, it might be felt, really has quite enough drama without extra claims being made for it. As for its ending, the site of Marlowe's last resting place is uncertain. He is like a person he apparently claimed to despise, Moses, in that 'no one knows where his sepulchre is to this day'. There may even be another parallel between these two. If Marlowe somehow lived on after the 1593 Deptford incident ... well, after all, Moses is traditionally held to be the author of the Pentateuch, which includes an account of his death!

The first person to make an impact in advancing Marlowe's claims was from North America. Calvin Hoffman in a 1955 book, *The Murder of the Man who was Shakespeare* (the British edition has a shorter title), found 'mountains of incongruity' in the orthodox view of Shakespearean authorship. He postulates that Marlowe did not perish in that brawl in May 1593. The death was 'arranged' in a scheme to save a prodigious talent from the fate that awaited him, via the almost certain outcome of those dire charges.

Hoffman saw the plot as being led by Marlowe's patron, Sir Thomas Walsingham (certainly Frizer was one of Walsingham's men), adding that Marlowe and Walsingham must have been lovers. An unknown – Hoffman suggests a sailor – was murdered in the latter's stead, Marlowe then being smuggled away to the Continent. There he lived on, an exile in Italy, sending the manuscripts of his plays to Walsingham for publication. Hoffman argues that the 'story' in the Shakespeare sonnets graphically illustrates the plight of one who had participated in some offences and was banished. Officially dead, he was doomed to perpetual silence as far as receiving the credit for the works was concerned.

We might, if at all sympathetic to such a theory as this, consider it a surprising coincidence that the birth of a truly outstanding literary talent (Marlowe) was followed, in just two months, by another (Shakespeare of Stratford). Coincidence is strained further by the fact that the name 'Shake-speare' first appeared so soon after the death of Marlowe, like a baton being handed on in a literary relay race. Hoffman draws attention to suggested close parallels between certain texts in the plays and verses of 'Shakespeare' and Marlowe. He offers much other detail; some is minor and certain items are clearly unsatisfactory. An example of the latter is reference to the analysis of word lengths in Elizabethan literature carried out, in the late nineteenth century, by Professor T C Mendenhall. Such checking of word patterns and associations in the writings of two authors, where we have a number of works by each, is nowadays potentially valuable, since it can be carried out by computer analysis. But, in Mendenhall's time, with only manual checking available, the 'results' can really tell us little.

Understandably cited by Hoffman is an interesting portrait; this is Elizabethan, and was rediscovered at Cambridge, in a poor condition, in 1953. He believes this to be one of Marlowe. Certainly the date (1585) and the subject's stated age (21) are right. If it is not a representation of Marlowe, we do not know who it might be. The Latin motto below it, translated as 'That which nourishes me also destroys me,' makes an apt commentary on Marlowe's talents. It has several echoes in Shakespeare. Hoffman also claims that several people to whom he showed this picture believed that it, along with the Droeshout portrait of Shakespeare, are of the same man at different ages. Another quite different point, known for years before Hoffman wrote, but picked up by him, is that a short collection of poetry, *The Passionate Pilgrim*, attributed to Shakespeare, contains an item known by all to be Marlowe's:

'Come, live with me and be my love'. Incidentally, this Hoffman version of Marlovian theory became the subject of an operetta.

There certainly were curious circumstances surrounding the death of Marlowe. Charges against the alleged killer and his companions, all servants of Sir Thomas Walsingham, were conveniently dropped. But, since Hoffman could not produce hard evidence that Marlowe survived after May 1593, the hypothesis was dismissed by the critics. Yet in many ways, for those prepared even tentatively to doubt received orthodoxy, it presents a fascinating, though rough-hewn, hypothesis. Parts of it have aroused amusement, notably the identification of the 'Mr W H' of the Sonnets as 'Walsing-Ham'. *The Times* offered the view that the theory was both fanciful and highly entertaining; this, in fact, seemed to be the general verdict. The florid phrasing of certain passages and the lack of an index alike contribute to heighten the impression that one is reading fiction. Hoffman was also guilty of a number of minor factual inaccuracies (mere molehills of incongruity?) which one anonymous reviewer in particular pounced upon most cruelly. Yet this book, whatever its stylistic or other defects, is very readable; I have vivid memories of my acquisition of it, in unusual circumstances, years after its publication; it was bought in a public library book sale in the Orkney Islands!

For the remainder of his days, until his death in 1986, Hoffman pursued the theme with great zeal. A short, but most interesting 1983 item, in the *Guardian* newspaper, tells of Hoffman's journey to Padua, made to follow up a rumour that an English writer named Marlowe had lived there as a recluse, dying in 1627. King's School, Canterbury, which Marlowe attended, now offers an annual prize for an original essay about him under a substantial bequest from Calvin and Rose Hoffman. It would appear that those to benefit so far from the prize are orthodox Marlowe scholars, despite the fact that this seems altogether contrary to Hoffman's intentions. But, apart from the annual awards available, there is a bigger incentive. Anyone providing 'irrefutable and incontrovertible proof and evidence required to satisfy the world of Shakespearean scholarship that all the plays and poems now commonly attributed to William Shakespeare were in fact written by Christopher Marlowe' can, to use a popular phrase, win the jackpot, taking all the remaining money in the bequest. Even supposing Hoffman's theory to be broadly true, anyone able to do exactly that would most certainly deserve the financial returns!

Back in 1956, Hoffman had received permission to open a 'tomb' relating to the Walsingham family at Chislehurst, since he hoped it might contain documentary evidence. He found there only fine sand. It must be said, in fairness, that what was actually opened was a chest in the Chislehurst church, resting beneath tablets commemorating the Walsinghams. The tombs proper are in the vault beneath. He returned to the fray later, with no more success. Sadly, unbelievers are often criticised for such initiative. In Hoffman's case, even F W Wadsworth, a normally fair commentator, did so. Yet they are often criticised too for failure to produce that 'irrefutable proof' in their cause! Nor is Hoffman alone in such quests. There was, for example, not many years later, a request by someone to find and open the tomb of Mary Fitton, hoping for evidence that she was the 'dark lady' of the sonnets.

Hoffman it was who ignited the touchpaper of the Marlovian cause, giving it a clear band of followers; perhaps we might call them 'Calvinists'! The most original has been William Honey (died 1990). Honey, clearly a man of wide cultural interests, grew up in Australia, but spent much of his life in the British Isles. He produced and privately published *The Life, Loves and Achievements of Christopher Marlowe, alias Shakespeare* (1982). This huge tome, on a theme which came to dominate his whole life, takes his story of Marlowe/Shakespeare to 1604 only. He worked at a second volume, which would have been equally large, but it was never completed. At Honey's death, the raw material was destroyed, at his own request.

Honey's style is very different from that of Hoffman: indeed, were it not for the fact that this latter-day 'Mr W H' mingles fact indiscriminately with what must necessarily be his speculations, one might describe it as scholarly. The work shows evidence of meticulous attention to the whole field of Elizabethan drama, is carefully indexed, and runs to over 1400 pages. Honey has one or two major departures from earlier Marlovian ideas; these apparently displeased Hoffman, although the two men never actually met. One such departure is the argument that the person murdered in 1593 and replaced by Marlowe was the actor from Stratford-upon-Avon, William Shakespeare. These men of the theatre were only two months apart in age. Honey believed they must have been equally close in terms of physical resemblance. Marlowe did not, according to this theory, go abroad permanently, but simply replaced the orthodox Shakespeare, encountering some blackmail from the family. It is Marlowe's remains, on this basis, that lie in that so famous grave without a name at Stratford.

The argument makes a little use of cryptograms. Honey tells us that we need the proper use of anagrammatic methods, using the system set out in William Camden's *Remains* ... (1605), remembering things like the fact that I and J, or U, V and W were interchangeable in Elizabethan days. That mysterious dedication at the start of Shakespeare's sonnets, then, becomes addressed to their recipient; not Walsingham but, as has been much more commonly supposed, Henry Wriothesley, Earl of Southampton. It is an essential part of Honey's case that Southampton supplanted Walsingham as Marlowe's special friend and lover and that he indeed is the fair youth addressed in so many of the sonnets.

According to Honey this is a tale of homosexual love. One aspect which will surprise the reader is that the mysterious 'Mr W H', 'only begetter' of the sonnets, whose identity has caused argument for the scholars over the centuries, could be merely part of an anagram. So too is the apparent signer of the dedication 'T T', always previously believed to be the publisher of the sonnets, Thomas Thorpe. It is worth looking at Honey's rendering of the oft-quoted epitaph on the grave of Shakespeare, although we do not know for certain that it was written by the great poet. Honey believed that its so-called doggerel, that so enraged Mark Twain, has a purpose; that the lack of a name is more apparent than real. Thus, the famous warning to the curious:

> Good frend for Iesvs sake forbeare
> To digg the dvst encloased hear
> Blese be ye man yt spares these stones
> And cvrst be he yt moves my bones

becomes, through William Honey's interpretation, 'converted into the fully Shakespearean':

> Good friend who wishes for Shakespeare
> To dig the dust: entomed here:
> Plays by the man, verses, his sonnets,
> And Christopher Marlowe's bones.

Well, it could appeal to some people; there is enough similarity to make it superficially attractive. Yet, apart from my deep suspicion of all cryptograms, I found I could not quite work it through using the method offered. I have modernised the spelling, but one of the problems is bringing down an 'arl' from the earlier lines to fit between the 'm' and 'o' of 'moves' in the last.

Those few who do see Honey's book may well only dip in, or scan the synopses of the introduction and 83 chapters. Hoffman is certainly a much easier read. Naturally, weaknesses in what is said are partly the same. The distinctive parts of Honey's argument may seem to strengthen the case for Marlowe in some respects, but have very real problems of their own. All in all, the argument that Marlowe helped to murder and then 'became' Shakespeare of Stratford seems a very wild, frothy, hypothesis. Yet Honey has a passion for thorough research and truth in seemingly minute details which sometimes serves him well. For example, at the date of Marlowe's supposed death, the dramatist was in effect on bail; obliged to attend daily at the Privy Council, an integral part of the court, because of accusations concerning his behaviour and beliefs. Honey indicates that the court concerned was the royal one, then 13 miles outside London, at Nonsuch. Travel was on horseback on relatively poor roads. It is thus reasoned that Marlowe could not attend the Council that day yet be in the sinister group – all the members of which, as the coroner's report stated, were at that Deptford inn from ten in the morning onwards. While not conclusive as to whether our dramatist was absent from the grim Deptford session or not, this is an interesting point.

Yet Honey can also irritate by presenting, alongside historical facts, so many speculations which are offered in exactly the same spirit of assurance. Actuality and assumption are indistinguishable in terms of the text's tone: allegory, metaphor, allusion in the plays (as seen through his eyes) lead him to speculative reconstruction of even the most precise details of week-to-week events. Honey also offers some curious descriptions and conclusions (Ben Jonson, when 24, was 'a pimply autodidact'; another great literary figure, rather nearer to our own time, wrote 'protoplasmic mush'). Believing that Shakespeare/Marlowe was homosexual, he illogically goes on to conclude that not merely the sonnets, but all poems written by one man concerning another (Milton's *Lycidas*; Tennyson's *In Memoriam*) must betray such tendencies.

Much could be criticised about William Honey, but not dedication. Indeed, an attempted summary of so long a work illustrates very ably my contention that to contract an argument considerably is to invite risk of distortion. He is not alone in arguing that Shakespeare of Stratford was murdered; we shall see that a few Stratfordians have claimed this. Honey's faults lie in some 'tunnel vision'; in the indiscriminate mingling of fact based on painstaking research with a massive degree of conjecture; and, strikingly, in a reluctance to examine the work of those with very different views, so strong that it might rival that of the most fundamentalist of preachers clutching his Bible. Honey deliberately chose isolation, or so it seems. Consequently, even many people who feel they have charted at least some part of the course of the authorship controversy may not have come across him. Did he write, one may wonder, simply from an overwhelming need to express the deep conviction he held, or did he believe his ideas would be vindicated eventually? We cannot say. I corresponded with William Honey on rare occasions; it was to my regret that he declined an opportunity to meet me in 1987. His work, although so striking, represents an avenue, or perhaps a cul-de-sac, off the main highway of Marlovian activity.

Currently, there has emerged a very different British advocate for Marlowe, Mrs A D Wraight, a devotee of this dramatist from her youth. In 1965, as joint author of a beautifully illustrated work subsequently reprinted, she had done no more than show some empathy with the 'heretics'. But some 30 years on, in *The Story That The Sonnets Tell*, fuelled by pointers in the apparent biography behind the poetry, she goes much further. Wraight insists that years of thorough research compelled this most controversial route. She chooses not to mention Honey at all, perhaps because of his view of Marlowe's personality, and her work is as vastly different from Hoffman's in terms of a scholarly approach as it is in style, although many of his contentions are re-packaged. The essentially original parts of the argument rest upon the idea of the sonnets being addressed to various persons – the poet's patron is one, the fair youth another. The official sonnet sequence is seen as needing rearrangement, interlocking strands being appropriately untangled. References to Freemasonry echo some Baconians, although there is no doubt in her mind as to Marlowe being the right candidate.

This author is a good deal more friendly towards orthodoxy than are many anti-Stratfordians. Acknowledging gross flaws and fantasy in the literature of doubt, she emphasises that Shakespeare lovers have no cause to worry over her conclusions. The rose of reconciliation, as mentioned in her text, seems especially apposite here. For she relies, optimistically in my view, upon the integrity of all Stratfordian scholars to examine fairly – and then hopefully accept – her revolutionary thesis. A major source of inspiration for Dolly Wraight has been the work of a Stratfordian, the late Dr Leslie Hotson. At one time discoverer of a major documentary find on Marlowe, his proposal of what seemed to many critics an unusual choice for the sonnets' phantom figure of 'Mr W H', is endorsed by Mrs Wraight. Two things at the very least can be said for sure of the sonnets, even without exploring her reasoning any further: one is that they most certainly *are* complex, as so many conventional scholars have found – yet not offering a consistent picture as to a solution; the other is that anyone at all inclined to think that Marlowe lived on after 1593 will find their poetic message most heartening.

Returning to the sixteenth century, notwithstanding his apparent defects in the realm of comedy, Marlowe was a stupendous tragic dramatist in his own right for his own, or indeed any, time. So, in the realm of the tragedies at least, he becomes a plausible alternative Shakespeare, always assuming we can take the giant stride to accept that he did live on after his official dramatic death. Admittedly, there are curious features about that. It was convenient for certain people. If the Marlovian theory is broadly true, it was most convenient of all at the time for Marlowe himself, although the enforced hiding, not to mention the official silence, would naturally become an increasing source of pain and frustration. Like Salman Rushdie in our own times, he would have to hide; unlike Rushdie, if he produced great writing, another would get the credit.

There are orthodox Marlowe Societies in both America and Britain, but Marlovians (in the sense of this chapter) within the USA also have an association (entitled 'Marlowe Lives!'), for which the enthusiast David More runs a lively newsletter. The theory that Marlowe was Shakespeare is a little different from others; could there be truth in it? Continuing research during the last decade or so has introduced some new elements on Marlowe's 1593 death, but without providing telling evidence to discredit the official story. So, basically, we still have to decide from our reading whether his living on could be fact – or is merely good fiction.

SCENE 7

GROUP THEORIES
(SLATER, EVANS, POWELL); SUMMATION

Marlowe had some advocates many years before the time of Hoffman; these included one or two who saw him as part of a group responsible for the Shakespearean output. Before looking at examples of group theory, it must be pointed out that this history of the controversy in the twentieth century is incomplete in two respects. I have proceeded by 'candidate' rather than strictly by date, only covering the major contenders; I have also greatly contracted each argument, indicating sources I think best equipped to give more detail.

It may be reiterated that the literature of 'heresy' is extensive, although but a very small fraction of the total published on Shakespeare. Clearly, the subject has attracted seekers of novelty as well as some good minds concerned for historical integrity. The work of the doubters also contains much repetition. Many names could have been added in this historical survey, but nearly all the arguments merely repeat, with minor variation, those illustrated. Several acolytes, although they may strive for originality, are near to being mere clones of the originator of the theory concerned. But this kind of overlapping, whether of biographical or critical comments, is also to be found in the orthodox literature concerning Shakespeare.

There is a 1962 casebook which unfortunately is now, in the United Kingdom at least, very elusive. Compiled by American writers George McMichael and Edgar Glenn, this provides an interesting collection of source material on the controversy. Numerous extracts from past literature are given about the debate or which may throw light upon it. These are left to tell their own story, the editors firmly declining to intervene. Some of these readings are from Elizabethan times, others are modern, or relatively so. Evidence both pro and con is provided: so, for example, advocates of Bacon are given space to have their say, but there is also an extract from the Friedmans' conclusions concerning their examination of ciphers.

McMichael and Glenn also seek to provide a comprehensive list of all the alternatives, including the most bizarre, ever advanced up to that time. This totals no less than 56 individuals (excluding the Stratford Shakespeare). The full range of advocated 'claimants', as listed by them, includes diverse and sometimes most unlikely candidates. For example, the first Queen Elizabeth has been advanced as the true Shakespeare by G E Sweet (this despite the fact that Sonnet 20 proclaims its author to be male). Anne Whately, Sir Walter Ralegh, Robert Burton, King James, are just a few examples of other candidates, equally unlikely or nearly so. The claim for Anne Whately, as an intended bride of the Stratford man, may be of especial interest, since, it is widely conceded, she may not even have existed. (She is quite likely a mere copying error in a register which should say 'Anne Hathaway'.) One of the two books about her is most curiously dedicated, with affection, to the ravens around the salt tower. However fair one tries to be, it may be difficult to resist an obvious rejoinder: this must be strictly for the birds!

To such a formidable listing can be added at least one 'minority candidate' first put forward only in recent times, William Nugent from Ireland. Others are being revived: an outstanding instance of this from the 1990s has been the work of Lillian Schwartz in the United States. Superimposing, by computer graphics, an image of the Droeshout portrait upon that of another (but, of course, the accuracy of such paintings is uncertain), she has argued that these represent the very same person. On this basis, Dr Schwartz takes up vigorously the Queen Elizabeth theme of Sweet, nearly thirty years on. Such writings or other expositions always astonish, often entertain. On occasion too, they inform. That 1962 listing also contained (amazingly) two organisations, the Jesuits being one, the Rosicrucians the other. Perhaps there are yet more individuals or societies one day to be cited as the true Shakespeare, preparation of their case being still in nascent form?

There also remains scope for various permutations of candidates, provided it can be accepted that the Shakespeare works – some of them most certainly extensively revised, recast, edited – were the product of collaboration. Clearly some doubters make a rash choice, then become over-credulous concerning any possible supporting idea, espousing it not wisely but too well. As *The Tempest* puts it: 'they'll take suggestion as a cat laps milk'.

All the diversity, let alone clear excesses, can scarcely help the cause of the disputants. Yet it does not prove their general concerns to be necessarily founded on error. Theoretically at least, one could be right, others relatively near. That would mean that the rest were right (to the extent of arguing that a historical deception had taken place). Anyway, taking up Shakespeare's simile, there are some cats, both discriminating and lucky, who insist on lapping only the cream!

Many of the names advocated, sometimes never having more than one supporter, may be thought fanciful or extreme. Psychologists, or others, could claim that there is a wonderful feeling associated with the very thought that one might reveal a great truth which has evaded good minds, even doubting minds, over the centuries. But the major claimants on offer might be seen as strenuous, often desperate, endeavour to find the right key or combination for revealing secrets long locked away. If such analogy is used, the problem is that we don't know if we have the right key, because there is a bolt as well as a lock on that very solid door. The 'bolt' represents the denial

117

of access into compelling, factual, final evidence for any of the candidates (this including the generally accepted author). So no key turns the lock. The compensation, if that is the right word, is that the existence of that very bolt is what enables speculation over the mystery of Shakespeare's identity to continue. What is more, neither guesswork nor wild excess is confined to the 'heretics', as we shall see.

This is certainly long enough by way of introduction to the 'group' theory which, like the Baconian one, was well established by the beginning of the twentieth century. These plays were seen as the work of a number of Elizabethan dramatists in combination by a Kentucky judge, John Stotsenburg, who was writing then. One particular strand of his argument certainly had later appeal: it was that no one person could have had the range of vocabulary to write these works unaided.

Many group theorists have been people of achievement in one area or another, as was the first choice for some emphasis here, historian Gilbert Slater. In his 1931 volume, *Seven Shakespeares*, Slater puts forward a case for Oxford as the key central figure, supported in various ways by Bacon, Derby, Rutland, Ralegh, Marlowe (still alive after his supposed death). The seventh person is female: Mary Herbert, Countess of Pembroke, the sister of a deceased courtly poet, Sir Philip Sidney. We know that Oxford received money from state funds for some unspecified purpose. Slater argues that this could have been for the organising of drama as a means of patriotic stirrings, basically war propaganda.

Certainly, *King Henry the Fifth* and parts of some other history plays could represent such wishes. Professor Slater also makes suggestions as to how the other six might have lent support. He is arguably weakest when it comes to explaining how these diverse contributions would be collected and unified to give the necessary coherence, but perhaps we should think of this book as a set of proposals for discussion rather than an emphatic final statement of the fact, or nature, of any plurality in Shakespeare. Slater, who died in 1938, is interesting not only for his theories, but for his attitude to what constitutes truth. He gives a fine rebuttal of the view that it is safest, in the interests of genuine scholarship, for orthodoxy to be assumed sound; to be handed on uncritically to posterity, until or unless proved absolutely wrong. For he asks: 'Would an engineer continue to use girders suspected of flaws?' He was, in one respect at least, like the first Charlton Ogburn in that he was followed down these paths by his son, in this case a psychiatrist of some international renown.

In *Shakespeare's Magic Circle* (1956), by A J Evans, we have a different version of the group theory. Evans, like Slater, had publications on other, quite different, themes. The two make an interesting contrast. We see Slater, sometime principal of Ruskin College, as a distinguished academic: 'Johnny' Evans, although he writes ably enough, was also very much a man of action (some, with an eye for biblical metaphor, might say with a wry smile that his life experiences prove it is easier to pass through the eye of prisoner of war camp barbed wire than to convince the unwilling that there is something radically wrong with the conventional kingdom of Shakespeare). Evans views the authorship as the edited input of the Elizabethan nobility; there is no place for Marlowe in his theory. While he gives a high position to Oxford, he feels that Derby was the essential Shakespeare, seeking to link him particularly closely with *A Midsummer Night's Dream*. His quite brief book ends with 39 key points of evidence. In essence, members of the Elizabethan nobility, closely linked by marriage, were able to provide William Stanley with ideas and raw material.

Evans naturally repeats some of the other 'Derby evidence'. He finds powerful arguments in Derby's continental travel; in his links with north Warwickshire as a child (concerning places mentioned in the plays); in the family's historical interest in the stage. He feels there is good reason to believe that Derby's tutor is ridiculed in the Nine Worthies interlude in *Love's Labour's Lost*. He is intrigued by some suggestions, published in a 1955 journal, from Lefranc's successor as the leading French Derbyite, Professor Lambin. These argue that *Measure for Measure* is linked to Paris in 1582, when Derby was there, the names of several characters being based on personalities of the Paris scene at that time. For any serious student of the group theory, one need have no hesitation in commending Evans along with Slater. Evans sums up the essence of such thinking very well. It means

> the combined wisdom of a group of outstandingly intelligent aristocrats, who met frequently, who had ample time on their hands, whose greatest relaxation in life was pursuit of the Muses, ... led by one master mind, formed a group – a magic circle, without which the divine works of Shakespeare could not have come to their full glory.

Groupists might style themselves as eclectic, although even other doubters could see their view as merely a dilution of the truth. Staunch supporters of the orthodox Shakespeare, on the other hand, would view hybrid versions of unorthodoxy as no better than any other form of that plant. The reply by such defenders of the received faith to the Groupists would include the assertion (to change from botanical to animal analogies) that such pluralists are but misguided 'magpies' or people with inherent 'mongrel theory' tendencies. Such ideas, the reply might continue, seem highly convenient. If one person died, for instance, at the wrong time to be credited with all the works, the solution is to provide one or more collaborators. Seeing all doubt as a form of rebellion anyway, Stratfordians might say that the idea that there could be as many as seven authors is but a route to complete anarchy. For what of all the other possible permutations? Why not eventually (to partly echo a scriptural text) seventy times seven such theories? Some critics of the group theory, in suggesting or pointing out these things, have also added emphatically that it would be most difficult for a committee to write the plays and poems.

But then, a committee is most decidedly not what Groupists have in mind, although Enoch Powell, entering the fray once more, is accused of just such in the introduction to an article by him. This item, as a sample of group theory, certainly has the merit of brevity, as well as being relatively recent. The normal modern concept of a committee – its agenda, debate and 'consensus' decision-making – when placed alongside Powell's view of a cluster of literati, in intimate, confidential co-operation, but with a clear leader, looks a quite different thing. Perhaps the article was really too short to do justice to the argument.

Summation

There are really two types of people who might be styled as Groupists, although at times the distinction becomes somewhat blurred. One kind believes in a key figure, who received varying degrees of support from others; the second type allocates different works by 'Shakespeare' to different people. Certainly, all members of any pluralist school of thought offer complex solutions, but then (if there are any shreds of validity at all in aspects of any doubter's case) there must be complexity associated with the Shakespearean enterprise. Of course, even if one has real misgivings about Shakespeare's identity, the attributions of the work of our supreme dramatist to someone other than the man from Stratford-upon-Avon may seem to be hopelessly conflicting. Most people would accept that some contain elements on the lunatic fringe; to use an Oxfordian-type pun, the veriest nonsense!

Yet be patient, for orthodoxy contains its share of nonsense also. Some alternative theories may seem most strange, yet one must be prepared, just possibly, to entertain an angel unawares. The fact that many attempts to provide evidence for one or another of the candidates overlap, is not necessarily a weakness in the general fabric of unbelief. The common thread is information, references, allusions, parallels that, whatever the verdict, must affect our view of Shakespeare. If some points merit serious examination, it will not diminish the suspicions if one writer thinks the signs – for example, constant references to hunting and hawking – point to nobleman A, another assuming they indicate nobleman B. If some indicators do conflict, that could indicate the cooperation upon which these Groupists would insist. Collaboration was common in the drama of that time. And if we can admit it as possible here under a pseudonym then, remembering that the nobles were emphatically restrained from writing for the theatre, it is likely to be collaboration largely, if not entirely, between themselves.

Some hints that the biography of English or foreign nobles of the time is in the plays may doubtless be exaggerations. This would also apply to events which one of the nobles is said to have witnessed, or the use of names in the plays being based on people they knew. But exaggeration, while it distorts factual accuracy, does not entirely negate it. There is so much offered, as further reading quickly verifies: the pointers stretch way beyond the normal boundaries of sheer coincidence. Some then acquire a remarkable ring of authenticity. Of course, certain of these events might have been subjects of general gossip, picked up by the Stratford man. But to others he would surely, without collaboration, not have had access. It would, anyway, have been greatly audacious for a commoner, without express permission, to use the biography of the contemporary nobles so.

From a Groupist point of view, there is too a certain charm, even if we may well be reverting back to the most highly speculative, in thinking that occasional sentences in the plays may touch upon the collaborative approach of the nobility, frequently perhaps in their evening table-talk. So, if such were conceded to be the case, a question put to a gentleman as he comes on stage in the final act of *The Winter's Tale* ('The news, Rogero?') could indicate an echo of a post-prandial request to Rutland for input, based on information gained from his travels or experiences!

This survey of theories can thus now be concluded by observing that the literature of authorship dispute, within the present century, covers a number of quite distinct personalities. The main thrust of the debate has been illustrated adequately, although at the expense of dealing with some points quite scantily. Bringing many 'sects' together so briefly like this may well serve to highlight differences between them, together with excesses or other adjudged misdemeanours. Yet there is much common ground, not only concerning the negative evidence from Stratford, but also in that a large number proclaim Shakespeare as a member of the aristocracy, accepting that he may have received some advice or ideas, in varying degrees, from friends. The issue then becomes one of, 'Who was the literary genius leading the group?'

Many disbelievers are, as their writings on this and other subjects show, by no means fools, cranky, or deranged. They are, on the contrary, earnest literary enthusiasts who admire Shakespeare's writings. The problem is all too evident to them, although its all-convincing answer has proved so tantalisingly elusive. It only needs one to be right to bestow respectability on the general thrust of their endeavour. Some, including many advocates of Bacon, Oxford or Marlowe, see their man as not only denied the credit for great literature, but also as unjustly tainted by history's official report upon him. These, like the others, all seek truth, although they may well be in error; their discovery of weakness and oddities in the traditional case can hardly be criticised. However, this is not the verdict of orthodoxy upon them, as we shall soon see.

For the moment, all that need be said further is that if the list of the attributes of Shakespeare, as revealed by the plays and poems, is to be seriously examined, there needs to be added one vital extra dimension: the span of mortality. We might postulate that he was born between 1550 and 1565, with probability favouring a relatively early date in this period, bearing in mind the maturity of some of the early works. That would be especially true if he had to go through an extensive programme of part-time, informal self-education. His visible work ended about 1612, but crucially important further work led to the collection of plays, many never previously published, for eventual release in the 1623 Folio. This suggests a date of death of 1619–22.

We may well ask which individual, of all those before us for consideration, meets these criteria. Some of our 'candidates' fare better than others; but, by the exacting use of such pointers, there is no one 'ideal' person. Shakespeare, as a writer, was once compared by one of his contemporaries to the classical author Terence, who some people think was a mask for two authors writing together. Could our great dramatist really have been plural? Some people, even those well prepared to doubt, do not like that idea at all. In the end it is possible, using the analogy of religion yet again, to remain agnostic if one so wishes. Essentially, the argument then becomes that we can never really know for sure who the author was. Yet, unlike religion, there can be no question of an 'atheist' standpoint. For, whether we actually indulge in literary worship or not, clearly somebody *did* do that great writing.

ACT 4
A FAIR HEARING?
TWENTIETH-CENTURY
COMMENTARY

Is not this excuse for mere contraries
Equally strong? Cannot both sides say so?
John Donne, ?1572–1631

SCENE 1

SOME OBSERVATIONS IN AND ON SHAKESPEAREAN LITERATURE (SUNDRY CRITICS OF THE DOUBTERS; A L ROWSE AND AFTERMATH)

The rapid display of the principal alternatives on offer may be seen only as a broad illustration of the anti-Stratfordian cause in our century. But it does span the distinct lines followed by doubters over the years: that the 'real' Shakespeare was a learned person of high birth; that he was a disgraced Marlowe; and the so-called group theory. Ideas, some admittedly most bizarre, have come forward steadily. But they have all always reached only a relatively restricted audience. One might think that those who deny the Stratford claim would see other unorthodox groups as being on the right trail – the less deceived (to borrow a Larkin title), with Stratfordians (like Ophelia) then being the 'more deceived'. Yet they have not been consistently kind in their attitude towards each other: there are one or two cases where a rival 'alternative', or adaptation of their own theory, can goad them to real anger.

But the real problem for them is the indiscriminating dismissal of all rival theories by the champions of orthodoxy. True, some wild ideas or strange, alleged messages are on offer, but one must seek to judge fairly in each case. It has been well observed that the existence of frenetic solutions can never, in itself, deter or undermine the possibility of doubt concerning the authenticity of the authorship message so commonly received. Notwithstanding all the excesses, it seems to me that there is something disconcertingly insecure in the speed with which certain supporters of the conventional authorship viewpoint use the broom of sarcasm to sweep away, not only dross, but any glimmer of possible gold in a rival argument. We know that someone, writing as Shake-speare, produced an unrivalled range of superb literature. Many, given the chance, will see that there are at least genuine gaps and problems in ascribing the works to their traditional source, despite the constant belief or assumption of most people that this must be so.

Although Sir George Greenwood's writings opened up the way promisingly for early twentieth century scepticism, the 'heretics' have not been well received within general commentary. Could this possibly be because of the paralysing fear that they just might carry and implant the seeds of decay for many a cherished reputation? Some various illustrations of just how expressed doubts have been received will show the extent to which charity, accuracy, and fair play alike, have frequently been absent in efforts to refute these dissenters. Examples of such illustration, now to be examined, inevitably add to the glut of names which arise in the course of nearly a century. But there is one that is outstanding; that of Dr A L Rowse, whose uncompromising stance will be treated in some detail towards the end of the discussion.

Charles Nicholl, as an orthodox modern writer on Marlowe, suggests that the Marlovian theories of Shakespeare authorship rely upon alleged numerous acrostics or hidden messages. But this is not usually so: really one thinks only of Honey's examples, and I beg leave to doubt whether Nicholl had those in mind. Another example of inaccuracy in the rejoinders is that Sir George Greenwood, writing relatively early in the twentieth century, frequently took pains to point out that he attributed Shakespeare's works to an unknown lawyer, not to Francis Bacon. Yet, as late as its 1966 edition, *The Oxford Companion to English Literature* continued to proclaim him a Baconian. This error is rectified in the current version of that standard work of reference, but only at the cost of his complete omission: to quote an appropriate sonnet line, 'from the book of honour 'rased quite'.

A further example of careless comment was in late 1987 when Hoffman was described by *The Daily Telegraph* as having opened a dramatist's tomb in 1956. As we have seen, it was technically not a tomb at all and did not directly relate to a dramatist. A striking instance of prejudice was highlighted in an excellent BBC 1987 radio broadcast, entitled *The Yankee Seeress*, on Delia Bacon. This pointed out that, when she voiced her doubts in the 1850s, the periodical *Punch* made the (possibly ever-so-slightly sexist?) remark that women do better to restrict themselves to the unfolding of table linen, rather than seeking to unfold the biography behind great literature! As for fair play in modern times, Joan Bakewell, as reported by *The Times*, speaks of the controversy as a folk myth for people (more interested in speculation than in scientific testing) who like to think there is a problem. The crucial point is that we have no scientific verification on either side of the fence, yet the unbelievers are frequently criticised for any efforts they may make to seek such! Without it, their freedom to speculate must surely be the same as that of Stratfordians.

The world of official imaginative literature provokes a more tolerant reaction to even the worst heresies. For, in that which is universally acknowledged as fiction, anything can be acceptable. There are, naturally, some good novels about Shakespeare. In *Nothing Like the Sun*, Anthony Burgess gave distinctive treatment to a literal interpretation of a theme in the sonnets, without ever straying beyond Stratfordian boundaries. Likewise, we may find fiction based on the account of Marlowe's death which scarcely scratches orthodox beliefs. But others have wandered further. Long ago, William Zeigler proclaimed the 'Marlowe didn't really die in 1593' theme in fiction. In our own century there are Baconian, Marlovian and Oxfordian works of fiction or drama; too many such exist for a full enumeration to be given but, as just one illustration,

129

Farrukh Dhondy, writing nearly a century after Zeigler, has a few echoes of both that writer and of Burgess in his lively novel *Black Swan* (1992).

There have also been, aside from one or two instances of brief references to the controversy in dialogue during films, some excellent radio and television documentaries on the controversy. Televised programmes in Britain during the last decade, for instance, bearing titles such as *A Midsummer Night's Mystery* and *The Battle of Wills*, have included many protagonists featured in this book. Another, simulating a new court hearing of evidence concerning the death of Marlowe, invited the 'jury' to judge whether he was killed accidentally in a brawl, murdered deliberately to ensure his silence, or spirited away from the scene. Such can be very entertaining: this does not mean that none of them can possibly hit upon the truth, or part of it. Once, in a newspaper article, commenting on a critic's review of *Nothing Like the Sun*, Burgess pointed out that first-rate imaginative work, just as much as any piece of researched scholarship, might reach, or come close to, the heart of events long past. But, although they do not come across to me as always being mutually exclusive classes of literature, we must return from the world of speculative fiction to that of general Shakespearean commentary, noting comments from works cited in the bibliography.

I do not wish to sound unfair to those who genuinely cannot accept any of the doubters' arguments and wish to refute them, but it is disturbing that Shakespearean criticism should abound with statements like that of G B Harrison, who argues that until now, scholars with first-hand knowledge of the Elizabethan age have never supported the anti-Stratfordian theories. This is an unacceptable shibboleth: it faults people for failing a test that they cannot possibly pass. It must be rejected on two distinct grounds. The first is that any persons supporting (or even seeming to tolerate) the claim automatically risk damaging their literary reputation. (Of course, certain poets or novelists have tolerated it. But these were merely creative artists, not 'scholars'!) The other reason for rejection of it is that I strongly suspect that such reference to first-hand knowledge in any counter-argument would only excite ridicule. It would be immediately equated with superhuman longevity – remember that earlier anecdote about Bacon still being with us and drawing his old age pension!

Most encyclopedias, including specialist ones, tend to reject any questionings. As for general introductions on Shakespeare, much in the same dismissive vein on behalf of the official cause is Martin Fido. He rightly speaks of many books from the orthodox presenting dubious theories as though they were accepted truth, and often indulging in special pleading. Yet he sees those who portray a nobleman as the true author as snobs, overreacting to the excesses of bardolators. Of course, he insists most strongly, people of real literary sensitivity have never believed anti-Stratfordian theories. Henry James, Walt Whitman, Daphne du Maurier, Mark Twain, hang your heads! The most unworthy thrust of the verdict is the all too frequent one – to deter doubt, even honest enquiry, by stigmatising it.

In the same vein is Ian Wilson (not to be confused with A N Wilson), following his book on evidence for the founder of Christianity with a similarly titled one on Shakespeare. This author is at times enlightening, at others exasperating. Do the extant signatures of the official Shakespeare make him seem near illiterate? That must be the effect of writer's cramp! No incongruity is seen in the fact that Shakespeare saw his work as immortal, yet expected his name to disappear. Commenting on the seventeenth Earl of Oxford being advocated as the true Bard, Ian Wilson cannot resist the story about him breaking wind in Queen Elizabeth's presence. This may well seem amusing. Yet it is curious to find it chosen for inclusion in what should be a dispassionate survey, when the writer finds only space for a few pages on the whole of the doubters' cause. In fact, it is neither an original remark in twentieth-century commentary (see under Schoenbaum in the next scene), nor is it edifying. It was tempting to substitute 'relevant' for the last word of my previous sentence. Alas, I sometimes wonder if there is a curious kind of relevance in such utterances: namely, that they just might, deep down, represent a defence mechanism, betraying awareness of the insecure foundation of much Stratfordian dogmatising. For Garry O'Connor also resorts to this lavatorial tale in his biography of the Bard, claiming a few other dubious Oxford 'qualities' for good measure.

Another commentator from the later part of the century, Gary Taylor, believes that the impulses of the Victorians may have given rise to the 'Baconian myth', but concedes that they 'also generated much of the best criticism and scholarship of their century and our own'. Yet he repeats the unreasonable barrier to unorthodoxy just discussed, saying that the heretics' arguments 'have never been persuasive by any logical, legal, historical, or rhetorical criteria. They have never persuaded specialists.' Ah, there's the rub – for the weight of specialist orthodoxy, with fear of tarnishing the image of established scholarship, ensures that such unconventional beliefs debar their holders from joining the ranks of those who can be recognised formally as having made Shakespearean study their specialism.

Karl Popper, philosopher of the history of science, once made a famous statement about non-falsifiability, which is echoed by Gary Taylor. For Taylor speaks of these unorthodox theories as being invulnerable; capable of being neither credited nor discredited. What is meant is that, in the absence of irrefutable evidence, they cannot be said, with complete certainty, to be right or wrong. If this is really so, it seems odd that the orthodox (as we shall see by reviewing some surveys from the past half-century) have worked so hard to discredit all the doubters. It seems unjust for the sceptics to be scoffed at, yet to have the onus of proof placed upon them in a matter in which Taylor, along with most others, believes proof can never be obtained! It also means that the orthodox view, so comfortably accepted by the vast majority, with or without due thought, is itself non-verifiable – so such doubters can never be finally silenced.

This may sound complicated, but it is important: essentially, we are simply back to the issue of scientific verification. Taylor is saying, in effect: 'There is no scientific way of proving anti-

Stratfordians wrong, but in our hearts we know that they are.'
But the doubters would say the very same thing about
Stratfordian belief! Final verification is denied to all alike on
two counts. These are: that the necessary degree of cohesion in
terms of sure, consistent testimony from historical evidence is
lacking; and that the whole question, as one relating to the
realm of culture rather than to science, may come, after due
investigation, to be seen as a matter for a critical, aesthetic
value judgement based on probabilities.

A few more examples merit review. Phillips and Keatman
are modern authors who, in *The Shakespeare Conspiracy*, stop
short of joining the doubters, although they do not altogether
lack empathy, being worried by the official Stratfordian life
and records to such a degree that their ambition might have
been made of sterner stuff. All that need be said here is that
they 'explain' the orthodox Shakespeare's career development
by creating an extra dimension of life for him within the world
of espionage. Eventually, they claim, he was probably
murdered, perhaps by Sir Walter Ralegh.

Some earlier theorists, although also within the Stratford
tradition, have wilder surmises than this. Charles Hamilton, a
handwriting specialist, offers a chirpy, conversational work
which is well illustrated. Certainly some anti-Stratfordians
have plenty of excess, even 'rubbish' on offer, but, for anyone
wanting entertaining nonsense to be distinguished by the stamp
of the orthodox faith, Hamilton's book may be just the one. No
matter, perhaps, that George Greenwood is yet again falsely
proclaimed a Baconian by it. Hamilton had, when young,
prayed to Shakespeare's ghost, in Stratford church, that he
might one day find a new example of handwriting from
orthodoxy's Bard. Years later, after hours of perusal in a
library, his eyes bloodshot by now (his secretary had warned
him about this), he decided that the famous 1616 will was in
his Shakespeare's own hand. Then he found more examples of
that hand in Bacon's 'Northumberland Manuscript', thus
breaking the silence of the reading room to shout, in his joy,
the Saviour's name (with the initial 'H' in the middle).

It need not surprise us that what follows in Hamilton's book is that Shakespeare of Stratford did some clerical work for Francis Bacon. (Hadn't he, according to orthodox belief, more than enough jobs to do?) Or that he wrote some of the works (in his extensive spare time, perhaps) attributed to Bacon. Nor does Hamilton's verve end with this. He has another joker of his own to add to the traditional pack of legend: that W S of Stratford fame was murdered, being poisoned by his son-in-law, Thomas Quiney! The taste of such stories may please, although the idea that there may be substance soon seems to melt away. Of course, the vast majority of orthodox Shakespearean scholars or believers are themselves not convinced by any of it. For of such is the kingdom of candyfloss.

One other 'voice' simply cannot be resisted in any sampling process; indeed, it should perhaps dominate this chapter. Most commentators pale into insignificance as critics of anti-Stratfordians, in comparison with the ultimate authority (in his own eyes), A L Rowse. In popular articles and broadcasts, he has proclaimed himself the greatest Shakespearean expert ever. Most students of the controversy, Rowse insists, are not qualified to hold an opinion; they should 'shut up'; they should accept the expert's verdict (these vary on many Shakespearean matters, but he means his own view). It is only reasonable to do so, we are told. For he, if he wanted his car repaired, would not dabble personally, but would go to a reliable mechanic. This is the essential gist of his stance and tone. The argument will not do, not simply because he is an 'expert' who is all too easily caught out in assertions or inaccuracies, but because nobody can, without incontrovertible evidence, demonstrate a solution to the authorship issue as conclusively as we might a leaking car radiator.

Now certainly there are, in our modern, complex world, many people who do pronounce on subjects on which they are not qualified to have an opinion. It is undoubtedly irksome to have investigated something in detail and to be told by someone ignorant of it that 'my opinion must be as good as yours'! We should all investigate before pronouncing a verdict. But for Dr Rowse it is anyone at all, no matter how well informed, differing from his good self, who is not qualified to state a view! He tells us that he has cleared up many deep-rooted problems in the work of Shakespeare, such as the identity of the Dark Lady of the sonnets. He is apparently unconcerned that many other orthodox scholars disagree with his 'solutions' or interpretations. That is their loss.

It is all self-evident to Rowse. This may be because his reasoning is perfect, at least in terms of circularity. We should take his word on trust since he knows all the answers; we can be sure he does know all the answers ... because of our complete confidence in his word! For some of us, his books seem to reek of vanity and vexation of spirit, as psychologist and Oxfordian Bronson Feldman once put it in a now sadly defunct periodical on the authorship question. We might charitably concede that some have found Rowse's eccentricities very endearing; likewise, we could assume, without accusing him of speaking out in his dotage, that he became more intolerant and dogmatic in his old age. But he certainly pontificates where he ought to seek to persuade. In him, we might, with regret, be reminded of another Sherlock Holmes passage, where it is said of brother Mycroft that others are just specialists, but his specialism is omniscience.

Speaking of people not qualified to have an opinion, one wonders how many of those rejecting Enoch Powell's 1993 article in *The Spectator* have ever investigated the controversy for themselves. Certainly, his views are not a denial of genius, nor could acceptance of them lead to the conclusion, as someone apparently supposes, that construction work on the Globe Theatre should cease. It ought not to be necessary to accept what Powell says to see that these reactions are wild misrepresentation. But, in the question of authorship, most people would vote against him; that is democracy ... or is it? Not only is Rowse called up as the doyen of critics of the heretics, within the UK at least, but an old political opponent of Powell, Lord Healey, also joins in. One sees that, for him, the very concept of an intellectual in that political shade comes across as a contradiction in terms. The effrontery of the group theory clearly demands a more serious rebuke than calling the perpetrator a mere 'silly billy'. Connoisseurs of expressive language may care to consult the newspaper report for the chosen expression.*

Even the periodical publishing Powell's article is, perhaps unwittingly, a little unkind to him. Apart from the reference to a 'committee' theory, a word he does not use, it proclaims that Enoch Powell does not believe in Shakespeare. Such terse statements can give rise, all too easily, to misunderstanding. He has, it is true, what I have called 'the will to disbelieve'. But, of course, he certainly believes in the quality of the works, which he acknowledges appeared under the name of Shakespeare; he also believes, quite distinctly from these things, that one, William Shakespeare of Stratford-upon-Avon, was a real flesh-and-blood person, alive from April 1564 to April 1616. It is just that he does not choose, despite the pressure from the orthodox, to believe that these two sets of beliefs must necessarily be united. However, rebukes were still coming in a few weeks afterwards. Robert Gore-Langton, contemplating who might be England's Bard if there had been no Shakespeare (Jonson, perhaps: Marlowe is contemptuously discounted simply on the grounds of his character as reported by enemies), sees Powell's 'committee' theory as junk – which yet, paradoxically, can beguile some people with a fine brain.

Nearly a year later, novelist and newspaper columnist Allan Massie, although admitting he has not had the benefit of Powell's complete analysis, is nevertheless prepared to dismiss what he thinks is the theory. But he picks up only a part of one facet of the argument. If you have a vivid imagination as a writer, as Shakespeare of Stratford had, Massie argues, you do not need direct experiences of the events you describe. After all, today's major crime writers have neither committed nor investigated murders in real life. Massie's short article is quite entertaining reading, although essentially it misinforms. In his

---

* This paragraph is based on comment as reported in *The Sunday Telegraph*, 31 October 1993. The newspaper report has some slight factual inaccuracy.

eyes, it is Dr Rowse, scourge of the heretics, who has spoken definitively. Ah, but one may ask Rowse-like, whether, without the full extent of Powell's arguments available to him, Allan Massie is as yet qualified to have an opinion.

There exists much more commentary, of course. Orthodox lives of the Bard, chock full of conjecture, continue to pour out, perhaps inspired in some cases by the slenderness of known fact. One might even suppose the author of Ecclesiastes to have had such as the Shakespeare biography industry in mind when he said, 'of the making of many books there is no end'. Some of these biographies, it seems to me, silently say: 'It is a pity we do not know more for certain; let us then compensate by choosing which of the legends we want to emphasise, as a charming truth-substitute.' In terms of mass or might, they represent a very solid pillar. Yet the picture they present of the Shakespeare they proclaim, the actor-dramatist from Stratford, is far from being a monolithic one. Like some other 'churches', Stratfordian adherents, either openly or covertly, embrace a surprisingly wide variety of views. But these other examples of general commentary often simply echo that of the more moderate examples (relatively speaking) shown in this selection. There are, in addition, specialised surveys of the controversy which are older, but in some cases more detailed, than mine. Let us see if the Shakespeare 'heretics' fare any better in these.

SCENE 2

PREVIOUS SURVEYS
OF THE CONTROVERSY
(CHURCHILL, GIBSON, SCHOENBAUM)

Five accounts of the authorship controversy have appeared in
the English language during the second half of the present
century; one, by Oxfordians Warren Hope and Kim Holston,
published in the United States (1992), is the first such to be
anti-Stratfordian. Some of the others may now seem rather old,
but they still represent a benchmark as the scriptures of
orthodoxy – perhaps not often consulted, but there to bolster
faith as needed. It is necessary to comment upon them in order
to illustrate, as it were, their degree of success in presenting the
issues of the debate objectively. Unfortunately, they tend to be
quite openly (at times, quite unnecessarily or even
inaccurately) hostile to all the doubters, even to the very
possibility of any kind of authentic doubt itself.

Those surveys, each mentioned briefly earlier and cited fully
in the bibliography, are from Britain, those of Churchill (1958),
and Gibson (1962); from the USA, one by Wadsworth (1958);
then, in a work that covers orthodox as well as unorthodox
Shakespearean biography, Schoenbaum (1970, new edition
1991). Examination of at least one of them, if at all possible,
will enable judgement of the degree of bias on my own part in

the brief, critical commentary that follows. At times, here and elsewhere, the debate spits and crackles like hot fat in a pan; I do not claim to be consistently courteous. But, with regard to Wadsworth's *The Poacher from Stratford*, nothing need be added to previous comment. He can hardly be described as a dove: sometimes he hits hard. Yet, while our conclusions differ, in my view he offers a survey less prejudiced than the others.

The three chosen for emphasis are most decidedly hawks. *Shakespeare and his Betters*, by R C Churchill, is a lively historical review of the controversy, which gives details of many 'minor' as well as 'major' claimants for the Shakespearean glory. It has a very useful bibliography. The book claims to recognise fully that the unorthodox are not necessarily cranks or half-educated people – but it sets out nevertheless to put them very firmly in their place! Churchill is introduced by fellow Stratfordian Ivor Brown (himself a very fair commentator), who says that it cannot be complained that he (Churchill) has treated discourteously the views with which he, like the great majority, disagrees. But can't it? I wonder! Are not words applied to the doubters like 'fairy tales' or 'daydreams' somewhat impolite? Nor does it promise a high degree of objectivity when Churchill claims that the very diversity of non-Stratfordian theories, despite their persistence, automatically implies a cancelling-out function – so none can possibly be correct. We may ponder whether he would be so lacking in culture and courtesy as to apply this blanket rejection formula to the myriad hues of the world's great religions.

It is self-evident that someone, writing as 'Shake-speare', produced an unrivalled range of superb literature. Considering the claims of the Stratford man most strongly, we are still entitled to ask: who among the many possibles? Fair examination of the situation shows that there is a surprisingly large degree of diversity in Stratfordian writings, some of it indicating genuine gaps or problems in ascribing the writings to their conventional source. The fact that, every year, hundreds of books, articles, broadcasts and newspaper references make or imply such attribution does absolutely nothing, in itself, to vindicate orthodoxy. It is always easy to accept uncritically and then to repeat a widely held view. What is more, if we can assume, even momentarily, that the view might be false, we must see that constant repetition certainly fuels mythology enormously, but does nothing to alter its actual status.

Returning to Churchill, it simply has to be said that he makes a few rather ridiculous remarks. A good example is his comment about Sykes, pressing the claims of the Earl of Rutland. We are told that Sykes is unfair in that he has made his choice of the true author before he began to write. Has not Churchill himself done this? Does not every writer on this controversy do it? It would only be unfair if the choice were made without starting to investigate (some Stratfordians please note). Churchill is prone too (and he is not alone in this) to criticise people in the ranks of the doubters who say, in effect, 'perhaps such and such happened'. Yet he constantly does it himself. The maximum probability is squeezed out of events or assertions which seem to favour orthodoxy, and the minimum possibility is attributed to those that pull in the reverse direction. So he claims, for example (brackets and emphases are mine), that:

> *The Metamorphoses* [of Ovid] was a fourth-form text in the grammar schools of the period, so it is *likely* that Shakespeare [if he went to one] knew a little of Ovid in the original. He *could have* borrowed a very nice edition of the original from his publisher, Field.

I do not say that it is quite impossible that the man from Stratford was (either solely or with others) the great author, or that he might have done what is suggested above; although, according to Churchill, he was borrowing books from Field constantly. I do say that it is totally unreasonable to confine speculation purely to theories that harmonise with received orthodoxy. Churchill, most interestingly, notes that, in a survey of the controversy much earlier in the century, the French writer Georges Connes had remained a Stratfordian, but had found it necessary to postulate that the Stratford man must have had contact with a core group in the aristocracy for ideas, sources and inspiration. Churchill will not tolerate such a thought: it can all be done by borrowing books, getting help with French (for instance) from one's landlord, and travelling England as a player – such input leading to instant glorious output. Yet it is most significant that Ivor Brown, who provides Churchill's foreword, has agreed elsewhere (in his 1949 book *Shakespeare*, p. 328) with Connes on this point.

The stance brought about by (subconscious?) bias is shown, alas, as early as Churchill's introduction. There he argues that the conventional authorship view

> is a fact at the present time and will continue to be a fact until it is definitely proved wrong. ... [Anti-Stratfordian] views are the theories and they will remain theories until one of them is accepted as a definite proof. When (or if) that day dawns ... the Baconian theory or one of its rivals will become the fact.

This argument, he continues, 'works in protection of Bacon as much as it does in protection of Shakespeare. If some writer in the future should deny Bacon's authorship of *New Atlantis*, that theory will remain a theory until it is definitely proved.'

Churchill picks here a work of Bacon's which has never had its authorship questioned. Then he says that, because he agrees with everyone that it is to be attributed to Bacon, all fair-minded people should reciprocate by refraining from asking awkward questions about who wrote those of Shakespeare! Furthermore, this is just the kind of argument that explains my earlier emphasis on factual, historical truth. Admittedly, the vast majority of people are convinced (and always have been) that the writer Shake-speare was William Shakespeare (1564–1616), author and actor, from Stratford-upon-Avon. But surely, if that is right, it will always be so. It is not a question that admits of its answer a temporary fact like 'today is Friday'. It is only our perception of what is fact that could possibly change; the author Shakespeare cannot (factually) be William from Stratford today, possibly Francis of St Albans tomorrow ... then eventually, perhaps, someone else! Such historical events must be, to use an Oxfordian-type pun, either ever true or never true! But Churchill is really proclaiming to us indirectly that what is 'true' is always what the majority, at any point in time, choose to believe. Would a long retrospective view of the history of science support that contention?

Of course, one may feel that neither Churchill, a man for whom historical truth appears to be potentially mutable, nor I can be trusted as completely impartial. He says, towards the end of his book, that the only really neutral investigators were a group led by a man named Topcliffe in 1601 (when the official Shakespeare and all the rivals for his 'crown' were alive). Topcliffe's men were investigating, on behalf of the Privy Council, a special performance of *King Richard the Second* as the circumstances of that performance might constitute a political offence against the queen. Churchill concludes that, if there had been a noble author behind the play, Topcliffe and his men, who were very efficient (how does Churchill know that?), would have discovered the fact. What they discovered was the man from Stratford.

Churchill's shout of triumph at this is entirely unjustified. Their findings do not constitute evidence either way: it could equally be argued that plausible cover would be essential for any secret 'Shakespeare enterprise'. One reason for a noble, or other secret author, to hide behind a very efficient screen was to have the freedom to write without the risk of imprisonment, or worse, for political or religious offences. There was a 'Shakespeare' for Topcliffe to find; he was duly found, doubtless protesting that he had used a historical source, and that certainly no offence was meant. No punishment ensued. Playwrights of the Elizabethan age, unless they went further than this, as one or two did, were small beer. But, in this instance, to refer to no less a Stratfordian authority than Chambers, it cannot be imagined that Shakespeare, in writing *King Richard the Second*, deliberately set out to make an analogy between Richard and Queen Elizabeth.

Such a summary, with emphasis on my points of

disagreement, can scarcely do justice to Churchill, who makes some useful points – on the use of Warwickshire dialect in the plays, for example. Many of his arguments set one looking for more information, which is what 'continuing education', in the best sense of the phrase, is all about. One statement which he makes against the Oxfordians is one with which I sympathise: it was observed when I presented, in summary, their case. Since Oxford died in 1604, some of the conventional dates for Shakespeare's plays mean that they were written when the Earl was no longer living. We noted that Looney sought to counter this by saying that *The Tempest*, for instance, is not a true Shakespeare play. Most modern Oxfordians would disagree, seeking rather to suggest that the plays were written earlier than is commonly supposed. Churchill points out that the stylistic characteristics of any short period do not affect just one author; the progressive traits are copied. Thus, because of the inevitable influence of an evolving style on other dramatists, it would seem certain, on such a theory as this, that we have to put back the dates for the writings of Shakespeare's contemporaries too. Furthermore, if this idea were true, way back in 1598 Francis Meres, citing examples of Shakespeare's work, could have included the tragedy *Macbeth*. Surely the fact that he did not was because it did not then exist? I have condensed an important argument here, but personally would never, if espousing an unorthodox view, use this particular line of reasoning anyway.

Churchill follows his very relevant criticism on this with an observation which constitutes my final comment on his work: 'A literary artist can no more go back to a style he has outworn than can an artist in paint or music. And he cannot crowd ten or twelve years' stupendous development into half that time.' I entirely accept this. But I am also intrigued, in the context of it, as to how Churchill and others can cram an exceptionally stupendous metamorphosis for the Stratford man into, at the most, the years 1585–91. In addition, in the light of this last quotation, can we honestly accept both that he could (and did) scale the highest cultural mountains; then voluntarily returned, at the end of his days, to a mundane, outworn lifestyle? It also

143

amuses me, incidentally, that Churchill himself has chronology problems. He accepts, not unreasonably, that the author of Sonnet 2 was at least forty years of age when it was written. Can we really date this at 1604 (when Stratford's Shakespeare was forty) or even later? Most specialists say most definitely not.

Now we must look at a slightly later survey, also British. *The Shakespeare Claimants* by H N Gibson (1962) concentrates on four main theories: those supporting Bacon, Oxford, Derby and Marlowe. It is a thought-provoking book. There is much there with which I would personally take issue: indeed, it concerns me that the spotlight Gibson throws on alleged Stratfordian objectivity might seem reasonable to a reader who went no further than his text and did not see that frequently facts are selected or presented in a way to suit the author's preordained purpose. Like Churchill, he insists that there is too much fanciful speculation in the history of the debate, but offers some himself. So, for example, he says: 'there might well have been many chances for the author of *Venus and Adonis* to have borrowed from Oxford'. He seems to find Oxfordians courteous and Baconians less so; perhaps that is why he says he sees the former theory as very attractive, although the latter has some good arguments. I have always experienced courtesy from both camps.

Baconians are sometimes prone to ridiculous extremes, but Gibson only matches this when he states (p. 205) that they do not generally accept title-page names as evidence of authorship, but that someone else's name in that position is, to them, 'proof positive that a book was written by Bacon'. How ludicrous, if thought through, such careless comment is! He had a valid point to make, but spoils it via massive overstatement. To take only two examples from the thousands possible, could he find anyone who thinks that Bacon was the poet W H Auden, or perhaps the power behind Agatha Christie?

Dr Gibson remarks also that the portrait found at Cambridge, claimed by Hoffman to be that of Christopher Marlowe, is unlikely to be so; yet Gibson (or his publisher) used it to represent Marlowe on the dust-jacket. He claims too that it was impossible that Marlowe's death was feigned and that he left behind *Venus and Adonis* to be the first work bearing the name Shakespeare because that work 'was entered in the Stationers' Register, with Shakespeare's name as author ... nearly five weeks before Marlowe was arrested'. It was certainly entered on the date stated by Gibson, 18 April 1593 – but anonymously!

It is suggested that heretics create the 'god' of Shakespeare in their own image – lawyers would have him a lawyer, soldiers a man of military experience, and so on. The assumption is that none can be correct. But some of the orthodox also do this: Rowse, so proud of his own grammar-school background, insists that it must be grammar-school people who do well. I do not wish to retread the ground of earlier debate, but have to suggest that the author Shakespeare could create the impression of a wide range of experience, travel, knowledge of various subject areas, better than his contemporaries. Notwithstanding his genius, it follows that, to achieve such effect, he must have had extensive experience and education. If his knowledge of the law impresses some legal specialists, we must remember that these people are as 'expert' in their field as literary specialists claim to be in theirs.

Before expressing other concerns, I should register some points where I am in agreement with Gibson. He is right to say that it is neither necessary nor wise to denigrate the Stratford man, if one doubts his right to claim the authorship, by suggesting that he was a dolt, a 'dummy', or a person who deliberately robbed the true author of a rightful place in literary history. If (of course, it remains a big 'if') there was subterfuge, it was surely at the wish of the true author. Moreover, the Stratford man must have appeared at least a tolerably credible candidate for some kind of authorship to anyone at the time who might ask questions. Gibson is right too in suggesting that the doubters have sometimes both stated that the real authorship was a closely guarded secret and then suggested that there are many clear signs of it, via cryptograms. Or they have argued that a significant number of Shakespeare's contemporaries knew, or half-suspected, the truth. If this were really the case, it would be impossible to present the actor from Stratford as the 'official' author to enquirers. It was either a secret within a relatively small circle, with only a few vague suspicions outside that, or was widely known. If the latter supposition were true, the purpose of a pen-name would be defeated and it would never have been possible for the works to come down to posterity as those of the Stratford man. The anti-Stratfordians cannot have it both ways on this.

But I have four main criticisms of Gibson's *The Shakespeare Claimants* still to make. One is that it states that the work of George Greenwood was totally discredited, his arguments reduced to rubble, in books by J M Robertson, especially *The Baconian Heresy* (1913). Gibson suggests that all anti-Stratfordians have feared to read, let alone cite, the fiery Scot. We have already seen that Greenwood, in fact, gave a detailed rejoinder to him; that the debate continued. Who is more right is for people to judge for themselves. Far from ducking away from Robertson, I have already urged those with the wish, time and access to a very large library to sample him. He is certainly, at best, a very mixed blessing for the orthodox camp. In fact, he carves up the Shakespeare of convention. To give only a few examples, he strongly queries the authorship of *Titus Andronicus*, thinks *The Merchant of Venice* was rewritten from a Marlowe draft, that *King Richard the Second* is Marlowe's and that work by George Chapman formed the basis for *Coriolanus*. He finds more evidence for Marlowe in *The Taming of the Shrew* and *The Two Gentlemen of Verona*, believing that some scholars 'can never recognise hands'. In his own distinctive fashion, Robertson remained a Stratfordian, but one suspects that if he had held as keen an interest in lifestyles as he did in literary styles, he might have moved much closer to the position of his good friend, George Greenwood.

A second major criticism of Gibson's survey is that he finds incidents in the plays to link, sometimes in a not very complimentary way, with the life of the Stratford man. Stratford itself, incidentally, is not mentioned in the dramas: some other possibly relevant places, like Francis Bacon's St Albans, are. But the limited biographical linkage noted might be explained equally well by postulating that the Stratford actor was a crucial collaborator in a literary enterprise. Gibson draws a few examples of linkage from a book by J Middleton Murry and gives the impression that this is a mere selection. Yet, if we take the trouble to consult his source, we find otherwise. For Murry, an author who is an impeccable example of majority orthodoxy, is at pains to caution us that the number of passages in the whole of Shakespeare's plays which may seem to point emphatically at actual incidents in the Stratford man's life is surprisingly small. A person relying solely on Gibson would never suspect this.

Another major charge against Gibson is that he tells us that many doubters, at least subconsciously, do not really believe their own theories. Perhaps some who read no book but Dr Gibson's on the controversy would accept such arrant nonsense. To reveal it as an extraordinary assertion, one need only cite the effort and erudition that goes into an anti-Stratfordian book like the one by Charlton Ogburn, or the zeal of Calvin Hoffman in visiting Padua in his last years in search of new and compelling evidence. Perhaps the most eloquent form of refutation can be found in a sentence or two from (Marlovian) William Honey, in a letter to me, early in 1987: 'I am now very old ... I go out but twice a week ... I live in dread of not being able to complete my work, so devote all my time to it.' Out-and-out unbelievers in the traditional assignment of the authorship might, in a spirit of pure mischief, suggest that it is Dr Gibson and others of his stamp who do not really believe the message that they proclaim! But the fair-minded, on either side, will not let the excesses of opponents determine their own conduct.

My final criticism of Gibson rests in examples of the orthodox themselves doing what they (sometimes rightly) accuse their opponents of doing: distorting evidence. Gibson does just this in relation to the discovery of the 1599 document suggesting that the Earl of Derby was found to be penning comedies. In a manner fit for the most extreme anti-Stratfordian, he pronounces that this may actually be a coded message, really meaning something else entirely!

147

But a more important indication of attitude, when confronted with something uncomfortable, may reside in Gibson's comment relating to the self-revealing Shakespearean sonnets. Lines 1 and 3 of Sonnet 125 read:

> Were't aught to me I bore the canopy ...
> Or laid great bases for eternity.

The poet goes on to suggest that such things would lose significance if he did not have the love and support of his friend. Gibson thinks it unreasonable to infer that the first line should refer to an actual event – like the carrying of a canopy over the head of the Queen, when she was taking part in a state procession. It cannot be so interpreted, he says. Why not? It may well be part of the autobiographical nature of the sonnets. When we find Gibson, who elsewhere complains about the denigration of an actor, saying the third line also can have no possible literal meaning, we may wonder who is really denying Shakespeare's glorious and lasting achievement.

It is true that Sonnet 125, its theme the familiar one of expressing the poet's regard for the young lord, is difficult in certain respects. Many other Stratfordian commentators take the first line to be literal, yet doubly conditional (i.e. Would it have made any difference to me *if* I had ever carried the canopy, *if* I were to lose your regard?) This is admittedly a possible interpretation, although it seems a weak, unsatisfactory one. There is a less strained view of the meaning available, embodying a single condition: 'Could the fact that I have had such outward honours as carrying the canopy make any compensation to me *if* I lost your regard? Pomp and circumstance matter little compared to the bond between us.' In any case, why would the poet ever think of such a ceremony as this, as a starting-point for the theme of this sonnet, unless the canopy *had* actually been carried by him?

Incidentally, back in the mid-nineteenth century, another orthodox writer, Howard Staunton, much better known in the history of chess, had tried a different interpretation of the opening line of Sonnet 125. He accepted that the reference to

148

the canopy related to an actual event, but suggested that it was the recipient of the sonnet, not the writer, who 'bore' it. However, on this occasion, his gambit is surely always destined to be a losing one, since the sense of the poem does not easily admit of this interpretation.

There seems a risk of becoming entangled in this canopy! But, before we extricate ourselves, please note that Dr Gibson's own stance is quite different from any of the above attempts at textual analysis. Shakespeare, he states, sometimes uses the word 'canopy' to mean the sky – this is what it must mean here. So the correct interpretation of line 1, according to Gibson, should be: 'Does it mean anything if I have held up the heavens?' Are we considering Shakespeare here, or Atlas?

The word is certainly sometimes used by Shakespeare and other Elizabethans to mean the sky, but they also use it in different ways. So, Shakespeare's near-contemporary, John Webster, writing about a ruined building and the dead that lie therein, says:

> They thought it [the building] should have canopied their bones
> 'Til domesday

and the meaning is clear – any appropriate shelter or kind of overhead covering may be seen as a canopy. It is a very strained interpretation that restricts it to the sky. We should maintain that it is up to biographers and critics, Stratfordian or otherwise, to explain it all much more reasonably than this.

These surveys can be seen to be weighted heavily in favour of orthodoxy. One might suppose that, in this respect, Gibson's excesses represent the nadir. But it is not so. Within *Shakespeare's Lives* (1970, new edition 1991), Samuel Schoenbaum, distinguished Professor of Renaissance Literature at the University of Maryland, makes a highly distinctive contribution. His book, as a whole, is actually a long and informative critical history of all biographies of the bard. Thus only one section, entitled 'Deviations', deals with heretics; in the 1991 edition this, although updated, is compressed to less than 70 pages of the work. From that sectional title and the sardonic tone of its very first sentence onwards, a heavy aura of predestination hangs over the verdict.

It is most unfortunate that what Schoenbaum sees as cruel hilarity or sneers in aspects of the history of orthodox Shakespearean biography becomes permissible for him when addressing the unorthodox. The jeering at all dissenters is pervasive. This is despite the fact that the account of orthodox Shakespearean biography in the rest of the book presents not only a record of painstaking endeavour, but also an unedifying tale of the frequent use of legend, fabrication, guesswork, desperate improvisation, even patent contradiction.

We have been told elsewhere that it is the high-born who want to view Shakespeare as one of themselves. For Schoenbaum, determined to explain these 'deviations' in terms of psychological disorder, the low-born are equally guilty. Thus, Delia Bacon is seen as wanting Shakespeare to be a noble person because she herself was afflicted by genteel poverty. Even in the new edition, where space is short, some is found so that her 'log cabin' beginnings can be emphasised triumphantly. As for the Earl of Oxford, Schoenbaum, like later commentators, is delighted to mention the story that comes from John Aubrey, an intriguing, but unreliable, seventeenth century gossip. Aubrey's tale is of how the Earl once 'let fart' in the queen's presence. One would see this as belonging to my earlier comedy section were it not for the fact that Schoenbaum's commentary (just as others were later to do, using the same Aubrey remark) takes a most unreasonable swipe at the logical method of trying to work out who Shakespeare really was by drawing on evidence in his writings: 'Looney does not include flatulence as another of his hero's special attributes' (1991, p. 432).

The American professor takes over Gibson's suggestion that a young woman named Katherine Hamlett, known to the Stratford actor in his youth – she drowned in 1579 – was the model for Ophelia. That is at least 'an interesting speculation'. But similar conjectures by the anti-Stratfordians are dubbed 'gossamer fancies'. To be biographically adventurous is permitted only when suitably restricted by the plaster coating of orthodoxy. In spite of this nod of approval concerning the drowning incident, Professor Schoenbaum, anxious to preserve that coating against all of doubt's possible chisels, is clearly worried on the whole rather than encouraged by the efforts of Churchill and Gibson – as he has every cause to be! The former is seen as an amateur, a word of dismissal in *Shakespeare's Lives*, the implication being that those who do not hold a relevant academic post are but well-intentioned meddlers. Writing later than Churchill, Schoenbaum is shrewd enough to contradict him over a denial of the illiteracy of the Stratford actor's daughter, Judith Quiney, since the evidence for it is clearly there. He thinks, too, that some of Sir George Greenwood's reservations, early this century, were understandable at the time: one can only wonder, in view of the paucity of archival evidence of significance, what striking new facts have since emerged.

Despite Schoenbaum's erudition, supported by his undoubtedly very extensive reading, some amusing little errors or inconsistencies creep in. Instances of these are worth citing. His index, in one entry, confuses dramatist Robert Greene with schoolmaster/clergyman Joseph Greene; in another, a twentieth-century orthodox Shakespearean biographer, J Dover Wilson, is muddled with a Wilson from over 150 years before. Could this be an embryonic Stratfordian counterblast to the near-immortality claimed, by some extremists, for Bacon? Alas no, merely an indexing slip! Professor Schoenbaum disapproves, because of references to the work of Hoffman therein, of the 1965 book by A D Wraight. But he also assumes, in citing it, that the author is male (she actually once played the title role in Marlowe's *Dido, Queen of Carthage*). In the 1991 edition he speaks of Canterbury archivist William Urry as not yet having completed his work, although by then Urry had been dead for several years and another author had completed it.

No complex text can be assuredly infallible: even Homer occasionally nods. So, in such a detailed, far-reaching work as Schoenbaum's, one would certainly let minor index errors pass as permissible, while other little mistakes which niggle would be seen to reflect the problems of keeping up to date on details across the Atlantic, in either direction – were it not for the fact that they lie most uneasily on one who is so swift to ridicule opponents for any error or excess (an example concerns the Groupist, Gilbert Slater, who is rebuked for a male/female error in his text arising from a slip in proof-reading). Schoenbaum also derides comments in the history of Shakespearean doubts which link the authorship issue to the techniques of detection. Yet, when commenting on the minute and exhaustive work of Dr and Mrs C W Wallace in examining historical records, he does not hesitate to congratulate them as archive sleuths. In any case, several other modern writers of firm Stratfordian persuasion, like Ian Wilson, also quite legitimately liken their quest to a 'detective story'.

The 1991 edition of Schoenbaum's book picks up the major Oxfordian writing, then relatively new, of Ogburn. Yet it ignores Ogburn's perceptive comments on aspects of its own earlier edition, including references to factual errors. This is surprising in such a scholar, since he is prepared to criticise mildly A L Rowse for just this sort of thing: 'nowhere does Rowse allude to past errors' (1991, p. 559). The detail of Ogburn's work draws forth a remark about lack of economy, similar to those made by him about Greenwood and Judge Stotsenburg (you not only have to prove orthodoxy wrong, you must do it in a form much more brief than many Stratfordian books, yet showing every scrap of evidence!). Doubtless, if it were rather brief, it would be criticised for that also. Perhaps it is as well that Schoenbaum seems not to have come across William Honey. On the subject of Marlowe supporters, we can see how Schoenbaum will go the extra mile for the heretics. Calvin Hoffman's colourful style is criticised as 'sweaty journalese', but when he disapproves of a Stratfordian passage by Ivor Brown, for instance, the 'crime' is only 'purple journalese'. One knows just what is meant in Hoffman's case, yet the phrase, although very memorable, must be deprecated. Indeed, those who use it should take care. A typical sentence in that vein is: 'Then, suddenly, in 1857 a streak of crazed lightning flashed across the spring sky.' This could well be Hoffman's, but it actually comes from the pen of a certain eminent Professor of Renaissance Literature (1991, p. 385)!

It is difficult to convey, succinctly, the all-embracing nature of Schoenbaum's unyielding prejudice. We know several doubters go to excess, that sometimes wild excesses occur. Yet surely that is no excuse for implying that all are in need of psychological help? Sigmund Freud himself (who, incidentally, had first read Shakespeare when aged eight) is a target. He was apparently found, immediately after his death, to have had more anti-Stratfordian than orthodox Shakespearean books. This is a sure sign of instability in Samuel Schoenbaum's eyes. A charitable Freudian rejoinder, one supposes, might be that Schoenbaum seems to suffer from some kind of cognitive dissonance: the inability to receive facts at variance with what one is determined to believe. After all, Freud did on one occasion refer to the narrow-mindedness shown by some of the best minds, commenting on their determination to deny most forcible arguments against their cause while retaining simultaneously a credulity which allowed them, if convenient, to accept the most disputable assertions.

Yet the contraction of that caustic section on the heretics, within the new edition of *Shakespeare's Lives*, leads Schoenbaum to the prefatory comment that 'some curious and wayward folk no longer recline on my couch'. It would be more reassuring, if this really were an obsession, for him to provide the cure of incontestible proof rather than mere diatribes. However, from his high academic position, he prefers an attempt to crush doubt by the sheer weight of orthodox opinion to its refutation by reason. One scents real fear in this; the writing, in a book covering a vast area, is usually superb, but the literary brilliance of the invective must not be allowed to obscure uncertainties in Schoenbaum's own position. Why descend to such virulent tactics, the academic equivalent to cricket's 'sledging', for the disbelievers? Some may think there can be but one answer, rather worse than any cognitive dissonance – the higher the academic status, the more painful the remotest risk of fall. Like A L Rowse, Schoenbaum proceeds by assertion rather than demonstration. Their stances are equally circular. Start with the insistence that *all* doubters of the received authorship tradition must be mad, perverted or deceived. Dismiss them on that basis: 'lunatic anti-biography' in Schoenbaum's terms. Then, as they have been so comprehensively dismissed by scholars of such rank, they must surely all be deceived, perverted or mad.

In sum, Samuel Schoenbaum detests the heretics, would hate to help them. They represent, to use religious analogy again, sin against the fundamental tenet of the orthodox Church. They would deceive, were it possible, the very *créme de la créme* of the Stratfordian elect. So they should be rooted out, to be hacked to pieces (metaphorically), as his namesake in the Old Testament once (literally) did to some captured enemies. Or, if you prefer New Testament analogy, they are dismissed by Schoenbaum as merely wild voices crying in the wilderness; yet, perversely, he wants their heads on a platter!

Curiously Professor Schoenbaum does, in a sense, assist the seekers of an alternative Shakespeare in two ways:

- his attitude – to put down opponents by ridicule – seems rather like the product of a siege mentality in that he is unable to refute doubt by reason and yet is unwilling to debate it seriously;

- his endeavour, in dealing, on the other hand, with Stratford records – seeking conscientiously to separate fact from legend – only shows how scanty the reliable material for the generally favoured candidate is. The word 'compact' in the title of another book by him on historical documents about the Stratford man is virtually a redundant one in view of their range and character.

That which has most nourished us (professionally) must never be put at risk of destroying us – as perhaps Ovid or Shakespeare ought to have said. So there is no doubt in Schoenbaum's mind that books querying the authorship should not be published by any means. When they are, they should be ignored: some might even be far too dangerous to be taken seriously. The best of the literature of disbelief really should carry the equivalent to a government health warning concerning the extensive damage it could do to certain academic reputations.

SCENE 3

THE CONCLUSION OF THE MATTER

In the surveys highlighted, erudition mingles with both entertaining remarks and harsh observations. Each reader who sees good fun in point-scoring pyrotechnics may be balanced by another wondering if these commentaries still deserve analysis. But, although they may not be available to all, their stance is an essential part of the history of the controversy since 1950. Its combative nature has, doubtless all too evidently, become two-way here. This has been brought on by the hubristic attitude of orthodoxy, which begets in me a moral obligation to follow a 'knock for knock' policy. Whether the combat is enjoyable or not, it is now time to bring this part of our 'drama' towards an end.

Perhaps there is some light in the tunnel of literary criticism. Another American writer, I L Matus, whose researches have both quality and originality, has recently produced his second book about Shakespeare. This specifically defends orthodoxy against one set of unbelievers – the Oxfordians. Irvin Matus makes good points about the dating of plays, but has other observations offering plenty of scope for debate. He ignores some important issues such as the autobiographical sonnets, while his explanation of how the conventional Shakespeare procured his source for *The Comedy of Errors* demands a high degree of conjecture. This might be deemed risible by conventional commentators if the cause supported were anti-Stratfordian. Matus is often selective in his argument, being most convincing when attacking Oxfordian excesses. To believe, as his apparent mentor Samuel Schoenbaum does, that this may be the mother of all books on the authorship question, is clearly wishful thinking. Yet at least Matus is fully prepared for serious debate: doubts and doubters are addressed in acceptable fashion.

Returning to the earlier surveys of the whole controversy, I have concentrated on perceived weaknesses, yet these volumes all give, in certain respects, a more detailed account than does mine. It should nevertheless be seen clearly why this 'Act' began with that Donne quotation. At times both sides in the authorship debate, in the words of Sonnet 117, 'on just proof surmise accumulate'. Neither camp has the exclusive right of access to truth; neither has the monopoly of fanciful speculation or wild excesses. Stratfordian and anti-Stratfordian biography alike have been battlegrounds for theorists, with much in-house contradiction going on. Thus, if we wanted to ponder the probable future of the warring between them by using a title of Freud's, from a different context, *The future of an illusion* (1927), we would still need to determine where 'illusion' resides.

The excesses of the unorthodox may be the fruit of overenthusiasm, or partly desperation driven. Every 'sect' mentioned contains some; more sober doubters can freely acknowledge them. After all, few would decry all alcoholic liquor simply because some people drink it to excess. However, the accepted majority view has a huge advantage simply because it *is* the view of the vast majority. A tendency to side with those sceptical of official history in this matter, as shown here, is not purely emotive, although the heart does have a say in these things. My conviction is that, although many doubters must, of necessity, be wide (even very wide) of the mark, there is at least a rather better than 50 per cent chance that one or another of the arguments on offer from them comes near to re-creating historical events. Even to think that the majority position *may* be right, or broadly so, does not mean one must concur with the oft-repeated assertion that there are no real problems. We should not be bullied into accepting it uncritically.

My critique of those three surveys probably sounds much more scathing than the last few lines would suggest. This is simply because I dislike tactics relying on smear or steamroller technique. Or for that matter, to digress briefly from the surveys, methods based upon insidious manipulation or distortion. Ogburn gives a good example of the practice of this, *vis-à-vis* the experience of his parents. A reviewer of their 1952 book, because he insists the writer Shakespeare must be William Shakespeare of Stratford, elects to employ a sleight of hand which capitalises on the fact that, in one sense, it is merely stating the obvious to say 'Shakespeare must have written Shakespeare'. Thus, when the Ogburns indicated that there was no clear reference to the Stratford man as the great author in his own lifetime, their critic points out indignantly that there are references, from 1598 onwards, to Shakespeare as an author. It is pretended, via some kind of academic autism perhaps, that the Ogburns make the error of ignoring these. They do not, of course: they simply say we cannot, for certain, link these references about Shakespeare the writer with the actor from Stratford of the same (or very similar) name. The critic knows this, but pretends otherwise: he may thereby fulfil his intentions of discrediting the Ogburns effectively as far as the unwary are concerned, but to stoop to such a deliberate misrepresentation is reprehensible in the extreme. To the discerning this can never denote a position of strength.

The doubters surely deserve (as a corrective) one or two general surveys such as this, rather more favourable to their cause. When Schoenbaum (1991, p. 451) writes of a supposed professor of English Literature being asked, while on holiday, whether Shakespeare of Stratford really wrote the plays, he suggests that nothing said by the expert 'will erase suspicions fostered for over a century by amateurs who have yielded to the dark power of the anti-Stratfordian obsession'. How can one react? My own response would be that nothing the doubters can say can apparently remove the unjustified dogmatism, fostered for at least as long, of some literary 'professionals'.

Ogburn hoped his book's approach could lead to resolution of the issue: this is one reason for its detail, which Schoenbaum affects to despise. But no argument as such, however cogent, eloquent or comprehensive, will ever fully resolve it. Without just such factual evidence it must remain an open issue. That no one can make a case secure from assault is acceptable. It is not acceptable to find criticism of doubts offered seemingly with a view to discouraging all investigation. If the orthodox had many more hard facts in their favour, they could repel doubts more moderately. As it is, quite apart from their fury, they are as full of inaccuracies and phrases such as 'it is probable', 'perhaps he had', 'it seems likely that', 'it could be', as most anti-Stratfordians. Amusingly, any book review of a new Stratfordian biography may chide its author for offering speculation as fact – yet, of these very same suppositions, ones which happen to support rather than irritate the reviewer's own thinking will be applauded. In the phrase of one of the reasonable writers in the vast camp of orthodoxy, Dr Leslie Hotson, Stratfordians are content to 'go a-maying': they really have to do so, because of the lack of facts. We all have to call on inference, conjecture, what is seen as probability.

Another reasonable Stratfordian commentator, Ivor Brown, wonders whether a particular passage in Shakespeare was composed by his man during a summer walk to the churchyard by the river in Stratford and asks whether to suppose such is to invite censure as a sentimentalist. No, it is not blameworthy at all. Surprisingly, there is a poem in like mood by none other than the usually unemotional Sir Edmund Chambers. His verse, imagining the retired Stratford man deservedly relaxing, eating apples, does not deserve criticism either. But any speculations of this kind certainly carry no more guarantee of accuracy (in some cases it would seem less so) than those of the unbelievers. As one commentator in *The Independent* newspaper put it, rather in the spirit of Mark Twain: 'We know as much of the historical Shakespeare as we do about the yeti, [and] biographies ... tend to be fanciful, cunningly padded affairs, peppered with "maybes" and "might have beens".'

Surely, then, neither side can justly claim to monopolise either the factual or the moral high ground? The phrase 'all things are possible to those who believe', applied here with some irony, can relate as much to orthodox as to the unorthodox Shakespearean biography. The former lies uneasily on just a few solid pieces of knowledge. There are huge gaps in the historical records of the Stratford man if he was indeed the great author. There are also huge inconsistencies. These two inescapable truths, between them, oblige his own commentators to speculate extensively. In summary, any well-read doubter would contend that Stratfordians have an insecure foundation for their belief, and that they frequently come up with contradictory theories in trying to plug gaps. Yet, although constantly resistant to any effort to find 'hard', possibly conclusive, new evidence they are determined to stamp out doubt.

On the anti-Stratfordian side, because of lack of sure facts, there is also extensive guesswork. Because of the volume of literature, the total speculations from the two sides are legion. Scarcely a book is free from them – certainly not the one now being read. Admittedly the unorthodox ranks have bias, but this is true of the orthodox too. It is particularly so in those three surveys. At least those who have doubted have the excuse that it requires some extra dimension of effort to row against such a mighty current of received and vehemently proclaimed opinion. If I ever lost patience with such people, I might regain it after re-reading Gibson, Churchill or Schoenbaum. I suppose to the last named this would suggest that I am in the grip of some 'dark power'. The true explanation is much more dull. It is simply that one looks for intellectual honesty, facts, reasonable presentation to go with the inevitable speculations. Yet any typical mix of academic Stratfordians may well condemn their cause out of the inherent contradictions that flow from their own collective mouths.

Because of that, we cannot content ourselves, for instance, by being simply amused by those excesses of A L Rowse in his pronouncements as a 'grand old man' of expertise concerning the age of the first Elizabeth. Expertise, always prone to be inflexible, has here ossified completely. Seemingly programmed to resist all opposition, he is too often intellectually offside. Still, as a professional expert, he should at least be reliable in matters of basic details. Yet he could not bother to spell Looney's name correctly; he also referred to this founder of the Oxfordians erroneously, not to say most curiously, as an 'American' – rather as though that were a fault. Never mind if Looney's contention may be supported by some good argument; surely you realise that several of the seventeenth Earl of Oxford's supporters do have the temerity to come from North America? No wonder that Schoenbaum is somewhat wary of Rowse.

One last thought in this context is that, if we believe William Shakespeare of Stratford to be the true author, his genius must have surely been augmented by much self-education, plus the snapping up of trifles of gossip wherever he could. The facts concerning the 'gossip' so used can be seen in the plays. They indicate that it came from various classes of society, much suggesting social intercourse with people of superior station, in the manner proposed by a few of the more moderate Stratfordians. If not, he seems more than a genius as a writer: rather someone with supernatural ways of acquiring knowledge and sophistication which he could not arrive at even by the most arduous of accepted routes. If this is really so, it then becomes very hard to see why those powers could not have anticipated the blot placed on his name (as his supporters will have it) by the authorship controversy, taking steps to nip it in the bud. It is his own behaviour that is one of the most compelling of all the reasons for doubt. This Shakespeare of Stratford might well have decided he had no concern with the future of the works: his biography supports such a claim. But the message of the author within those works is so very different. It shows awareness of their durability in speaking of humanity's condition and aspirations, then contrasts their undoubted permanence with the seemingly certain disappearance of his own name.

Whenever we sift those strands of testimony; weighing the

certain facts, likely truth, legend and supposition, seeking to incorporate it all into a coherent theory, we simply have to look at a key matter such as the indication in the First Folio that the author Shakespeare was our man from Stratford-upon-Avon. But the disturbing features of that man's chosen lifestyle and lack of educational opportunity are equally key matters, as are many other of the issues raised by those who remain thoroughly sceptical. Somehow, for any honest enquirer staying with orthodoxy, these things must be explained.

At this point, as an observer with strong anti-Stratfordian leanings, I could easily leave various readers (after consulting the Epilogue) to make their own decision. It seems better, however, to 'stiffen the sinews' by putting forward, as the final 'Act', the kind of alternative that seems most satisfactory to me. This is not meant to be presented as though I regard it as inevitably true; it may, if one wishes, be considered as another interlude, this one being at least partly of a fictional nature. Even if the general thrust of it were correct, some elements of reconstruction must be inaccurate. There is one particular problem (or is it a delight?) of studying, at some length, the question of who Shakespeare was. It is that the uncertainties, the lack of scientific verification, allow anyone to put out such hypotheses for the critical scrutiny of others.

ACT 5
'TO FIND WHERE YOUR TRUE IMAGE PICTURED LIES'?

So he that takes the pain to pen the book,
Reaps not the gifts of goodly golden muse; ...

For he that beats the bush the bird not gets
But who sits still and holds fast to the nets.

From the introduction to the poetry anthology, *A Hundred Sundry Flowers*, first published 1573

SCENE 1

PROUD FULL SAIL

The shaking of the very foundations of English drama began
with the dawning recognition, in the age of the first Queen
Elizabeth, of two things. One was the enormous potential of
plays. These were principally to entertain; but in so doing they
might also put forward for mass consideration, if the author was
able and so wished, profound thoughts eloquently expressed,
historical pageantry, human dilemmas, or even propaganda. The
other factor recognised was simply the realisation that drama
could rise so very far above the primitive blank verse efforts that
had hitherto prevailed. The people who grasped these
opportunities, in Tudor times, fall basically into two categories.
One group was the university men, most prominent among them
being Christopher Marlowe. The other consisted of people
seemingly less well educated, in the formal sense. Its
contributions apparently began with Shakespeare.

Yet there was a third group who, in terms of knowledge and
education, had an enormous amount to offer the drama if it
cared, or dared, to do so – the Elizabethan nobility. They were
patrons of men of literature, but we have seen that there are no
dramatic writings bearing any of their own names that have
survived. There are, on the other hand, allusions suggesting
that Derby and Oxford, at least, did so contribute. 'In Her
Majesty's time', we are told in *The Art of English Poesy* (1589)

'are sprung up another crew of courtly makers – noble men and gentlemen of Her Majesty's own servants, who have written excellently well as it would appear if their doings could be found out and made public with the rest, of which number is first that noble gentleman, Edward, Earl of Oxford'.

Edward de Vere (1550–1604), the seventeenth Earl of Oxford, a man given every educational advantage, had written poetry, as an accomplished youth, under his own name. These poems have survived, but his efforts apparently ceased. A good example of this work, which also shows his liking for the use of his name, or variations on it or its 'true' meaning in word play, is the so-called 'Echo' poem:

> Oh heavens, who was the first that bred in me this fever? Ver.
> Who was the first that gave the wound whose fear I bear for ever? Ver.

The echo is continued in some more lines.

He it is who is offered here as the originator of a pen-name, Shake-speare. If de Vere, or another of his rank, had wanted to contribute to the drama, a pseudonym would certainly have been an absolute necessity.

Shakespeare's plays abound with just the kind of knowledge and familiarity of noble houses that the earl might have provided. Oxford would naturally take advice, as well as encouragement, from a small circle of friends. In the case of one early play at least, he may have had rather extensive advice: *Love's Labour's Lost*, 'augmented and corrected' by William Shakespeare, may owe something to Derby's help in the first drafting. As for Shakespeare's familiarity with the law, to take just one example of a major field of interest, Oxford's Gray's Inn training would provide him with the knowledge which is so evident (as distinct from mere interest in the law, also evident, but which we may accept as a reflection of a general interest within Elizabethan society). The Gray's Inn habit of dining in groups of four may well be reflected in *King Henry the Sixth Part I*, where Plantagenet says 'Come let us four [go] to dinner' – following legalistic-type debate in the Temple garden concerning the houses of the red and white roses.

De Vere clearly had the necessary breadth of interests. He was, by the late 1580s, of an age when, if he was to write so, there was no more time to lose. He had the maturity to write the comedies which so gloriously decorate Shakespeare's early career; hunting and hawking references would come naturally to his pen. Moreover, the choice of name would be an ideal one for this earl. Had not Gabriel Harvey written of him, in 1578, 'your countenance shakes a spear'? And was his crest not that of a lion shaking a broken lance? We have relatively few writings bearing his name, but the full text of the passage by Harvey indicates that there were a not inconsiderable number.

This man, vigorously proclaimed as the real Shake-speare by his modern advocates, has been dismissed by some of their twentieth-century commentators as a fop or a libertine. But we do know that Oxford was enthusiastic for literature and music; that he was impetuous and quick tempered, at least when young; that he travelled in Europe, sometimes being mocked for Italianate habits and dress; that he was relatively careless, even extravagant, in money matters. Shakespeare the writer seems to mirror at least some of these things. Surely he *knew* Europe, one country being known especially well?

> I am arrived for fruitful Lombardy
> The pleasant garden of great Italy
>
> *The Taming of the Shrew*

We must postulate, in the 'story' now unfolding, that de Vere kept Harvey's phrase in mind for some years, although discarding the attendant advice to abandon the pen. Then, having finally decided to write for the stage, he looked for a suitable pen-name and found a remarkable coincidence in the name of an aspiring young actor who had come to London from Stratford.

That actor would have been willing, even eager, to take the credit for dramatic and poetical work produced by another: very much wanting to make his way in the world, he would be paid well for his part in the enterprise. Oxford, together with some fellow peers, would be eager too: a flesh and blood 'author' was crucial to the scheme, as its visible, outer representation. Such a surface appearance of 'Shakespeare' provided an ideal means for de Vere. Assisted by ideas from the minds, experiences, or even verbal expressions of others (including, on occasion, the Stratford actor), the writing aspirations could be fulfilled without a stigma falling on de Vere's name. We need not, as many Oxfordians do, contend that the Stratford man 'stole' the glory. It was, rather, deliberately thrust upon him because of circumstance. However, whether he was meant to retain it indefinitely is much more difficult to say.

Well, then, might secret author de Vere remark that he was 'never less idle than when alone'. For, urged on by friends to use his evident talents to achieve the highest standards, the aspirations were dauntingly severe. They demanded considerable skill and creative power: in modern 'mission statement' terms, they were to create a corpus of literature comprising classic poetry, drama which encompassed great tragedy, courtly comedy, a tapestry of English history. And, in both drama and poetry, to express human thoughts, fears, longings, in the most eloquent way possible. This might mean taking up some others' efforts which might be susceptible to moderation, to be fine-tuned or remoulded under the banner of the spear-shaker.

Let it be repeated: all this needed – simply had to have – a plausible, trustworthy 'shop front' for public consumption. We need not consider that such marginalises the man from Stratford completely. He was that figurehead, also one of those with the right to offer ideas for possible input into the dramas. Every 'spirit' in the world needs a visible outer form, but Shakespeare the writer surely had 'that within' which surpassed the outer show. 'Shakespeare' was one of the variations of the Stratford person's name to which he could justly answer; his greatest acting role was this titular one – as the author. There was, of course, nothing remotely like the volume of curiosity one might expect nowadays over such an author. But, if anyone did query his involvement, he could offer assurance. Or, if necessary, dart away with an enigmatic smile. If pressed, he could always dissemble or gloze (this fine Shakespearean word is in good modern dictionaries).

Contemporaries were extremely unlikely, in any case, to come to grips with the complex reality. The hidden 'Shakespeare', about to be described, would be especially difficult to prove. A few people only knew the secret, or even part of it – though some others may have harboured suspicions, as the Hall–Marston satires suggest. Ogburn points out that when the Earl's second wife died in 1612 (curiously about the time the Stratford man retired) she left an unspecified sum to an unspecified man – apparently for holding his tongue about an unspecified subject! But, of course, were this our 'honest Will', it would be in his best interest to remain silent!

It is not the intention to repeat here too much of the ground covered earlier concerning de Vere. If this present argument appears to be simply a reiteration of Oxfordian theory, a crucial difference will soon emerge. Not only does the greatest weakness in the case for him (the date of his death) have to be combated, I also do not accept that his very considerable literary ability, along with his life experiences, could alone account for the genius or nature of the Shakespeare that has come down to us.

However, for the present, it suffices to say that I believe that the weight of probability suggesting that the origins of 'Shakespeare' lie with the English nobility of the late sixteenth century is irresistible – this despite the fact that the evidence is essentially inferential and circumstantial. Edward de Vere (Oxford) has the most compelling case, in my view, to be considered the originator of the pseudonym, but he doubtless had the counsel and input of a small circle of friends to draw upon (though never a 'committee' as such). Indeed, through marriages, his family forged close links with the houses of both Derby and Pembroke.

So it was that an 'invention' (the pen-name) first appeared in 1593, denoting the author in the published version of *Venus and Adonis*, dedicated to the Earl of Southampton. It has sometimes been alleged that a noble of Oxford's rank would never have used such flattering language as the dedication of this classic poem to Southampton employs. That claim misses the whole point: such wording, feigning an inferior position, was absolutely imperative. The poem was supposed to be by the Stratford man; it was also the very earliest use of the 'deception'. That dedication would bolster the intended illusion.

The plays, some of which are earlier than *Venus and Adonis* in their origins, include the re-working by Oxford of existing dramas like the *King Henry the Sixth* trilogy. But we need not doubt that the published editions of comedies such as *All's Well that Ends Well*, *The Merry Wives of Windsor*, *The Two Gentlemen of Verona*, represent versions of works originally conceived and drafted by Oxford who, as we earlier noted, headed Francis Meres' 1598 list of 'the best for comedy'. As a member of the aristocracy, Oxford would want to keep this activity well hidden. To continue such endeavour required the pseudonym. Of course, Meres mentions Shakespeare too; nor does he cite any dramatic works by Oxford. Perhaps he knew of none. He was summing up only what he had heard. What he certainly had not heard was that, in the context of these comedies, Oxford was the essential Shakespeare. (In some ways, it would be better for Stratfordians if Meres did cite de Vere's plays. As it is, we must assume them all either lost or 'concealed' under another name.)

Such a theory explains so much. It gives a hidden reason why the Stratford man, to the astonishment of some contemporaries, could apparently revise, with impunity, certain plays that people knew had been available (anonymously) for some time and claim them as his own. It explains why Henry Chettle, as the publisher of dramatist Robert Greene's abuse, would be advised (without being fully informed) to tender such a handsome apology; far from smashing the idea of a hidden noble author, that apology supports the notion that there was more to the 'Shake-scene' than met the eye. The theory accounts for the education, travel, culture, that is so abundant in the early Shakespeare plays. It provides authentic justification for the dramatist ridiculing Lord Burghley (capable of having over 200 words in a sentence!) as Polonius in *Hamlet*. He was Oxford's unpopular father-in-law. The famous soliloquy in which Hamlet ponders sleep, death, dreams, is an echo of a passage by philosopher Jerome Cardan of Milan, a translation of which was produced by Thomas Bedingfield, published by commandment of the Earl of Oxford.

Incidentally, Oxford's mother, like Hamlet's, pained her son by remarrying in some haste after his father's death. In that same play, there is a reference to 'a falling out at tennis'. It is a fact that de Vere quarrelled with Sir Philip Sidney over who had prior claim in the use of a tennis court. They were later reconciled. The memory of Sidney, of course, who died young on the battlefield, is held up as the model of a perfect gentleman. But there can be no doubt that both he and de Vere had a volatile side to their character. They knew each other well: in fact, had been contemporary law students.

Of other plays, *All's Well that Ends Well* has, most justifiably, been seen by Oxfordians as containing much that appears to be their man's biography. In it Bertram is ready to 'shake my sword' – the waving of a weapon being, in a metaphorical sense, of the essence of the Shakespearean enterprise. The theme of that is, of course, picked up by Ben Jonson in his glowing tribute within the First Folio of 1623:

> ... he seems to shake a lance,
> As brandished at the eyes of ignorance.

There are various similarities between Bertram and the young de Vere. Both left home very soon after their father's death. Strikingly both, when alienated from their wives, were brought to sleep with them unknowingly – in each case a pregnancy resulting! This seems too odd to be mere coincidence. Someone may protest that you do not need to experience something to write about it. True, but how many would know, or have the power to use, such an incident from the life of the seventeenth Earl of Oxford? Then there is the comic incident concerning the robbing of Gadshill and others in *King Henry the Fourth*. The source of this relates, not to Henry's reign, but to a letter addressed to Burghley from two of his servants claiming that (as in the play) they were attacked (in their case by Oxford's men)

171

when riding from Gravesend to Rochester. Another echo may just possibly be plays on words like 'ford' and 'ox' in *The Merry Wives of Windsor*.

If we can see 'Shakespeare' as a piece of entrepreneurial activity, initiated by one nobleman, but encouraged by some of his peers, then surely Oxford has the best case to be credited with the leadership and the supreme honour of 'inventing' the writer Shakespeare. There are, of course, many more alleged parallels offered in Oxfordian works concerning his life being mirrored in the plays. These are of mixed merit. But a significant point may be that de Vere had helped to bear a canopy (Sonnet 125) in a very real sense. This was carried over the Queen in the procession which marked the triumph of defeating the Spanish Armada in 1588.

Shakespeare the writer obviously knew several parts of Britain, not simply London and Warwickshire. For instance, saffron, the rare crocus used in cooking and noted by him, was known by relatively few people in the sixteenth century. It grew in Cornwall, but predominantly in Essex at Saffron Walden, near the Earl of Oxford's Hedingham Castle. That is an example of a very minor pointer; more significant are the many personal associations. In the list of the original actors in Shakespeare's plays, shown in most copies of *The Complete Works*, there is the name of an actor who played many jester roles, Robert Armin. This man was actually, for a time at least, a servant of the seventeenth Earl of Oxford. Then there is the question of those who influenced Shakespeare. The chief source for *Venus and Adonis* was Arthur Golding's translation of Ovid. Golding was a great influence elsewhere in Shakespeare, for instance in *The Tempest*. The most prominent example of this is in Prospero's 'farewell' speech beginning: 'You elves of brooks, hills, standing dales ...' Here, Shakespeare takes up Golding's exact words. The key point is that Golding, who was Oxford's uncle and tutor, had encouraged and praised his literary leanings.

Then, we might consider that Burghley's expert gardener, John Gerard, produced a work entitled *Herball*. The 'cuckoo' song at the end of *Love's Labour's Lost* undoubtedly reflects a section of this. Another influence was the contemporary writer of comedies, John Lyly. The stamp of this can be seen in *The Tempest*, plus passages like 'hark, hark, the lark' in *Cymbeline*. Although such examples are only presented very briefly here, the clear indication is of an accumulating mass of curious 'coincidences'. Of course, Stratfordians will understandably defend by pointing out that Oxford was dead when some of these plays were completed. But he could well have initiated them, largely developing their theme, to be completed (necessarily so, as circumstances were to dictate) by another. The point of bringing in John Lyly is that Oxford had a particularly close association with him, as his literary patron. A passage by Lyly in his *Endymion* encouraging fairies to pinch a human appears almost verbatim in *The Merry Wives of Windsor*. It would not be impossible for Stratford's Shakespeare to use these sources, but far less natural that he should be able to take them up so freely.

Besides, we would then have an extreme oddity: that of him drawing on *several* persons so very close to Oxford. In fact, there is at least one other such 'coincidence': it concerns Shakespeare's Sonnets 1–19. These have a persistent theme, urging a young nobleman (the consensus favours the Earl of Southampton) to marry, to 'make you another self for love of me'. It seems a little strange that the young Stratford man could address the lord so intimately; more strange that he should make, let alone constantly reiterate, such a request for the young lord to become a parent. The sonnets relate to events in the early 1590s. We know that, at that time, the person Southampton was being generally encouraged to marry was Oxford's daughter.

Oxford's copy of the Geneva translation of the Bible, now in the Folger Shakespeare Library at Washington, has many highlighted passages. A study of it, conducted by Roger Stritmatter, has suggested that several of these were used as sources by Shakespeare. A number of the marked passages relate to Falstaff. For instance, but for his bright nose, Bardolph (so Falstaff says) would be 'the son of utter darkness'. This is seen as a clear allusion to 1 Thessalonians 5:5, a passage which

Oxford had highlighted. There are apparently numerous such endorsed passages in that Bible, relating not only to speeches by Falstaff but also to those of other characters in the Shakespeare dramas. This could be most crucial evidence. Demolition of such would only happen if, for instance, it were to be shown that the Bible concerned was not Oxford's, or if the highlighted passages were to be proved as later additions. Unless such contentions can be made justly, we have here a major problem for Stratfordians.

Much that is in the sonnets is, of course, autobiographical – far more so than the plays, since the sonnets were meant to be, for the most part, Shakespeare's side of a private correspondence. The author speaks in one instance (Sonnet 3) of the young man's mother as a near contemporary; if, as most believe, the youth is to be identified with the Earl of Southampton, his father was dead. Certain sonnets take an avuncular attitude to the youth. Their author hints at his own age in some cases (Sonnets 2, 22, 62), at his interests, or background, in another (Sonnet 91). The age mentioned in Sonnet 2 is the one that de Vere, rather than Stratford's orthodox Shakespeare, would be when these sonnets were written in the early 1590s. There may be play on his name in some cases (Sonnets 76, 82). The essential philosopher within him also shows preoccupation with time – its fickle nature, relentless flow, inexorable destruction of human aspirations (see Sonnets 12, 15, 16 and 19, for example).

I have sought in this account to complement rapidly what was said earlier about de Vere as a possible alternative Shakespeare. His is the credit for conceiving, initiating, the Shakespeare enterprise. The plays all owe much to him, the comedies most especially. However, I cannot agree with all the ideas of the Oxfordians. What is more, I must reiterate that I do not believe that the Earl could, largely unaided, have given us the Shakespeare we now know. But, quite unexpectedly, there was added to the enterprise a jewel of inestimable price: the greatest professional Elizabethan dramatist, officially reported as having been killed in a brawl over payment of a bill, Christopher Marlowe.

Before we examine the phenomenon of such an astonishing addition, it may be useful to look at some suggested similarities between the writings of Oxford, in his own name, and those of Shakespeare. These comparisons have to be applied with care, since there are echoes of many Elizabethans in Shakespeare. This is partly because they had good ideas which he developed: essentially, to use a Robertson comment, 'inlaying their webs with his thread of gold, lifting their often halting verse ... to the utmost altitudes of song'. Another reason for caution is that Oxford's work (as Oxford), although more has been discovered in recent times, still represents a relatively thin sheaf: about 32,000 words at most, including much prose, compared with over 800,000 words comprising Shakespeare's plays and poetry.

SOME OXFORD–SHAKESPEARE PARALLELISMS

(NB: The Oxford quotes are all earlier in date than the Shakespeare ones)

(1) Three times, with her soft hand full on her left side she knocks
And sighed so sore as might have moved some pity in the rocks.
Edward de Vere, *A Vision of a Fair Maid*

And now she beats her heart whereat it groans
That all the neighbour caves as seeming troubled
Make verbal repetition of her moans.
William Shakespeare, *Venus and Adonis*

(2) What plague is greater than the grief of mind?
The grief of mind that eats in every vein
In every vein that leaves such clots behind,
Such clots behind that breed such bitter pain
Such bitter pain ...
Edward de Vere

175

She is not hot because the meat is cold
The meat is cold because you come not home
You come not home because you have no stomach
You have no stomach …
William Shakespeare, The Comedy of Errors

(3) Love's a desire, which for to wait a time
Does lose an age of years and so does pass …
Leaving behind naught but repentant thought
Of days ill spent on that which profits naught.
Edward de Vere

[Love] made me neglect my studies, lose my time
War with good council, set the world at naught,
Made wit with musing weak, heartsick with thought.
William Shakespeare, The Two Gentlemen of Verona

(4) And let her feel the power of all your might
And let her have her most desire with speed
And let her pine away both day and night
And let her moan and none lament her need.
Edward de Vere

Compare this with Shakespeare's Sonnet 66. Consider also:

Let him have time to tear his curled hair
Let him have time against himself to rave
Let him have time of Time's help to despair
Let him have time to live a loathed slave.
William Shakespeare, The Rape of Lucrece

(5) But when I see how frail these creatures [women] are.
Edward de Vere

Frailty, thy name is woman!
William Shakespeare, Hamlet

(6) That never am less idle lo! than when I am alone.
Edward de Vere

I ... vow to take advantage of all idle hours [to honour
the Earl of Southampton with further work].
>> William Shakespeare, Dedication to
>> *Venus and Adonis*

I, measuring his affections by my own,
That most are busied when they're most alone.
>> William Shakespeare, *Romeo and Juliet*

(7) ... if our friends be dead ... we make them live as it were
again through their monument. But with me behold it
happens far better; for in your lifetime I shall erect you
such a monument.
>> Edward de Vere (to Thomas Bedingfield)

Not marble, nor the guilded monuments
Of princes, shall outlive this powerful rhyme.
>> William Shakespeare, Sonnet 55

Your monument shall be my gentle verse ...
You still shall live ...
>> William Shakespeare, Sonnet 81

And thou in this [the verse you are now receiving] shalt
find thy monument
When tyrants' crests and tombs of brass are spent.
>> William Shakespeare, Sonnet 107

(8) Patience perforce is such a pinching pain.
>> Edward de Vere

Patience perforce with wilful choler meeting
Makes my flesh tremble ...
>> William Shakespeare, *Romeo and Juliet*

(9) For truth is truth, though never so old, and time cannot
make that false which was once true.
>> Edward de Vere

For truth is truth to the end of reckoning.
>> William Shakespeare, *Measure for Measure*

SCENE 2

ONE WHO COUNTED NONE

... the danger that might come
If he were known [to be] alive.
Measure for Measure

In presenting the case for Marlowe as a collaborator, it is necessary to touch upon argument made by Hoffman or later Marlovians. This certainly does not mean that all they say is accepted. However, earlier observations in this context may be reread since I try not to repeat them overmuch. Those unfamiliar with the meteoric career of Marlowe, as it is officially recognised by scholars, may wish to have a very swift recapitulation here of his background, deeds, main writings. He was born in Canterbury, the son of a shoemaker. Then he had (we know rather than merely assume this) early education at the excellent King's School, which is still to be found in that city. He went on, via a generous scholarship for able boys, to Cambridge University. There, at Corpus Christi College, he spent over six years in all. Incidentally, we know that the college had an excellent library, as had King's School. His burgeoning talents, coupled with a zest for bridging gaps in social status quickly – via his intellectual capacity finding its outlet in bold expression – brought him success. He was seen as a genius, a literary innovator.

Besides his enormously successful writing (great literary achievement with promise of greater to come), he was also active in espionage on behalf of the government. Apparently he performed some specific service of value on behalf of Queen Elizabeth. But his eloquent, audacious prose was matched unwisely by a habit of challenging convention in his day-to-day conversations. He was an outspoken freethinker, which was rash. Admired by many, he had enemies as well as friends. There were aspects of his life, either real or attributed by these enemies, which added up to very great danger in that day and age: violence, cruelty, atheism, the commendation of homosexual practices. Some modern commentators insist that these traits were present; others see him more as a much maligned free spirit, a leading pioneer of the Renaissance in England.

As for his literature, we have an epic poem, *Hero and Leander*, neither finished nor (like some of his other works) published in his official lifetime. There is the lyric 'Come, live with me and be my love'. There are, perhaps, above all some very fine, if uneven, plays. All agree that these foreshadow Shakespeare's work in history and tragedy. The plays are: *Dido, Queen of Carthage*; *Tamburlaine the Great*; *Doctor Faustus*; *The Jew of Malta*; *The Massacre at Paris*; *King Edward the Second*. The revolution which these brought to the drama can only be appreciated by those who know what preceded him. Marlowe also translated classics. That of Ovid's *Amores* was natural in view of his admiration of its author. More surprising was his choice of the first book of Lucan's *Pharsalia*, concerning the effects of civil war.

The intellectual credentials of one who must be counted a literary giant of his, or any, age are impeccable. At least, they are if we discount his temperament (or was it largely cruel circumstance?) leading him into desperate trouble. The brilliance of Marlowe's restless mind was indisputable. 'Tell Kent she has lost her best man' (*King Henry the Sixth*) can evoke memories of him without necessarily thinking that he might have been the real Shakespeare. However, there were at first rumours, then open allegations, of homosexuality,

179

blasphemy, scoffing at Holy Writ. Official history insists that he died, in May 1593, at the age of barely 29. It tells us that, while bound over by the court, reporting to it daily (in effect on bail), facing accusations which could lead to torture or even execution, he was stabbed by Ingram Frizer, in a public house at Deptford, dying during a dispute with his three companions over settling the bill.

The curiosities surrounding that 'death' have haunted English literature. It was, in fact, no common tavern, as had for long been generally believed. The proprietor, the widow Eleanor Bull, was a woman of some standing, with court connections. The official verdict of the royal coroner, of accidental death in a brawl (with the Queen's pardon ensuing for Ingram Frizer, the man alleged to have killed Marlowe) was highly convenient. Those present for this event on 30 May 1593 were all Sir Thomas Walsingham's men, connected with the espionage network. Meanwhile, informer Richard Baines had collected from witnesses, some of whom were clearly anxious to protect themselves, a damning set of testimonies about Kit Marlowe. Curiously, Marlowe 'died' just before these could be used against him. Some modern writers, like Charles Nicholl, have argued that it was not accidental death, but planned murder. But did Marlowe really die at all in 1593?

Taking up the theory that he might have lived on, three significant comments can be made straightaway. First, the idea of a substitute corpse was not unknown in those times; interestingly, the theme is picked up by Shakespeare in *Measure for Measure*, where the body of the pirate, Ragozine, is sufficiently like Claudio to be offered as the latter, while he survives. If this happened with Marlowe, he would have to be mute, at least as his old self. He would also have to 'lie low' ('not show my head', as Sonnet 26 puts it).

Second, as has been suggested earlier, many of those obviously autobiographical sonnets of Shakespeare tell a tale of disgrace, banishment, remorse, hiding, the holding of secrets (even the half-threatening to tell them) which perfectly fit such a situation. If we postulate, as I do here, that Marlowe survived the crisis of May 1593, to be subsumed in the Shakespeare enterprise as a talent far too valuable to be ignored, then it is easy to see *Venus and Adonis* being written largely or wholly by Edward de Vere, almost in competition, if one likes, with another fine classic poem, Marlowe's unfinished *Hero and Leander*. The former was dedicated to the Earl of Southampton, by Shake-speare, being the 'first heir' of the use of that name. Then Marlowe responds by writing the bulk of a new poem, *The Rape of Lucrece* – but Oxford has the power, a right that became a hallmark of their ensuing joint endeavours, to add or edit. In that second epic poem by 'Shakespeare', the warmth of the dedication to Southampton is greater. It is very much in line with Sonnet 26, which I believe to be Marlowe's.

But a third point is: why might the idea of a false death be effected? We would have to assume that the answer to this question, the whole reason for Marlowe to escape the most serious charges, rested on appreciation of his literary achievement by 1593 – still more on the recognition of the potential contribution to come under the bland cover of 'Shakespeare'. Intellectuals at court had read his work; he had powerful friends, such as Thomas Walsingham, as well as enemies. They would be well capable of special pleading on his behalf. There was a recent event, a secret known to very few, a noble deciding to mask his authorship behind the figurehead of a person with strong theatrical connections. Why not have two great hidden talents working together? It was the perfect way to ensure that a literary wonder was not lost.

For such a wonder Marlowe undoubtedly was. As contemporary dramatist Thomas Nashe was to say: 'no leaf he wrote on but was like a burning glass to set on fire all his readers'. Again, as the nineteenth century poet Swinburne remarked of him, in comparison with competitors when he began to write, he was not like the eagle to the wren, but more like the eagle compared with frogs or tadpoles: the difference was not of degree, but of a fundamental kind. The introduction of Marlowe into the concept of Shakespeare, providing diversity (in the tragedies, even enhancement) would inspire Oxford to the highest standards. Indeed, it was a necessity to create what resulted. The two must have been a constant spur to each other.

181

THE ALTERNATIVE SHAKESPEARE

We can safely surmise that Marlowe's work in the dramas had to be submitted for editorial vetting and for careful integration with that of Oxford. Most interestingly, as recently as 1993, there was report of the auction of a curious document from the 1590s. This appears to be a short passage written for, or else based upon, the plot of *King Henry the Fourth Part I*. Was it someone copying Shakespeare or a draft prepared for Shakespeare's play? The commentator in the newspaper favours the first solution which, although unlikely, seems more probable to orthodoxy than any kind of proto-Shakespeare hypothesis, in which the dramatist made use of someone's drafts. But what if one person were submitting copy to another for scrutiny, the latter being the head of their corporate endeavour?

What were the respective contributions of Oxford and Marlowe? The poems *A Lover's Complaint* (if Shakespeare's at all) and *The Phoenix and the Turtle (Dove)* were probably de Vere's. Both men contributed substantially to the history plays, but Christopher Marlowe's work, only slight in the comedies, became very substantial in the great, dark Shakespearean tragedies. There was certainly very much of de Vere in the relatively early tragedy produced by the partnership, *Hamlet*; quite a lot of him also in *Othello*. But, thereafter, Marlowe was the main, often almost exclusive, contributor to them. Gradually, after Oxford's death in 1604, Kit's faint hope of eventual recognition may have been extinguished. The growing intensity of his despair at his secret existence, with the credit for his writing going to another, flowed over into the plays, at times putting pressure on sanity. In two (*Timon of Athens* and *King Lear*) this seems very much the case, as Sir Edmund Chambers observed. A person often criticised by Chambers agreed with him on this particular point, for J M Robertson once remarked of the author of *King Lear*: 'to reach those heights, he had looked into madness'.

Well over half of the sonnets too are, in fact, Marlowe's. Examples include numbers 20, 23–26, and those many which follow that can be explained only as the tale of his having escaped the death described in 1593; recollecting hints of his wild escapades in verse; living on in hiding, full of bitterness because of the lack of personal recognition for his contributions.

These statements may all seem, at first glance, as remarks which simply must be complete fiction. But they are the 'story' of much of Shakespeare's sonnets: in what other way, or in whose biography, can we explain that story? Remember that these sonnets were not intended to be published like Shakespeare's other work. Their 1609 release was unexpected. Only an ersatz Shakespeare might safely ignore them. It must have caused someone 'behind the scenes' consternation, followed by a lasting dismay. Those sonnets have come down to us in quite good order of date sequence. They clearly had been written over a period of time, from approximately 1592 to, just possibly, as late as 1607. Sonnets such as 29, 34–35, 44, 87–89 offer an account of banishment, remorse, anger, but continuing love; a desire to be remembered – even still loved – by the fair young lord; this last mixing, as moods alternated, with a command to 'forget me quite'.

It is only in the context of a hidden Marlowe, suffering mingled yet intense emotions, that the 'autobiography' of much of them can make sense. The complex story of the sonnets is compounded by the fact that, after the start of the sequence with Oxfordian ones, more by de Vere are occasionally interwoven with those by Marlowe. As in the other Shakespearean poetry, there is an element of competition between the two. Little wonder that they have confused critics down the ages. Writing in 1923, H T S Forrest picked up the element of competition as being within the sonnets themselves, but postulated a host of unlikely competitors.

Like the majority of literary critics, I have taken the youth addressed in many of these 154 sonnets to be Henry Wriothesley, Earl of Southampton. The words 'love' and 'lover' can confuse, since they were used for friendship as well as for intimate relationships in those days. Oxford's regard for the young man was that of a friend towards a peer of the younger generation. Marlowe, Southampton's near-contemporary, is a different matter altogether. Marlowe, of course has been accused of homosexuality; one of the plays he produced (as Marlowe) certainly treats of that theme. It may or may not have happened with the fair youth but, if not, they came very near in their 'night of woe'. Sonnet 20 is suggestive of past physical intimacy, although showing that the writer (Marlowe) has now accepted that the youth is 'for women's pleasure'. Several modern commentators on Marlowe insist that he must have been homosexual (often adding that Shakespeare of Stratford was not); others, including members of the Marlowe Society, assert (with equal insistence) that the only reason we suspect this is because of the slurs cast by his enemies. They see him as a stupendous poet, a great freethinker, whose character has been much abused. But, in the theory here expounded, the young lord's relationship with Marlowe was undoubtedly intense (Sonnets 20, 27, 34, 48, 88 and 120, for instance).

Sonnets by Oxford include the sequence 1–19, imploring the young man to marry and have a child; Sonnet 62, which is by an older person; Sonnet 125 concerning the canopy; probably some that seem to play on words like 'ever' or 'truth'. Sonnets 153 and 154, placed at the end (despite an early date of composition) because they are a literary exercise so different from all the rest, are also to be attributed to him. Numerous commentators have queried who might be the particular rival poet, mentioned in some of the sonnets, who was praising the young Earl of Southampton too. Marlowe's great rival is, of course, Oxford. What has clouded the issue is the complex intermingling. Despite continual analysis and criticism concerning these sonnets, it has not been realised that this rival poet is there in the sonnets themselves, the author of some of them, the 'other half' of Shakespeare! So Marlowe could write to Southampton about 'both your poets', without the world recognising that Shakespeare spanned both. Several commentators have accepted that Shakespeare's main rival, as mentioned in the sonnets, was Marlowe – yet this entirely without grasping either that he was one of two contributors to them, or that it should be strange for orthodoxy to see him as an actively competing rival since he was supposedly dead when several of them were written!

Here is an extract from Sonnet 86, penned I believe by Marlowe, with my offered explanation in brackets.

> Was it the proud full sail of his [Oxford's] great verse,
> Bound for the prize of all-too-precious you [Earl of
>   Southampton] ...?
> Was it his [Oxford's] spirit, by spirits taught to write
> Above a mortal pitch, that struck me dead?
> No, neither he, nor his compeers [fellow nobles] by night
>   [at the dinner table?]
> Giving him aid, my verse astonished:
> He, nor that affable familiar ghost [William of Stratford?] ...
> As victors of my [Marlowe's] silence cannot boast ...

And the spirits encouraging Oxford to write so well are as shadows in the background: the compeers, the fellow nobles. If that last point seems strange, note that the rival poet (the nobleman Oxford) is also mentioned as a 'spirit' or 'better spirit' both here and elsewhere – Sonnet 80, line 2, for instance.

There are two or three other sonnets which may just possibly give different kinds of pointers towards Marlowe. Look at Sonnet 112:

> For what care I who calls me well or ill,
> So [if] you o'er-greene my bad, my good allow?

The obvious meaning is that the poet does not mind being criticised by others, provided Southampton glosses over the faults and emphasises his (Marlowe's) good points. But this painting metaphor, the only use of the word 'o'er-greene' throughout Shakespeare, is an interesting one. Why is green the chosen colour? Could it be an oblique reference to the criticisms of the dead dramatist Robert Greene? He had criticised Marlowe on numerous occasions. Of course, we are repeatedly told of the one occasion it is believed he also criticised Shakespeare. However, that was surely wiped out by the most handsome apology of the age, given posthumously via his publisher, so why this lingering reference? Perhaps because all Greene's strictures about Marlowe were still 'on the table', as it were.

Then there is Sonnet 121 where the poet is seeking to justify his own character. The daring direct reference to oneself, using God's words as recorded by the Book of Exodus, 'I am that I am', has the authentic stamp of a hot-blooded, defiant Marlowe. Stronger than such, of course, is the most pointed, indisputable, reference of all in Sonnet 74:

> ... my body being dead;
> The coward conquest of a wretch's knife.

This allusion to Marlowe's alleged death is generally acknowledged by many of the orthodox, who take it as some strange kind of analogy that Shakespeare wanted to make. But if the sonnet were anonymous, with Marlowe known to have survived the Deptford murder attempt, we would never doubt the true author for one moment. Doubtless, if orthodox opinion wanted to affirm that Marlowe wrote this sonnet, the line would be pounced upon as avidly as Robert Greene's reference to a 'Shake-scene' is so regularly flaunted as 'evidence' for the upholding of conventional belief.

There are also the so-called 'Will' sonnets, numbers 134–136. These are certainly by Marlowe. We need not take the 'my name is Will' too literally. Would a man given at birth the name of William really indulge in so much sexual innuendo about 'wills'? It is more the ironic comment upon an imposed pseudonym, being an attempt to use it to poetical advantage. As a hidden person, Marlowe would need to take on a name for his low-key day-to-day life. Perhaps the name assumed for that was, say, 'William Hews'. This would certainly explain the puns on 'hues' in the sonnets.* And if, perhaps, in growing frustration, he eventually put those sonnets on the market for 1609 publication, it would explain the mysterious Mr W H, their 'only begetter'. But 'my name is Will' can be explained anyway simply in terms of the pen-name. Likewise, the release of the sonnets in 1609 might have had nothing whatsoever to do with the hidden Marlowe. They might have been pirated, just as *Troilus and Cressida* was the same year, with 'W H' being the phantom figure who obtained them for the publisher. A Mr W H is also mentioned gratefully in a 1606 dedication by another publisher: he might have been simply a contemporary procurer of material.

King Henry the Sixth, the play containing the famous line intentionally misquoted by Greene about a tiger's heart, is thought by many critics of the drama to have originally been by Marlowe and others. Many modern critics with no anti-Stratfordian leanings accept that Shakespeare took on for development an earlier play from which he retained large sections, including the 'tiger's heart' section. Soon after the line used by Greene, we have direct parallels to the first line of one of the 'Will' sonnets (Sonnet 135). The wording shows the clear influence of Ovid, as translated by Marlowe:

> Bid you me rage? Why, now you have your wish;
> Would'st have me weep? Why, now you have your will,

and the sonnet says (words in brackets being my own interpretations):

> Whoever hath her wish, thou hast thy Will [i.e. Oxford]
> And Will [of Stratford] to boot, and Will [myself, Marlowe]
>   in over-plus.

---

* There has been, over the years, speculation by many, including Oscar Wilde, about an imaginary William Hews in the sonnets, because of frequent puns on the word 'hues'. In Marlowe's case, if he had wanted a name for day-to-day use, he at least had a real example on which to draw. Research by archivist William Urry of Canterbury in the 1960s revealed that Marlowe's father had an apprentice of that very name. But the pun might also – or instead – refer to the (loose?) pronunciation of Southampton's family name Wriothesley as 'Roseley'.

Beyond this play on words in the various 'Will' sonnets, with the clear sexual implication that is there too, there is the essential message (in Sonnet 136) that the poet is well hidden in the group:

> Among a number one is reckon'd none

which is, as we shall see in looking at parallels, an echo of Marlowe. We can say safely, in fact, that these are all Marlowe lines.

The bond between these close contemporaries surely goes way beyond the obvious link that *The Jew of Malta* has with *The Merchant of Venice*, or the connection of *King Edward the Second* with *King Richard the Second*. Shakespeare was more than Marlowe, but Kit was more than just a powerful external influence on him. Throughout the plays, the Marlowe voice is extensive, almost pervasive. The organic relationship can only be truly explained by confessing the dramatist said to have died in 1593 to be 'in' Shakespeare. J M Robertson, among others, has seen the hand of Marlowe clearly within so many Shakespeare plays: *The Taming of the Shrew*; *King Lear*; *Romeo and Juliet*; *Titus Andronicus*; *The Comedy of Errors*; *The Merchant of Venice*; *Macbeth*; *King Richard the Third*; also, of course, *King Henry the Sixth* being among them. Then there is the likely use of Marlowe's translation of Lucan as the source of Ulysses' 'degree' speech in *Troilus and Cressida* (some have seen hints of the same theme in *Macbeth*). Robertson finds a similar passage in both *King Richard the Second* and *Julius Caesar*. He feels, being a Stratfordian of sorts, that they tell of one pre-Shakespearean hand – Marlowe's.

But, it may be objected, Robertson was always to be seen as a maverick, a law unto himself. Very well, let us turn elsewhere. Extremely orthodox Stratfordian commentator J S Smart suggested that the source play *The Taming of A Shrew*, from which Shakespeare drew his play of very similar name, has lines pillaged from both *Tamburlaine* and *Dr Faustus*. To deny or dismiss the inference of all of these things in accumulation is, in a sense, simply to denigrate that great writer, Shakespeare: to assume him to be a gross imitator, even a stealer, sometimes of quite insignificant detail.

We may consider, very briefly, a variety of other pointers to Marlowe as part-Shakespeare. He was a close friend of poet Thomas Watson, who died in 1592 when in his mid-thirties. Watson certainly had links with de Vere, who was his patron. He may have contributed to the anthology of poetry, *A Hundred Sundry Flowers*; if not, he was certainly influenced by it. His sonnet sequence must, in turn, have influenced Shakespeare's. Watson is also the only poet, apart from Marlowe, to be quoted by Shakespeare, notably in *Much Ado about Nothing*. In addition, there was at one time a street brawl in which Marlowe and Watson fought a man named Bradley. This has been noted by commentators as not only a precursor, in some of its details, of Marlowe's alleged death, but also as a source for a fracas concerning Mercutio and Romeo in *Romeo and Juliet*.

What other miscellaneous items might be quickly raised as being of possible significance concerning the grafting on to 'Shakespeare' of that cut 'branch which might have grown full straight'? One could be the testimony of fellow dramatist Thomas Kyd, who had lodged with Marlowe, mentioning the latter's intent to visit Scotland. This may reflect an interest that was to contribute to a play that is very much Marlowe's: *Macbeth*.

Another point concerns the play *As You Like It*. Down the years, unbelievers in the orthodox Shakespeare have found in the curious words of the character Touchstone encouragement to believe he is acting as the voice of a hidden author in addressing a rustic character named William, with phrases such as 'to have is to have', or 'You are not ipse, I am he.' Touchstone has been claimed, by these authorship dissidents, to represent all too many alternative Shakespeares, including Marlowe. It may be wishful thinking. What must be noted is the fact that Marlowe is undeniably very present in this play. There are two references in it from the poem *Hero and Leander*, one of them a direct quotation. It is very thought-provoking, especially when Touchstone also, most curiously, refers (obliquely, but most unmistakably) to Marlowe's supposed

189

death: 'When ... verses cannot be understood ... it strikes a man more dead than a great reckoning in a little room.' The seventeenth century was dawning when this play was penned. Was Marlowe kept silent by means of threat or other coercion? Could he have been trying to slip in a hint, as he became increasingly fretful over his continuing obscurity, not to mention the uncertainty of even long term recognition for these plays?

Perhaps ... or, most certainly, perhaps not. But *King Lear* is also a significant drama in making a case for Marlowe. Within this play there is a statement by Lear, 'to scant my sizes'. This, perhaps a subconscious utterance by its author, comes from a Cambridge University phrase, which Marlowe would know well, meaning to cut down on a student's rations. It has lingered on in a few universities, but is otherwise obsolete. Its appeal at the time would be to the knowledgeable. We would have to assume (I think totally without evidence) that it was in wide general use in the Elizabethan age in order for it to spring so readily to the mind of a person who had not attended Cambridge. *King Lear* is, throughout, a very Kentish play. There is one scene in particular where Edgar looks down over the cliffs (several commentators accept this to be the cliffs of Dover, a town the Kent-born Marlowe knew and where his mother was born). The authenticity of the scene certainly suggests most strongly that its writer had first-hand knowledge of looking down from them.

In the context of that same play, Leo McDonald gave fellow members of the (British) Marlowe Society a talk in 1994 concerning an Elizabethan law case in which a woman named Cordell pleaded against her elder sisters who questioned the sanity of their father, Brian Annesley. The similarities with Shakespeare's play are strong, including his use of the name 'Cordelia'. So there is, once again, in this further 'coincidence', the suggestion of people close to Shakespeare, picking up real-life events to feed in ideas for his consideration. Who could it have been in this instance? Some knowledgeable Stratfordians may say that they know about the Annesley case, that the fact that he may well have been 'fed in' to Shakespeare to become the model for Lear is not disputed, but how can this possibly help Marlovians? The answer is that this law case was brought in Marlowe's county, Kent. Most interestingly it was also presided over by his patron, Sir Thomas Walsingham.

MARLOWE–SHAKESPEARE TEXTUAL PARALLELS

The Latin motto *Quod me nutrit me destruit* (That which sustains me also destroys me) appears under the 1585 portrait of a young man, alleged to be Marlowe. The portrait, found at Cambridge University, now hangs there in Corpus Christi College. This motto finds a clear echo in *Pericles*; there are several more variations on its paradoxical theme within Shakespeare's sonnets, for example:

Sonnet 73: Consum'd with that which it was nourish'd by.

Sonnet 80: My love was my decay.

Sonnet 29: With what I most enjoy contented least.

To the comment that the portrait might not be Marlowe, one can retort that it is most certainly not Shakespeare of Stratford, who had no Cambridge link. How would he ever come to know of it with its quotation? In the light of the portrait's Ovid-like remark, consider some commentary on Marlowe's *Hero and Leander* by orthodox critic J B Steane: 'the sense, always present in the poem [is] that there is a destructive, painful element strong in the love which is nevertheless the best thing that life offers to man'. Steane, incidentally, also finds echoes of Marlowe's translation of Lucan in Shakespeare.

Here I must voice my agreement with Calvin Hoffman that the young man shown in this portrait indirectly became, when in middle age, the model for the Droeshout illustration of 'Shakespeare'. I suggest that this was copied – perhaps from the 1609 'Flower', suspect though that portrait is – and that the so-called 'Grafton' one, the history of which has been well described by Thomas Kay, is also a portrait of a young Marlowe. These (there are also others, of course, purporting to be Shakespeare) do all look like the same person at different ages – 21, 24, 45 and older, although anyone opting to investigate further will find, in comparing them, that in the 'Grafton' the face is thinner and the eyes of a rather different colour. Droeshout's engraving is really so unsatisfactory, especially with regard to posterity's intensive demands. In any case, if we cling to orthodoxy, a model was surely used for it: Martin Droeshout was only fifteen when the Stratford man died!

There are many other parallels to be found in the work of Shakespeare and Marlowe, aside from clear links between the epic poems. Some of these might be expected; to be explained in the context of authorship orthodoxy, by borrowing being done, whether unconsciously or otherwise, by the conventional William Shakespeare. Others are merely common phrases which we would expect to find in plays close in their date of composition – or those which will be repeated each time certain similar circumstances occur, for example, 'I arrest you for high treason'. But still others give more rise to concern. Just a few close likenesses may be usefully quoted here, the Marlowe one (always earlier in date) being shown first in each case:

(1)   I ... hold there is no sin but ignorance

The Jew of Malta

I say there is no darkness but ignorance.

Twelfth Night

(2)   Over my zenith hang a blazing star.

Tamburlaine

My zenith doth depend upon a most propitious star.

The Tempest

(3)   These arms of mine shall be your sepulchre.

The Jew of Malta

These arms of mine shall be your winding sheet.
King Henry the Sixth

(4)   Mortimer … as a traveller
Goes to discover countries yet unknown.
King Edward the Second
The undiscovered country from whose bourn
No traveller returns.
Hamlet

(5)   Ah, cruel brat, sprung from a tyrant's loins!
Tamburlaine

O tiger's heart, wrapped in a woman's hide!
King Henry the Sixth

O serpent heart, hid with a flowering face!
Romeo and Juliet

(6)   O my girl, my fortune … !
The Jew of Malta

My daughter! O my ducats!
The Merchant of Venice

(7)   Blush, blush, fair city.
Tamburlaine

Bleed, bleed, poor country.
Macbeth

(8)   My swelling heart for very anger breaks!
King Edward the Second

The venomous malice of my swelling heart.
Titus Andronicus

(9)   Cut is the branch that might have grown full straight
And burned is Apollo's laurel bough.
Doctor Faustus

O, withered is the garland of the war
The soldier's pole is fallen.

Antony and Cleopatra

(10) O soul! Be changed into small water drops.

Doctor Faustus

To melt myself away in water drops.

King Richard the Second

(11) But, stay! What star shines yonder in the east?

The Jew of Malta

But, soft! What light in yonder window breaks?

Romeo and Juliet

(12) One is no number; maids are nothing then,
Without the sweet society of men.

Hero and Leander, Part 1, Sestiad 1

Among a number one is reckoned none.

Sonnet 136

(13) My mistress has her wish; my wish remains:
He holds the palm, my palm is yet to gain.

Marlowe's translation of Ovid's *Elegies*, Book 3

He pays the whole and yet am I not free.

Sonnet 134 (last line)

Whoever has her wish, you have your Will.

Sonnet 135 (first line)

(14) Nor in my books shall one but you be writ
You do alone give matter to my wit.

Marlowe's translation of Ovid's *Elegies*, Book 2

You are so strongly in my purpose bred
That all the world besides methinks are dead.

Sonnet 112

(15) Their fingers made to quaver on a lute
Their arms to hang about a lady's neck
Their legs to dance and caper in the air.

Tamburlaine

He capers nimbly in a lady's chamber
To the lascivious pleasing of a lute.

King Richard the Third

(16) And faintness numbed his steps there on the brink.

Marlowe's translation of Lucan

Yet are these feet whose strengthless stay is numb.

King Henry the Sixth

(17) Leading a life that only strives to die.

Tamburlaine

Where life has no more interest but to breathe.

Titus Andronicus

(18) People may see the likeness in sentiment or intent in other lines: for instance, the requests for a temporary denial of natural laws:

Stand still, you ever-moving spheres of heaven,
That time may cease and midnight never come.

Doctor Faustus

Stars hide your fires;
Let not light see my black and deep desires.

Macbeth

Hoffman cited more than this, some of dubious value to say the least. The latter may be simply oft-repeated figures of speech, or direct quotation, for instance. Yet his natural capacity for overreaching, born of enthusiasm, does not invalidate the general case. Such parallels as those shown above may well sometimes be subconscious; if they were deliberate borrowing by a Shakespeare of which Marlowe was not a part, they show us a reliance on the earlier dramatist which is embarrassing. They constitute, by any definition, in any age, clear borrowing. Such would nowadays be viewed as blatant plagiarism.

Lastly, let us look at a curiosity about Marlowe's poem *Hero and Leander*. The official position is that Marlowe wrote Part 1, which was not published in his lifetime (that is, before May 1593). The poem was subsequently completed by George Chapman, the two parts being published together in 1598. Since Marlowe was supposedly dead, we can (even if my theory is believed) accept that someone else had to be brought in if this poem was to be completed. Fellow dramatist Chapman, who like Ben Jonson had friends at court, was as good a choice as any. But, when first published, the completed poem contained a very warm, moving dedication to the wife of Marlowe's former patron, Sir Thomas Walsingham, a dedication which was destined to be removed from subsequent editions. This is attributed to George Chapman. Yet it seems to make no sense in relation to him, neither would it, nor *Hero and Leander* for that matter, have anything to do with the William Shakespeare officially recognised by the world. Here is an extract from the conclusion to this dedication, the offered explanations in brackets being mine:

> ... [Sir Thomas] my honoured best friend, whose continuance of ancient kindness [former favours] to my still obscured estate [condition], though it cannot increase my love to him, which has ever been entirely circular [please do not get the wrong impression about our friendship!] ... shall ... make my hearty gratitude speak; to which the unhappiness of my life has hitherto been uncomfortable and painful dumbness.

There is an edition of Shakespeare's sonnets that has on the cover a picture of an unknown man in flames. Those here claimed to be written by Marlowe convey the very spirit of that; the emotions vary a little, but the fundamental tone is one of extreme unhappiness. Compare, then, the end of the dedication of *Hero and Leander* to Lady Walsingham with the comments of Shakespeare to Southampton in the sonnets. Some examples of such 'painful dumbness' are Sonnet 85, 'my tongue-tied muse ... my dumb thoughts'; Sonnet 86, 'as victors of my silence cannot boast'; the reference to 'being dumb ... being mute' in Sonnet 83; Sonnet 89, 'in my tongue/Thy sweet beloved name no more shall dwell,/Lest I, too much profane, should do it wrong,/And haply of our old acquaintance tell'; Sonnet 120, 'if you were by my unkindness shaken,/As I by yours, you've pass'd a hell of time'. Conspicuously, there are portions of Sonnets 23 and 140:

> Oh let my books be then the eloquence
> And dumb presagers of my speaking breast.

>   do not press
> My tongue-tied patience with too much disdain;
> Lest sorrow lend me words, and words express
> The manner of my pity-wanting pain.

There was, of course, the awful hell (for him) of recognition that the sonnets would endure; that the youth of the sonnets would be immortalised; yet that one vibrant, crucial part at least of the true Shakespeare 'once gone, to all the world must die' (Sonnet 81).

The connection between the emotions of these sonnets with the dedication in *Hero and Leander* is surely there. It so clearly cannot fit the man from Stratford-upon-Avon, nor for that matter, George Chapman, but matches so well the idea of a silent, hidden, personally and artistically frustrated, increasingly desperate, very much alive – Christopher Marlowe.

SCENE 3

GRAND POSSESSION

As it is the care of a faithful servant to wipe away the dust which time has heaped on the tombs and escutcheons of the illustrious dead, so it is the duty of those who devote themselves to the service of literature to preserve a just remembrance of the departed.

Gentleman's Magazine, August 1845

There are, of course, accounts which provide more detail about Marlowe as a possible Shakespeare. For the seventeenth Earl of Oxford, Edward de Vere, there are many such accounts. In the case of neither do these other advocates see 'Shakespeare' as essentially a duality; a scholarly gentleman amateur enabled to work, through unusually propitious circumstances, with an exceptionally gifted professional dramatist. But some Oxfordians do accept that their man died before his work was completed, giving rise to the need for supervention by a collaborator who must have been of equal social status. For most surely several of Shakespeare's great works, especially the tragedies, were completed, or even largely written, after Oxford's death. Who, we may ask, effected this continuation with the necessary quality assurance? Marlowe, I must insist, certainly did much to ensure it: his great tragic genius, not to mention his mounting despair, came to full fruition in the Shakespearean tragedies. But the overall control continued to be exercised by the manuscript guardians; a coterie of supportive nobles, from whom a new key person emerged to take on the crucial lead involvement of composing, integrating, editing, evaluating – just as the original spear-shaker had previously done.

The 'other' who took Oxford's mantle had to possess great literary skill and enthusiasm; it would be a person who had played a support role from the early stages. Someone with deep empathy as well as zest and flair for the necessary extension and completion; who, with carefully applied skill, would ensure that eventually the works, including some apparently unknown before 1623, were available for posterity. They could thus be received, not quite 'without blot' as was stated, but reasonably whole and sound. There are certain key factors, including the timing of publication, to be seen as crucial concerning the enormity of the First Folio. These (once Oxford be accepted as the Shakespeare initiator) point irresistibly to who this person, bringing 'William Shakespeare' to the fitting quietus originally intended for him, must have been. It was Mary Herbert, Countess of Pembroke, whose literary brother, Sir Philip Sidney, had died so tragically early. Several of the courtly families were linked by marriage, and her younger son was the husband of de Vere's daughter.

If we look for signs that Mary Herbert was involved in the editing of Shakespeare, we find not proof, of course, but merely pointers. Certainly, she had the necessary interests and had been praised by her contemporaries as, for example, one 'who sets to school our poets everywhere'. A reference of dubious reliability concerning a letter (now lost, if it ever existed) to her son, in which it has been alleged that she says 'we have the man Shakespeare with us', cannot of course mean that she was 'the woman Shakespeare'. It might allude to Marlowe or to the actor, Shakespeare of Stratford, being at the Herbert's home at Wilton. However, it may be a small sign of what we may believe was her considerable interest in Shakespearean drama.

With regard to literary credentials, she had completed and

revised *Arcadia*, originally the work of her brother, after his death and had produced a metrical version of the Psalms. She was also involved in the translation of the Book of Psalms for the 1611 Authorised Version of the Bible. As for pointers, she had links with Wales early in her life, a country in which Shakespeare shows clear interest; there is some fine characterisation of women, particularly in later plays, and some sentences might seem to have been penned by a female. We need neither succumb to emotion, such as that which comments on the intelligence one sees in the slate-grey eyes of her portrait, nor necessarily argue (as has been done by a few) that Mary Herbert could have been the model for Sylvia in *The Two Gentlemen of Verona*. More significant is the fact that several contemporaries expressed considerable admiration for her high abilities. Her epitaph, even making allowances for the fact that eulogy was common in the seventeenth century, is perhaps the best example of the many verbal garlands brought.

The publication of various individual Shakespeare plays in good faith after 1616, by others ignorant of the facts, added to the need for an authoritative complete edition via the representative of the official possessors. When she died (on 25 September 1621) the work of publishing the great Folio had either begun or was about to begin. The great event of 1623 was long after the Stratford man, who made no provision for publication because it was not his concern, had himself left this world. This First Folio contained many plays hitherto unperformed or unknown. Most significantly, it was to the Pembroke brothers, Mary Herbert's two sons, that it was dedicated. This was safe enough in view of the effort made to safeguard the secret.

There are various signs of links between Mary, Countess of Pembroke, and Christopher Marlowe. The manuscript copy of his 'Come, live with me and be my love', along with Ralegh's reply, appeared in the commonplace book of the chaplain to the Earl of Pembroke. A pastoral by Thomas Watson appeared posthumously with a warmly expressed Latin dedication to her, commenting on her virtue, her literary interests and her 'glorious name'. That dedication was written and signed by

Watson's friend 'C M', who sought her patronage, here expressing himself as desirous of doing her some honour via his own writing.

The Shakespeare 'romances' (*Cymbeline, The Winter's Tale, The Tempest*) may be seen as plays which best demonstrate some examples of some literary creativity of her own, although we need doubt neither that the ideas behind, even first sketches, of these three were something she inherited, nor that she edited many of the other dramas for the great Folio. She certainly did some work on the three 'Roman' plays. It is possible that she was still editing some, including these, at the time of her death.* In *Coriolanus*, she perhaps found scope for the introduction of some feminine psychology. She had the privilege too (in a sense, a dubious one) of working with Marlowe. His brilliant, but perhaps increasingly erratic, talent for tragedy had to be sustained through some very difficult years; copy received from him had to be checked, even revised on occasion, before weaving it into the attempted seamless dress of the total Shakespearean enterprise.

We could only believe that the First Folio was edited by Heminges and Condell, honest actors, by accepting blindly, at face value, what the Folio introduction tells us. It is not only the considerable reasons for doubting the conventional author that lead one to say this; we know, indisputably, that the plays were not originally in the hands of these two men, but rather 'grand possessors'. Heminges and Condell can scarcely be conceived to have the time, the finance, even the intelligence for such a major enterprise as this Folio. So it was surely true that the great legacy of this collection, without which much of the Shakespearean canon would have been lost, was handed down to us, by one most certainly determined to devote herself to major literary service.

---

* Scholars have various theories about the timing of the production work for the Folio. One is that it did not begin until 1622. The more favoured theory is that work commenced in the late spring of 1621, but stopped in October, resuming only after a year's delay.

Perhaps Mary Herbert was Oxford's choice in the event of his death before the completion of the enterprise, perhaps the choice of the background group. We cannot know. The more we press for precise detail in a theory such as this, the more we risk driving points far too hard. But the strong family link is clear, the Earl's daughter being the wife of one of the Pembroke sons. Incidentally, Mary Herbert was also connected, through a sister-in-law, to the Walsingham family. If the ability to make a smooth transition after the death of Oxford is doubted, we should consider that many of the later plays had been drafted; that they awaited filling out, together with any necessary revision, coalescence or validation; that Marlowe was available to assist considerably with this; that the essential Shakespearean 'template' had already been set up. Problems came later, notably in 1609, when the sonnets were released for publication without official approval. It is most noteworthy that they are omitted from the 1623 Folio. Indeed, if the secret of this plural Shakespeare was for ever sealed, as may have happened, it could well have been their publication in 1609 that ensured that this simply must be so. (Why, people might even assume that 'Mr W H' was the elder son of the Countess!)

In due course, one supposes, the world might have been told of Oxford's involvement; of the fact that he had a professional collaborator, even possibly of the defiance of convention (in Elizabethan and Jacobean times, at least) by having a woman to complete and extend the contributions. It just might conceivably have been eventually confessed that one such bestowed with gifts, in Edmund Spenser's words, most 'wonderful and rare', had been so involved.

But those sonnets changed everything. It seems reasonable to believe that their 'begetter, Mr W H', may or may not have been the writer, but certainly the one who supplied them to publisher Thomas Thorpe. The remarkable dedication, Thorpe's not Shakespeare's, is very like one made earlier by Thorpe for an edition of Jonson's *Volpone*. Thorpe had published a work by Marlowe in 1600, after the official date of Kit's death. If Marlowe released the sonnets unilaterally to

Thorpe in 1609, as he may well have done, he doubtless would obtain some temporary satisfaction to atone for the intense depression occasioned by his prolonged isolation and enforced silence.

If so, it was a Pyrrhic victory. It may only have made sure that every effort would be made to preserve the secret in perpetuity, to see that the key part in the true Shakespeare played by a supposedly dead man was permanently hidden. Indeed, we might reason that soon after this Marlowe was banished from England, his work in the enterprise of Shakespeare done. For the purpose of an illustration within the great First Folio, one or more portraits of him were shown to the young artist, Martin Droeshout, who was told that the man he saw there was now dead, but was invited to depict him as he might have looked when aged about 50.

Thorpe, as publisher, would know next to nothing of the details; the omission of tell-tale lines here or there (Sonnet 126 apparently lacks two lines, Sonnet 96 has been given the same ending as 36) would thankfully minimise any scandal for him, as well as for others, which the revelations might have prompted. He did not know about the real Shakespeare. Indeed, I must again suggest that, if it were proposed that the truth about the composite Shakespeare was to be ultimately revealed, the intended outcome would be that posterity would never see these sonnets. A few were intended for strictly limited circulation and eventual publication: Francis Meres had heard of these. Others were not intended to be seen by anyone except Southampton. Paradoxically, then, while these sonnets, more than any other part of the literature, suggest that there was a secret Shakespeare, they may be mainly responsible for the preservation of that great secret. Perhaps the very high price of their unauthorised publication in 1609 is an eternal seal on Shakespeare's true identity!

Let us consider, for a moment, Ben Jonson's glowing tribute to Shakespeare in the 1623 Folio. How much did Ben know? Not all, but something for sure, since he later made an enigmatic comment concerning 'one who was desirous I should not name him'. He picks up the potential value of

'Shakespeare' as a pseudonym, referring to shaking a stage in one part of the tribute; to shaking a lance in another. He also refers to the sweet swan of Avon. Since there is more than one River Avon, the reference might well fit the Countess of Pembroke too, for she lived by one of them. Jonson was under instructions: he had to be guarded and ambiguous in praising Shakespeare in the preface to the collected works. The substrata were not fully revealed to him, but he was presumably told that the man from Stratford had a great collaborator. On the basis of things Jonson said at different times, such an admission would hardly be such a colossal surprise to him.

The clearest hint Jonson gives as to the plurality of Shakespeare is near the end of his tribute in the Folio:

> But stay, I see you in the hemisphere
> Advanced, and made a constellation there!

Yes, Shakespeare could be seen as the star of poets; but in another, very real sense, could be viewed as a cluster, or constellation. As for Jonson, he is often cited as the main plank in the defence of the orthodox Shakespeare because of his glowing attribution to his contemporary in the First Folio (rather at odds with some comments he was to make later). But his 1623 stance is well explained in Greenwood's observation: 'Ben Jonson might have seen nothing in the least objectionable in the publication by some great personage of his dramatic works under a pseudonym and if, being a friend of that great personage, he had solemnly engaged to preserve the secret inviolate, then without doubt he would have remained true to his solemn pledge.'

Perhaps about 30 people knew something of the Shakespeare secret. Fewer than this knew about Marlowe. Even the Stratford man himself, the visible embodiment of the author Shakespeare, may well not have known about Marlowe's involvement, while Ben Jonson would guess naught of the still living Marlowe. As for Heminges and Condell, we can safely say that they were well employed to give the tale an extra air of veracity. They accepted what they were told. Of the reality, they knew nothing.

The method of de Vere was to draft plays, to fill them out after discussion, to take on board massive inputs from Marlowe (with the right to edit or amend), then to revise and polish the outcome. Sometimes this was done after they had been first acted. The task of the collaborators from 1604 (Marlowe working away and the Countess editing, dovetailing the parts, adding ideas or some infrastructure if necessary, certainly taking the final decisions) was not to supersede the work of Oxford, but rather to ensure its fulfilment: the fabric of later Shakespearean plays owes much to the use of his conceptions and beginnings of plays – the 'bones' or first sketches that lead into the full expression of what Coleridge, much later, was to call Shakespeare's 'oceanic mind'. Building on the pearls of Oxford's ideas, draftings, suggestions, making too its own immense contributions, this new partnership was able to create the finest 'coral':

> Nothing of him that does fade
> Undergoing a sea change
> Into something rich and strange.

It is assuredly strange enough to make 'Shakespeare', as here presented, quite distinct in all literary history. So much so that this unusual, complex, theory may seem almost totally impossible. Yet it seems to me the best to fit the known facts. And it should surely be realised, in the light of all the alternative speculations made over the years, by both orthodox and unorthodox commentators alike, that the reality about Shakespeare, whatever it is, must be complex and unusual.

So we have here a theme of successful literary fusion, in which the nobility as scholarly amateurs combine with a great professional. It is certainly a most romantic one, but that is completely beside the point: judgement must be according to probability as suggested by the various pointers. Obviously, good sense would crush any idea that there could be a host of Shakespeares. But two writers at any one time, backed up by a small 'ideas input' team which included the Stratford man on occasion, is certainly feasible. Indeed, in modern computer parlance, the facts suggest that this is the 'minimum configuration' required to obtain the breadth, the glory, of the known end product.

Without Oxford, or without Marlowe, we would have a much lesser Shakespeare. Mary Sidney Herbert took on the mantle of the former. Determined to perpetuate the glory of fled times and bring admirable enterprise to its intended culmination, she built, with assiduity, on de Vere's 'shells' of plays. She incorporated Marlowe's work appropriately as Oxford had done; she ensured that dramas planned and begun, though not yet known to the contemporary stage, were not abandoned. To speak of a committee or board of directors is to use false analogy, but (supported as necessary by a small group) for over a decade she was the executor of what could be called, in more senses than one, a literary 'Will'. Essentially, she ensured the bringing of 'Shakespeare' from the Elizabethan to the Jacobean age. Perhaps, towards the end, as Marlowe was now seen as totally unreliable, there was some commissioning, via her Stratford agent, of a little work from a dramatist such as John Fletcher or George Chapman (they would assume their collaborator to be the Stratford man). In addition, although in quantitative terms Mary Herbert's textual input was much smaller than that of her male colleagues, her editorial overseer skills were vital to the continuity. Without her commitment while the dramas were in the 'grand possession' of a small group within the nobility, some half of the Shakespearean output would have been lost to posterity.

Any such theory as this, without compelling new evidence, will be resisted by orthodoxy. It is, of course, also easy to deride it; much harder to face the facts, searching for the version of history which most closely corresponds to them. If the situation expounded here (or something close to it) be true, it certainly represents a unique kind of literary synergy. But, then, it must be repeated, Shakespeare undoubtedly was unique.

We may observe that the lady editor excluded *Pericles* from the Folio that she planned for publication. It is most unlikely that the omission was an error. I can offer three alternative possibilities: that perhaps Oxford's contribution had been altogether too slight; that it was written entirely by Marlowe and another professional dramatist (who would believe his collaborator to be the Stratford man), and thus was not seen as truly Shakespearean; that she had not edited it to her contentment before her death. I favour the middle solution of the three. (The anonymous play *King Edward the Third*, with its Shakespearean overtones, I also consider to be by Marlowe and another.) Of course, for more obvious reasons – could there be any question whatsoever of the memorial Folio containing those sonnets?

The answer has to be a most emphatic negative! They had appeared some 14 years before the First Folio; it was perhaps thought that by omitting them from it their long-term impact could be minimised.They were seen by the Folio editor as so intensely embarrassing, not because they mention wills and pricks (there are plenty of 'bawdy' references of that kind elsewhere in the canon), but because the unequal, unconventional friendship of a reckless young lord with a commoner of great impetuosity was viewed as a source of great shame. This, the theme that underlies all the sonnets contributed by Marlowe, was meant to be an eternal secret. So it was never the intention that all be published. This was despite the fact that, as we know from the 1598 testimony of Francis Meres, a small selection were circulated to friends (among the high-born) soon after they were written. I believe these to be the earliest, Sonnets 1–19, written by the seventeenth Earl of Oxford.

The intricate assemblage of this composite Shakespeare represents a threefold cord so carefully intertwined that it has proved impossible to break it down: 'which three 'til now never kept seat in one', as one of the sonnets might put it. Originally there was to be one 'hidden' Shakespeare; circumstance enabled him to be unexpectedly joined by another; then the first died, yet another taking his mantle as organiser and editor. Yet, despite the input of ideas and advice from a select few who knew the secret, there were never more than two 'modes' of Shakespeare at a time – in the end, after the banishment of Marlowe, only one. Perhaps there was some clue left somewhere for posterity, perhaps not. That message, if it is really meant to be one, at the end of *The Tempest*, sounds so dreadfully ominous.

Even if it is so, any vision such as that sketched above is not necessarily a mirage. It may be that we can broadly reconstruct, as I have tried to do, arguing like the soothsayer from *Antony and Cleopatra* that even 'in nature's infinite book of secrecy a little we may read'. I postulate that Marlowe went back to Padua, one of the places visited during his original banishment, eventually dying there in 1626 (as alleged in the story reported by the *Guardian*); that William of Stratford, neither a knave nor a nonentity, but an essential part of a planned deception, did what those prosaic archives concerning him show that he did. He returned to the place of his birth well content, having made his way in business, able to fulfil his ambition to be a respected property owner.

The members of writer Shakespeare's small advisory group were aesthetic in temperament, yet the endeavour was also intensely entrepreneurial. The range as well as the versatility of the end-product testifies most eloquently to the value of bringing to fruition what Oxford had planned and begun. To his creativity, curious circumstance added an unexpected but enormous bonus, Christopher Marlowe. Together the two successive leaders of the group, with considerable input from their hidden professional associate, formed an enterprise which grasped all available opportunity. These names were well hidden behind the visible William Shakespeare.

Enforced hiding clearly frustrated the ego of the professional contributor who, even more than the others, simply had to remain unseen. Yet he participated to the full in the creative potential of the work. To be such mighty 'movers and shakers' was no easy task: the course of their glory is inevitably much compressed here. It required supreme literary ability; also planning, management skills, extensive cultural and experiential qualifications. Along with this was encouragement, plus various stories or ideas coming from a small 'backstage' group. But, through sustained endeavour, the successive lead people could satisfy their literary aspirations. In their hands (and Marlowe's) it became a vehicle for displaying an unmatched pageant of stirring history, moving tragedy, and sophisticated comedy, all in ways which greatly transcended the immediate limits imposed by the Elizabethan or Jacobean stage. The audience sought was not only a contemporary one: the works, proudly 'brandished' like a lance to show what was possible in literature, were meant to stand up to the ravages of time, to endure long beyond the confines of the lives of those creating them, to cascade down numerous generations, to be acclaimed throughout posterity.

For each person contributing to a composite but incomparable Shake-speare, his or her contribution well concealed by the chosen outer guise, these things constituted the essential mission.

THE CASE IN MICROCOSM

The seventeenth Earl of Oxford, using an assumed name to reach the full sail of his literary aspirations, responsible for the first dynamic of Shake-speare; succeeded by the Countess of Pembroke; both augmented, virtually throughout, by Christopher Marlowe. The latter was responsible for about half of the total Shakespearean input. A few others offered ideas and encouragement, but there was no committee. The noble authors integrated the contributions, having the final say on what appeared. William Shakespeare of Stratford-upon-Avon was the outer representation of this secret enterprise. The fact that it came down to us in his name was not what might have been originally intended; neither was it theft. It might best be regarded as enforced capital transfer, effected by a person committed to preserve a just memory of the departed, lest the sonnets taxed great reputations much too heavily.

Such is a summary of the alternative hypothesis I tend to prefer. It emerged as the one that seemed, in my eyes, to fit facts best. But within it there are various possible 'forks', or 'mini-sequences'. I have chosen to follow just one or two. For instance, one is the assumption (which might not be true even if my macro theory were to be broadly correct) that it was Marlowe who released the sonnets in 1609, being banished abroad again as a consequence. I have likewise assumed how Jonson may have been 'briefed' for his role.

Before having the audacity to endorse any seemingly very far-fetched theory, we have to recall the numerous points which suggest weakness in the traditional authorship ascription. Can *all* be shot down? If so, it would have to be believed that, (Marlowe not being alive after 1593 to be involved in the Shakespeare enterprise) England possessed not one but rather two men of exceptional literary genius, both relatively lowly born during the first half of 1564. It would then be assumed that both of them had an intense interest in Ovid; that both at least flirted with homosexual practices.

We would have to suppose that the autobiography behind many of the sonnets, fitting the concept of a hidden Marlowe so well, can somehow relate also to Stratford's Shakespeare. It would be necessary to brush aside most of the apparent references in the plays to the life and relations of de Vere, not to mention some that seem to indicate an ideas input by a person or persons of his rank. In sum, then, we have to explain a whole series of 'coincidences' relating particularly to de Vere and to a surviving Marlowe. We would also have to regard as coincidence the fact that the First Folio of plays, said to be in the hands of 'grand possessors', was released not to mark the death of Shakespeare of Stratford but rather relatively soon after the death of the Countess of Pembroke. What is more, it was dedicated to her sons. Among these diverse matters, some points may well be suspect and capable of refutation; but, to deny all – could any 'coincidence-chain' stretch so far?

Remember, too, the accumulative value of the doubts: that to reinstate the Shakespeare of tradition and common acceptance, one has to surmount not some but all from a series of remarkable facts. If, in the absence of precise 'measures', we use the concept of performance indicators to mean who was responsible for the Shakespearean performance rather than how good the achievement is, we might use a 1–6 scale, 6 being best. We might then decide to ask a comprehensive range of questions, 'scoring' the candidates on each one. The Stratford man would certainly score an emphatic 6 on the face-value evidence of the 1623 Folio. He might score 6 in that title-pages carry his name, though not in one of its more usual spellings. He would score badly in many other areas. But remember: performance indicators, although not all equal in value, are meant to be used in clusters; we have most confidence in them by finding an overall, mutually supportive trend, offering, as it were, a consistent probability graph or curve. These one or two important indicators are so very positive, as they would be either if he were the author or we were meant to think so. The other indicators, in the context of his candidature, are in conflict with it, but support each other remarkably in pointing us elsewhere. The combined effect of their intimations sends a very powerful negative message down the corridors of time.

Of course, for every anti-Stratfordian, there are to be found scores of people who would never want to doubt that the writer William Shakespeare is the man who was born in Stratford-upon-Avon, dying there in 1616. At an impressionable age, they were taught this, probably by an authoritative figure at school. But mere direct or indirect repetition of such an assertion cannot, in itself, make that assertion true. Moreover, nearly all among these hosts of people have never examined the alternative case. Thus, as Rowse might say (would most certainly say, if only he were himself an unbeliever), they are simply not qualified to offer an opinion.

Lastly, I indulge myself a little by returning to the first part of the quotation with which this Act began, this time adding two previously omitted lines. I identify the author of it too by one of the 'posies' he used, in 'signing' contributions to that sixteenth-century poetry collection entitled *A Hundred Sundry Flowers*:

THE ALTERNATIVE SHAKESPEARE

So he that takes the pain to pen the book,
Reaps not the gifts of goodly golden muse;
But those gain that, who on the work shall look,
And from the sour the sweet by skill shall choose ...

Ever or Never

EPILOGUE

Many theories within orthodox Shakespearean scholarship, as well as anti-Stratfordian ones, have been put forward too dogmatically as though they were a new, undeniable revelation of actual events from previous centuries. Having hopefully demonstrated earlier that the concept of a possible 'alternative Shakespeare' is feasible, I have simply sought within 'Act 5' to give voice to what would be my own preference. Let me reiterate that my great leap into speculation, although stated there as if it were clear revelation of a most extraordinary historical combine or nexus, is not meant to be read as something I claim as indubitable truth. Nor is it something I decided to believe before investigation. At the broad level, it is merely a sketch of the most likely or consistent 'alternative' explanation, as it appears to me, from all that we can know at present. As it seeks to go into more detail, so the guesswork factor inevitably increases. Of course, in terms of sharp-edged factual precision, it can be neither proved nor disproved. But then, there is relatively little worth knowing concerning the author Shakespeare about which we can be incontrovertibly sure.

I accept, for example, that one particular statistical analysis of word usage and word clusters by computer, showing Shakespeare's language to be somewhere between that of Oxford and Marlowe, must necessarily be inconclusive. I also accept that mine is a theory which (although it may seem to offer an umbrella under which a number from the broad church

213

of doubt could possibly shelter) could well displease some Marlovians or Oxfordians – not to mention nearly all Stratfordians! Some of its strands could be much expanded, but the potency of the argument is most unlikely to be increased by a longer presentation: there is a fallacy, to which many in life regularly succumb, to suppose that the more extensive or eloquent the debate, the more chance there is of inevitably resolving the issues. One will either reason that my hypothesis (or something reasonably close to it) is, or could be, right – or feel certain that such ideas are uncongenial.

Where is the reality behind all of the speculation? My view (and this Epilogue, along with 'Act 5', is really the most personal part of the whole book) is firmly that truth either must reside within a heavily modified version of Stratfordian tradition, or in something quite like the theory just put forward. This is, in its essentially exploratory nature, quite similar to theories that might be encountered in philosophy or economics. As with a philosophic theory, it is based on its exponent's perception of probabilities, and upon the argument arising therefrom. Another parallel rests in the idea that there may be a hidden essence, behind what is visually obvious; such an idea is at the very heart of the metaphysics expounded by several philosophers.

But there is an important difference with regard to economic theories. Their 'truth' might feasibly depend upon local or temporary circumstances. Any unusual Shakespeare authorship theory, on the other hand, is either permanently true, or permanently false, since it deals with historical events. And, to an extent quite unlike many economic or philosophical speculations, it has to contend with the colossal burden of denying the generally received 'expert' views of truth (and the incalculable attached vested interests) without the benefit of factual proof positive.

Is my theory nothing but moonshine, or a largely insubstantial vision; a fantasy spree, or merely a different flavour of what I have elsewhere called candyfloss? Well, as William Wordsworth wrote in another context altogether:

If this be error and another faith
Find easier access ...

then so be it! Indeed, designed as it is to complement the preceding account of the controversy, my own reconstruction attempt, interweaving facts with inevitable guesswork based upon them, must necessarily contain some fiction. Critics may think much of it to be like a novella or the raw material for one; that is their right, always provided they are willing to shake off any mythological presuppositions of their own. For those who disagree with me wholeheartedly, there is an onus to marshal a counter-argument in the light of facts and probability, rather than by mere assertion. My primary intent has been to stimulate thinking rather than persuade towards acceptance of any one theory as irresistibly 'the whole truth'.

However, we would not suppose our Shakespeare to be over-dependent on his predecessors. So consider the alleged use of incidents from the lives of the nobility or parallels in wording between Shakespeare and Marlowe, for instance. Some of the latter claims may seem born of desperation, some achieve the status of the (largely subconscious) influence of one writer upon another, some thrust upon us the insistence that we are listening to the very same person. We need to decide upon the right category. But if even a few compel us to the last conclusion ... !

Studying the Shakespeare authorship problem has put me in a position as a Groupist or Dualist, in that I lean strongly to the theory stated in 'Act 5'. Of all the twentieth-century 'heretics' mentioned, Slater's is the stance that comes closest to it. But I contend that the focus must be much sharper than he presented it; there were only two people constituting the essential Shakespeare at any one time, supported, in terms of advice or encouragement, by a small group of 'spirits' which may have included the actor from Stratford. My conviction remains that there are only two alternatives as to the truth. One is along the lines of the story above: the other would be that the Stratford man was, in a sense, the author, but that he had very extensive literary help, ideas, encouragement from the aristocracy of his time, being perhaps a close 'friend' of noblemen. I applaud those orthodox commentators like Ivor Brown and Georges Connes who have given some support to a scenario of such a kind. Personally, my considered opinion is that this second option, though not impossible, bristles with difficulties. How, for example, does it explain the sonnets, or the apparent reliance on the 'Marlowe factor'? Yet it merely stretches my credulity to the full; only travelling further towards the orthodox position would snap belief altogether.

Of course, nobody is driven purely by reason in these matters. There are the fruits of imagination, emotional yearnings. I acknowledge these. One may just love the idea of an earl being the Bard. Some may see, for instance, a picture of a sunset over Oxford's Hedingham Castle (built by one of his ancestors in 1140) and dream of him as Shakespeare. Or, listening to moving music, they might feel attuned to hear a plaintive voice of 400 years ago, coming through the deeply frozen crust of others' indifference, looking for justice, saying 'to have is to have', or complaining over his 'still obscured' state. If my own expressed theory seems a moving one, that is irrelevant to the burning issue of whether it is true. But such sentimental feelings can just as much affect the supporters of Stratford-upon-Avon, as we have surely seen.

Somewhere between pure reason and such outright emotion, there is also the question of where one is comfortable in terms of intellectual honesty. I have no doubt that such, as well as rational factors, is at work when I say that I must prefer the unorthodox alternative. It would not have been too difficult to have diverted the path of this book into becoming a new survey of the controversy which avoided all risk of stigma by siding firmly with convention. Being on a collision course with majority belief means that several 'experts', if they even deign to read any contrary view, would insist that a proper understanding of the Elizabethan age and Shakespeare would put paid to any vestige of doubt. Such an understanding, they would contend, must show that disbelief is all superfluous breath, essentially flaccid stuff employing a thought process which is but scratching 'the poor itch of opinion', or akin to drunken, tuneless scat singing breaking in on the sacred concert of literary scholarship. But then, having their carefully accumulated past reputation to defend, they would, wouldn't they?

There is really no point in emphasising enthusiasm for historical truth (or, if necessary, probability based on thorough searching) only to let expediency override mental comfort in the quest. In fact, integrity in this matter is very important. Quite apart from my own preference in terms of a theory, the stance and technique of many Stratfordians in dealing with doubters is something I often find appalling. So perhaps, as well as belief, a wish to redress the balance means that unhesitatingly, whenever I come off the fence, I feel happier to be counted standing with Slater rather than Schoenbaum; with Greenwood rather than Gibson; even, if necessary, with Carr rather than Churchill, or with Robertson rather than Rowse.

Yet this book has also been prepared to criticise aspects of the anti-Stratfordian views too. Generally speaking, this quest for a legitimate alternative author, over its total history, has been badly served by adherents in at least four ways:

- Overreliance on cryptograms and ciphers.
- Supporting (often with very flimsy 'evidence') a candidate much more likely to be original than genuine.
- Excesses such as arguing that the true Shakespeare was a descendant of Queen Elizabeth or wrote most of the literature of Elizabethan and Jacobean times – even later works.
- Insisting that the secret was an open one; that, by the beginning of the Jacobean era, quite a large number of people knew, or guessed, who was 'behind Shakespeare'.

It is tempting to add to the list, 'also by too much circumstantial evidence', but then what other kind is available, with positive new facts seemingly impossible to acquire? The route to truth is not necessarily trackless, but we have to rely on pointers. Many of the narrow paths offered soon peter out; answers end, although the asking does not. So feelings, sympathies, or (for some) prudence take over where reason is forced to break off. The magic book, which would enlighten us conclusively with a revelatory identification, is seemingly drowned; the key or staff broken and buried many fathoms. We reach into a void, trying to grasp historical certainty, but touch only a freezing silence. What we have are the shards or suggestions embedded in the huge total literature of doubt. These are of very mixed merit. Their opponents would doubtless use for them an alternative (Shakespearean) meaning of 'shard'. There most certainly is an ample share of dross, sometimes born of overenthusiasm or desperation to press home what is seen as important truth. But (to adapt Hilaire Belloc's delightful phrase) although when taken as a whole their sins sometimes be scarlet, several of these books deserve to be read!

There have, across the years, been various simulated 'court trials' of the Shakespeare authorship case. 'Verdicts' have differed, but most have erred on the side of caution, favouring the conventional authorship ascription. Yet the right verdict in this controversy must be the famous Scots one of 'not proven' – by either side. Bardolators really worship an unknown god. An Anti-Stratfordian museum, which might even be located at Stratford-upon-Avon, has been proposed. Naturally, there has also been pressure to search for documents. The Stratford bust apparently contains nothing. Ah, but is it the original? And then there was an incident in the 1970s when an attempt to explore it was either made or feigned: as Ogburn reports, there were curious features about that.

The dominant Shakespearean view may be adamantine, impenetrable, as far as changing most people's views are concerned. The alternative theorists may all then be dismissed by most people as, to use my own earlier title, 'a comic interlude'. Yet there will remain a few independent souls who will resist absorption into orthodoxy, daring to 'be a Daniel' in the den of the lions, or refusing to 'bow the knee to Baal'. For, although books by doubters are often written off as part of the history of delusion, it is instructive to see how the Stratfordian case (however desperately propped up) itself rests, in terms of rational justification, on a flimsy floor. It merits, at the very least, a gentle scepticism. Its supporters, when faced by doubts, are certainly forceful in seeking to repel these. If they sometimes seem omnipotent, it is for an ignoble reason: the argument being that, in the case of a lack of proof positive, the onus is all on those who challenge – the *status quo* must, until proved false, be taken as final definitive 'truth'. The doubters are expected to produce effective rather than merely quixotic lance-waving. Yet the means to do so may now seem to be permanently 'screened-off', perpetually inaccessible.

But remember Slater's comment about continuing to use girders suspected of flaws. Or, to use a crude sporting analogy, if a world boxing champion faces a challenger and the result is a draw, he retains his crown. Yet such deadlock hardly creates an impression of a convincing holder of the title. It might be better, then, if Stratfordians would support, rather than seek to block, endeavours to obtain all-convincing new data. If the orthodox would be less obstructive, admitting more readily the genuine difficulties in their case, there would be more energetic talent released to look for facts. There is scope for inter-party discussion: the academic and popular debate highroads are alike broad enough to tolerate some two-way traffic.

There are, as we have seen, comic strands in the history of the controversy, but also cause for sadness. There is a great Shakespearean contrast in modern times, although it is well hidden from most people through the suppression of unorthodoxy. On the one hand, the plays can reach their full scenic potential by availability on video; they have been 'translated' into modern English at enormous cost; one can obtain the Shakespeare text on CD ROM for detailed searching of it, or explore via interactive video programmes. Electronic conversation about 'Shaksper' (this term is a concession not to a spelling sometimes used by the doubters, but to a computer's liking for truncation to eight letters) is available via Internet. Shakespeare the writer is constantly applauded, being idolised on a massive scale; has long been in the syllabus for so many literature courses; generates an abundance of critical works; has been translated into numerous languages; has inspired great music; is drawn into other fields, his characters becoming brand names for products; is even cited, for example, as a supreme example for management expertise of a kind that is relevant in the present day. Yet, on the other hand, it really may be that we cannot be sure of who this person was!

Remove a large top slice of extremist disbelievers and there is nothing much to choose between the rest and orthodoxy in terms of necessary reliance on speculation. In both camps, guesswork is essential. For the doubters it is so because they must construct what they think is the most reasonable alternative case without full evidence. For the orthodox because their man, after the most extensive searching for new historical data, offers nothing that suggests literary splendour. He seems surely what sober historical minutiae, based on a degree of searching beyond compare, show him to be: a man aspiring to property owning and gentility; pressing for the payment of debts; having trouble with his taxes; selling commodities; acting and play-brokering. It is facts, not some form of snobbery, that proclaim him such. There must surely, therefore, be a genuine case for exploring an alternative to the official Shakespeare of history, notwithstanding the fact that there have been such differing views as to that alternative's identity.

In terms of general grounds for doubt, there are so many straws in the wind that, even discarding many, we end with a veritable haystack. Of course, the needle of final proof takes some finding. This does not mean that doubt's haystack is a mirage. Perhaps some who have come this far are almost persuaded: remember that point about accumulative probability? As it is, the finding of a new, telling portrait; the evidence of some newly discovered document; or, much more dramatically, opening up a grave or monument to good purpose, would be the only ways to obtain vital new evidence. The odds are stacked against success; as Germaine Greer, for instance, once argued in an article, the assumption that the actor and the Bard were the same person could theoretically be overturned by a great discovery. She rightly added that, as so much document-hunting has already taken place, this is scarcely now likely.

It becomes even more unlikely because orthodoxy has steadfastly opposed the searching of the most promising locations. (What about that unnamed grave in Stratford with its doggerel curse discouraging admission?) Some would say we should revere any such places by leaving them alone. Yet what are the possibilities if such a search took place? There are really only three:

- the most likely one, that the search would yield nothing;
- new information, supporting the traditional Shakespeare, might be found;
- information revealing Shakespeare as a pen-name might be discovered.

Happenings over the last decade or so have generally suggested that Stratfordian fears concerning the third greatly outweigh both their interest in the objective quest for truth and their hopes in the second category. Of course, we have to face the fact that not only is there a distinct possibility that there was never any documentary evidence hidden away, but also that, if it was, it may have decayed by now while awaiting posterity's response to the challenge. Documents might need to be in expensive lead caskets to still survive. Since searches of known records are now unlikely to offer information more significant about the Stratford man than requests to or by him for payment of a bill, the doubters should collectively continue to bring pressure to bear on authorities to permit investigation for conclusive evidence, via searches in more monuments (or other locations) to be made. This can be done with due care and reverence. By means of electronic scanning, for example, it is possible to minimise the literal use of chisels, or other implements, in doubt's quest.

Will there be a change in the position by the end of the twentieth century? Or (about two decades from my completion of this) by the next major Stratfordian commemoration in 2016? Will Stratford-upon-Avon be replaced by another 'Mecca'? It seems to me most unlikely. Sublime vaticination would be needed to be really confident of such. That is why any anti-Stratfordian should be cautious: there has been too much pain or disillusionment in the story of this controversy, by hopes being set at far too high a level. Remarking earlier that some of those who disbelieve in the Shakespeare of Stratford have been over-optimistic about the acceptance of their case, I used my three chosen Oxfordians to illustrate that point. They are far from being alone in their optimism, even in their own camp. In upbeat mood on one 1993 occasion, another prominent advocate of the Earl of Oxford, encouraged by the surge in recent activity, expressed with some confidence the view that the year 2000 would be recognised as the 450th anniversary of the birth of (the true) Shakespeare.

Perhaps he really meant 'eventually so recognised'. Barring a sensational supportive 'find', any change in majority belief by then will seem most unlikely to 'neutrals', although certainly we need never doubt that all committed Oxfordians will mark that date as the one they suppose accurate. Since not even gradualness is inevitable in securing progress for the dissenters, these statements are rather like those of evangelists fervently proclaiming the imminence of a Messiah's second coming. There have been allegations, at various earlier times during this controversy, that the 'last trumpet' is soon to be heard, and these have not all come from one group. Nevertheless, it may be safely assumed that newcomers to the debate can explore safely, secure in the fact that any delving will not be overtaken by fulfilment of such invocations of the apocalyptic vision. The end of all things is not yet.

It should be admitted that, until or unless there is a momentous discovery, all that can be relied upon is what we see as probability. In terms of more extensive general belief in an author other than the supposed one, time (or is it human nature?) is apparently in no hurry 'to calm contending kings'. Moreover, in the context of academic recognition, time does not seem so much to ignore them as to go out of its way to avoid them. Theologians are prepared to believe or examine many things that average churchgoers would shun (if they knew or understood them), yet there is no obvious equivalent niche for

222

this Shakespeare identity debate in higher literary circles. Will we, one day, have a professor of English Literature, liberal and bold as any modern churchman, prepared to admit that the authorship is an open issue?

Unfortunately, for most people, the present state of affairs encourages blithe compliance with repeated daily assertion, quite devoid of any personal exploration of the options. As for change in such attitude, Twain was much more realistic about it than most. His strong views about the difficulty of removing ingrained, treasured beliefs may be recalled. In his 1909 book, he felt sure there was no chance 'that Shakespeare [of Stratford] will have to vacate his pedestal this side of the year 2209. [Widespread] disbelief in him cannot come swiftly ... it took several thousand years to convince our fine race – including every splendid intellect in it – that there is no such thing as a witch.'

Even those who totally disagree with my attempted reconstruction will surely accept that we are in a situation where we should be judging by the weight of probabilities, unless a documentary treasure trove does come to light. To come to the end of a zealous quest for accurate historical truth, only to be left with mere likelihood, may seem disappointing to the point of total anticlimax. Yet, if probability becomes the only legal tender, it becomes all the more important to have made this investigative journey. Consolation for lack of certainty may be found in the realisation that the issues remain for enjoyable exploration by oneself or others, or perhaps the elusive nature of the final step may add to the attractions, so that one may borrow a line from one of Marlowe's characters to say: 'that like I best that flies beyond my reach'. After all, Shakespeare himself, according to the later great poet John Keats, had an enormous 'negative capability'. This unusual, perhaps difficult, phrase means that one may bask in uncertainties, mysteries, doubts, without perpetually insisting on reaching for solid facts. Anyway, to believe that one has found certainty may merely inhibit the reception of further ideas.

People who have duly done some investigation should feel left to decide for themselves whether this great controversy is merely an eristic, although enjoyable, arena for speculators, all recreating Shakespeare in their own image. Is unorthodoxy a candle for truth or merely a phantom, an irritating 'ghost in the machine' of today's vast conventional Shakespeare industry? Is it but some sort of simulation of what might have been historical truth, but was not; a cyber-world type of 'virtual reality' pleasing only to its adherents?

Reading this volume will, at the very least, have meant some enquiry; a subsequent view, orthodox or otherwise, must be the better for that. It is also, whatever the degree of prior knowledge, an approach to Shakespearean studies in a most valuable alternative way, alas all too frequently ignored by the formal curriculum at school or college. It may be that some will feel that the Stratford ceremonies and celebration can be seen as giving glory to Shakespeare the author – whoever that author was. Although he may actually have half wanted to provoke us, let us take a portion of Ben Jonson's tribute at its face value. Can we then not see, or be content with pretending to see, the face from one of the 'Shakespeare' portraits as representing the true father for the 'issue' of these works?

Such a stance would never do for the true, indomitable, out-and-out 'rebels', who feel that the best books in their cause are much chewed by opponents, yet all too rarely digested. They continue to push at the seemingly immovable, often faced with a climate redolent with resentment. Yet they journey on, possessing a radiant faith. For there is, they contend, a concealed truth which abuse, browbeating or perpetual repetition of the 'official' line can never snuff out. There is no wavering in these ranks concerning the traditional William: he surely belongs to 'green in judgement' salad days. For them the majority view is defunct, however frequently or vehemently proclaimed.

Surely, they would say, the real parent of these publications was a man with a provocative past as shown in the sonnets. Surely the 'children' show him to be saturated in culture; urbanely philosophical; immured in a world of exciting words, sensitive to their flow, cadences, impact? Indeed, disbelievers might unite to argue that, if they held their peace, the very works would cry out – probably using a speech from the most memorable character in *King John*, when proclaiming that Sir Robert Falconbridge is not his real father:

> [He] might have ate his part in me
> Upon Good Friday and ne'er broke his fast ...
> Could he get me?
> [He] could not do it.

My own views are more flexible than those of many of these sceptics, but are unlikely to change from those expressed unless compelling new argument or, preferably, new evidence appears. It must be reiterated that this is unlikely. If there are no documents to be found (or one is denied the chance to search because orthodoxy fears the shadows or spectres that might rise from the disturbed dust), what options are left? How interesting it might have been if the authorship had been queried almost immediately; if, say, Francis Bacon or William Stanley had been interviewed in 1625 – or even a surviving person from the family of Shakespeare of Stratford had been quizzed then. For it must be reiterated that, if there was a carefully planned 'imposture', the years immediately after the publication of the First Folio were the crucial ones for sustaining it.

If we had immortal powers, we could discuss these things with such personalities in the future. On that basis, let me suppose that in an after-life, several people (myself included) were to be (very briefly) given the privilege to meet the writer Shakespeare, to be allowed just one question each. If, this being so, I found to my surprise he was the very man always proclaimed by the literary specialists, what would my choice of question then be? Probably a wordy one: 'Why did incredible genius, that which brought you almost instantaneous culture, along with knowledge of experiences apparently beyond your reach, have a perverse dimension, which ensured that the most exhaustive searching of archives by posterity would show you consistently in an entirely different light as essentially of mercantile inclinations, even to come across to some as an upwardly mobile huckster?' Of course, to find the real author to have been someone else would confer upon me the right to ask a completely different question. It might leave many others, offered that same privilege, speechless!

As it is, at times in the stormy twentieth-century history of this debate, appeals have been made to those long dead, voices from the spirit world being (apparently) produced to testify for supporters of Oxford or Bacon. This is perhaps no stranger than the imaginary interviews some Stratfordians have with, say, the conventional Bard's father or son-in-law. Yet for me such witness, on behalf of authorship dissenters, ranks with the cryptograms. But its very existence (again, perhaps, born of desperation in the absence of the compelling proof really sought) leads on to one last biblical analogy. Down the years, in this great controversy, there have all too obviously been some false prophets with very curious messages. But the best of the doubters – people of intellectual stature, with clear concern in the matter – ought not to be dismissed so glibly. They should be seen as the genuine enquirers they are, worthy at least of respect. The orthodox have the testimony of these people as to 'William Shakespeare' being a pseudonym. It seems to me that, if they are not honest enough to give even a fair hearing to such prophets, they likely would not listen were an authentic voice to rise from the dead.

APPENDIX 1: BIBLIOGRAPHY

(*Note:* All works were published in Britain unless otherwise indicated. Where a book has various editions, the one cited is usually that consulted by me. Details of shorter monographs, and of periodical, pamphlet or newspaper references mentioned in the text, are given in the second section of this bibliography.)

1. BOOKS AND OTHER SUBSTANTIAL MONOGRAPHS

General

The Complete Works are, of course, essential. A separate text of the sonnets, with impartial annotation, is useful.

Surveys of the Authorship Debate

Churchill, R C, *Shakespeare and His Betters*, 1958.
(This includes an account of pre-1900 debate, as do some of the other surveys.)

Gibson, H N, *The Shakespeare Claimants*, 1962.

Hope, W and Holston, K, *The Shakespeare Controversy: an analysis of the claimants to authorship and their champions and detractors*, 1992.
(Published in the USA, this is anti-Stratfordian with Oxfordian conclusions. History of the debate is followed by an extensively

annotated bibliography. The former ends in 1975 in this book, although the bibliography continues to 1991.)

Schoenbaum, S, *Shakespeare's Lives*, 1991.
(There is a longer section on the 'heretics' in the earlier edition of 1970.)

Wadsworth, F W, *The Poacher from Stratford*, 1958.
(Published in the USA.)

Orthodox Shakespearean Commentators

Boyce, C, *Shakespeare A–Z*, 1990.
(An encyclopaedia.)

Brown, I, *Shakespeare*, 1949.

How Shakespeare Spent the Day, 1963.

Chambers, Sir E K, *William Shakespeare: a study of facts and problems* (2 volumes), 1930.

Connes, G, *Le Mystère Shakespearien*, 1926.
(Published in France.)

Epstein, N, *The Friendly Shakespeare*, 1993.
(A 'popular' rather than academic work in which an American author vindicates her belief that Shakespeare deserves a wider audience.)

Fido, M, *Shakespeare*, 1978.

Hamilton, C, *In Search of Shakespeare: a study of the poet's life and handwriting*, 1986.

Harrison, G B, *Introducing Shakespeare*, 3rd edition, 1977.

APPENDIX 1: BIBLIOGRAPHY

Hotson, J L, *Mr W H*, 1974.

Shakespeare's Sonnets Dated, 1949.

Kay, T, *The Grafton Portrait of Shakespeare*, 1914.

Lee, Sir S, *The Life of William Shakespeare*, 4th edition, 1925.

Matus, I L, *Shakespeare in Fact*, 1994
(An American writer examines and rejects Oxfordian arguments.)

Muir, K, *Shakespeare's Sources* (2 volumes), 1957.

Murry, J M, *Shakespeare*, 1954.

O'Connor, G, *William Shakespeare: a life*, 1991.

Phillips, G and Keatman, M, *The Shakespeare Conspiracy*, 1994.

Smart, J S, *Shakespeare: truth and tradition*, 1928.

Taylor, G, *Re-inventing Shakespeare*, 1989.

Wilson, I, *Shakespeare: the evidence*, 1993.

Wilson, J D, *The Essential Shakespeare*, 1932.

The Selected Twentieth-Century Anti-Stratfordian Theorists

Amphlett, H, *Who was Shakespeare?*, 1955.

Evans, A J, *Shakespeare's Magic Circle*, 1956.

Greenwood, Sir G, *The Shakespeare Problem Re-Stated*, 1908.
Is there a Shakespeare Problem?, 1916.

The Vindicators of Shakespeare: a reply to critics.
(Reprinted in the USA, 1970.)

Hoffman, C, *The Man who was Shakespeare*, 1955.
(Also published the same year in the USA, with a slightly different title.)

Honey, W, *The Life, Loves and Achievements of Christopher Marlowe, alias Shakespeare*, Volume 1. Privately published, 1982. (The planned Volume 2 was never finished.)

Lefranc, A, *Sous le masque de William Shakespeare.* (2 volumes), 1919. (Published in France.)

Looney, J T, *Shakespeare Identified*, 3rd edition, edited by R L Miller (2 volumes), 1974.

Ogburn, C, *The Mysterious William Shakespeare: the myth and the reality*, 1984. New edition, 1992.
(Published in New York. Also published in Britain in an abbreviated form, edited by Charles de Vere, Earl of Burford. Those wanting an update on Oxford's case, in concise form, could try another American writer: R F Whalen, *Shakespeare – who was he?* 1994.)

Porohovshikov, P S, *Shakespeare Unmasked*, 1955.
(Previously published 1940 in the USA.)

Slater, G, *Seven Shakespeares*, 1931.

Sykes, C W, *Alias William Shakespeare*, 1947.

Theobald, B G, *Enter Francis Bacon*, 1932.

Titherley, A W, *Shakespeare's Identity*, 1952.

APPENDIX 1: BIBLIOGRAPHY

Twain, M, *Is Shakespeare Dead?*, 1909.

Wraight, A D, *The Story that the Sonnets Tell*, 1995.
(A sequel is promised.)

Other Anti-Stratfordian Books Cited in the Text

American Bar Association. *Shakespeare Cross-examination*,
1961.
(A collection of ten articles which had appeared at intervals in
the Association's journal, together with the correspondence
which they provoked. These articles are mostly, but not
exclusively, anti-Stratfordian.)

Anderson, V, *The de Veres of Castle Hedingham*, 1993.
(A good modern account of de Vere biography and history
through several generations.)

Driver, O, *The Bacon–Shakespeare Mystery*, (USA), 1960.
(Argues that Anthony Bacon, elder brother of Francis, was the
writer Shakespeare.)

Hutcheson, W J F, *Shakespeare's other Anne*, 1950.

Stotsenburg, J H, *An Impartial Study of the Shakespeare Title*,
(USA), 1904.

Sweet, G E, *Shake-speare: the mystery*, (USA), 1963.

Ward, B M, *The 17th Earl of Oxford*, 1928.
(The official biography, now dated in some respects.)

Orthodox Works on Marlowe Cited in the Text

Nicholl, C, *The Reckoning: the murder of Christopher
Marlowe*, 1992.

Robertson, J M, *Marlowe: a conspectus*, 1931.

Steane, J B, *Marlowe: a critical study*, 1964.

Urry, W, *Christopher Marlowe and Canterbury*, 1989. (Published posthumously, edited by Andrew Butcher.)

Wraight, A D and Stern, V F, *In Search of Christopher Marlowe*, 1965. (Reprinted 1993.)

Other Works Cited

Friedman, W F and Friedman E S, *The Shakespeare Ciphers Examined*, 1957.

A Hundred Sundry Flowers (1573). 2nd (modern) edition, edited (in the USA) by R L Miller, 1975.
(The interest in this edition is in the seventeenth Earl of Oxford. Some standard Oxfordian works have been reissued in new editions, enhanced by Mrs Miller's annotation and commentary.)

McMichael, G and Glenn, E M *Shakespeare and his Rivals,* (USA), 1962.

Robertson, J M, *The Baconian Heresy*, 1913.

The Shakespeare Canon (2 volumes), 1922, 1923.

The Genuine in Shakespeare, 1930.

Literary Detection, 1931.

Wilson, A N, *Jesus*, 1992.

2. NOTES ON SHORTER MONOGRAPHS, ARTICLES AND NEWSPAPER REFERENCES

These are provided below in the order in which the items concerned are cited in the text.

Act 1

Pares, M, *A pioneer: in memory of Delia Bacon*, 1959.

The letter concerning word coincidences within Psalm 46, as shown in the text of the Authorised Version of the Bible (1611), appeared in the *Guardian*, 18 August 1984. It seems kindest not to cite other items offered here as examples of comedy.

Act 2

J Enoch Powell's views are taken from the substance of the text of his address to the Shakespeare Club, Stratford-upon-Avon, 13 April 1971. (Subsequently reproduced as a pamphlet by the Shakespeare Oxford Society.)

The article by Hugh Trevor-Roper appeared in *Past & Future*, January 1964.

The booklet mentioned concerning all documentary records on Stratford's Shakespeare is *Shakespeare in the Public Records*, 1985. (Public Record Office.)

Archie Webster's article, noted in the text, was published in *National Review*, September 1923.

·The quotation concerning accumulative probability comes from a short story by Arthur Morrison, first published in *The Strand Magazine* in 1894.

Act 3

Baconians: Thomas Bokenham's booklet *A Brief History of the Bacon–Shakespeare Controversy* was published by the Francis Bacon Research Trust, 1982.

Penn Leary's contribution, an article on ciphers, appeared in *Baconiana*, December 1991. He is also the author of a book on this theme.

Examples of articles concerning Francis Carr are those in *The Sunday Telegraph*, 24 April 1983, and the London *Evening Standard*, 17 March 1986.

Derbyites: The news item mentioned was in *The Independent*, 26 April 1988.

Marlovians: The anonymous review of Hoffman's book mentioned appeared in *The Times Literary Supplement*, 27 January 1956; the news reference to his visit to Padua can be found in the *Guardian*, 11 July 1983.

Group Theorists: The article by Powell mentioned in my text appeared in *The Spectator*, 30 October 1993.

Act 4

The statement about Hoffman opening a dramatist's tomb appeared in *The Daily Telegraph*, 5 December 1987.

Joan Bakewell's observations are as reported in *The Times*, 22 April 1990.

The article by Anthony Burgess, which includes comment on fiction as a possible illuminator of truth, appeared in *The Observer*, 8 August 1982.

A sample spread of articles from the 1980s which show the views of A L Rowse are: *The Telegraph Sunday Magazine*,

6 September 1981; *The Spectator*, 30 March 1985; *The Weekend Telegraph*, 20 August 1988.

Feldman's remark about Rowse arises during his article in *The Bard*, Vol. 3, Part 1, 1980.
The Gore-Langton and Massie comments concerning Enoch Powell appear in *The Daily Telegraph*, 16 November 1993 and 30 August 1994 respectively.
One paragraph in my text, concluding with the reference to Lord Healey, is, as stated there, based upon a report in *The Sunday Telegraph*, 31 October 1993.

The remark quoted about knowing as little about Shakespeare as we do about the yeti appeared in *The Independent*, 15 November 1991.

Act 5

The implications of Roger Stritmatter's study of de Vere's Bible are well described in *The Shakespeare Oxford Society Bulletin*, 28(2) 1992, and 29(4) 1993.

The report about an auction at Sotheby's of what appears to be a draft of a Shakespeare play appeared in *The Daily Telegraph*, 18 July 1993.

Epilogue

The statistical analysis suggesting that the style of Shakespeare stands between those of Marlowe and Oxford was by L S Penrose and appeared in *Shakespearean Authorship Review*, Winter 1972.

The article by Germaine Greer mentioned in the Epilogue was published in *The Observer*, 28 November 1982.

APPENDIX 2: SOME SOURCES OF FURTHER INFORMATION

(Because orthodox Shakespeare societies are easily found, the emphasis below is anti-Stratfordian. 'Contact' names shown are correct as of early 1995.)

The Shakespeare Authorship Information Centre

Disseminates information via a newsletter showing recent newspaper extracts on Shakespeare, with particular reference to authorship questionings. Director: F Carr, 9 Clermont Court, Clermont Road, Brighton, BN1 6SS.

The Shakespearean Authorship Trust

Seeks to promote scholarly examination of authorship issues. Chairman: Dr L L Ware, 11 Old Square, Lincolns Inn, London, WC2A 3TS.

The Francis Bacon Society

Maintains a library; publishes the journal *Baconiana*. Secretary: T D Bokenham, 56 Westbury Road, New Malden, Surrey, TK3 5AX.

Objectives: 'To encourage, for the benefit of the public, the study of the works of Francis Bacon as philosopher, statesman and poet; also his character, genius and life, his influence on his own and succeeding times, and the tendencies and results of his writing.

To encourage, for the benefit of the public, the general study of the evidence in favour of Francis Bacon's authorship of the plays commonly ascribed to Shakespeare, and to investigate his connection with other works of the Elizabethan period.' The equivalent organisation in the USA is **The Francis Bacon Foundation**, 655 N. Dartmouth Avenue, Claremont, CA 91711.

The Shakespeare Oxford Society (USA)

Publishes a regular newsletter. Current 'contact' address for membership information: Greenridge Park, 7D Taggart Drive, Nashua, NH. 03060-5591

Purpose: 'To document and establish Edward de Vere, the seventeenth Earl of Oxford (1550–1604) as the universally recognised author of the works of William Shakespeare.'

In 1993, the **De Vere Society** was revived in Britain to work as the British arm of increased Oxfordian endeavour. Current secretary: Christopher H Dams, 8 Western Road, Henley-on-Thames, Oxon., RG9 1JL. A booklet stating de Vere's case concisely was produced by this society in 1995. The two Oxfordian societies work in close association.

Edward de Vere Newsletter (Canada)

Published monthly. Contact: The Editor, 1340 Flemish Street, Kelowna, British Columbia. V1Y 3R7.

Marlowe Lives! Association (USA)

Purpose: 'To investigate and propagate Christopher Marlowe's claim to the authorship of the Shakespeare canon.'
Publishes the newsletter *Marlovian*. Contact: David A More, 1602 Montview Boulevard, Greeley, Colorado 80631.

The Marlowe Society

Purpose: '...a historical society to commemorate Christopher Marlowe as a poet and dramatist, to extend interest in his life and works, and perform his plays.'
Organises outings, theatre trips and other events as well as encouraging research and debate; now some 40 years old, it 'combines the functions of a learned society and that of a popular organisation within the grasp of the average person interested in Tudor times.' Publications include a quatercentenary booklet marking the official death of the dramatist Christopher Marlowe (1593–1993).

Note: This last-named society honours Marlowe as Marlowe. It is emphatically *not* an anti-Stratfordian organisation, although *some* members do hold such views. Current secretary: Michael Frohnsdorff, 6 Beech Close, Faversham, Kent, ME13 7SL.

INDEX OF REFERENCES TO
SHAKESPEARE'S WORKS

239

THE ALTERNATIVE SHAKESPEARE